ericonhisbike

A HOME
TO HEAD FOR

eric olverson

A Bright Pen Book

British Library Cataloguing Publication Data.
A catalogue record for this book is available from the British Library

ISBN 978-0-7552-1343-6

Authors OnLine Ltd
19 The Cinques
Gamlingay, Sandy
Bedfordshire SG19 3NU
England

This book is also available in e-book format, details of which are available at www.authorsonline.co.uk

Acknowledgements

I must start by enthusiastically thanking my wife Carole: without her support I could not even have contemplated achieving what I accomplished.

My family and friends – wherever located – provided constant and continuous encouragement, both while I cycled through Africa and then while I wrote this book. From these I would like to single out: Matthew Cohen and Susan Moorhouse for their design and regular updating of my blog site (www.ericonhisbike.com) and for always being available to assist; Charles Brett for insisting, in his editorial capacity, upon a professional approach, while still managing always to encourage; JD Moorhouse for providing the original illustrations; Peter Butcher who spent long hours preparing the maps and creating the book you now see; and Kelly Walsh who designed the cover.

Fellow Tour D'Afrique riders Dana Farrell, Rick Wasfy Bill Nelems and Gerald Coniel kindly allowed me to quote from their blogs. This I feel has enhanced the book. Dan Spasojevic, through his generosity, stands out as having given me the impetus to start writing.

Despite the efforts of all of the above, and the many who are not individually named but who each in their different ways contributed, the errors and mistakes are all mine.

Tunisia
Morocco
Algeria
Libya
Egypt
CAIRO
Western
Sahara
Mauritania
Mali
Niger
Chad
Sudan
Eritrea
Djibouiti
Senegal
Gambia
Guinea
Burkina Faso
Nigeria
Central
African Republic
Ethiopia
Somalia
Sierra Leone
Liberia
Ivory Coast
Gana
Togo
Benin
Cameroon
Equatorial
Gabon
Republic of
The Congo
Democratic
Republic of Congo
Rwanda
Burundi
Uganda
Kenya
Tanzania
Angola
Zambia
Malawi
Namibia
Zimbabwe
Botswana
Mozambique
Madagascar
Lesotho
South Africa
CAPE TOWN

Kilometres

0   1000   2000

CONTENTS

MAPS

One of the sayings in our country is Ubuntu – the essence of being human. Ubuntu speaks particularly about the fact that you can't exist as a human being in isolation. It speaks about our own interconnectedness. You can't be human all by yourself and when you have the quality – Ubuntu – you are known for your generosity.

We think of ourselves far too frequently as just individuals, separated from one another, whereas we are connected and what we do affects the whole world. When we do well, it spreads out; it is for the whole of humanity.

Archbishop Desmond Tutu

CHAPTER 1
WHY?

Priesthood was not for me. After several years at the seminary, I realised this at the age of 15 and told the Rector. He persuaded me to at least stay until I had finished my "A" level exams. This I had now done, but I did not want to go to university.

"What are you going to do now then?" my father asked me. We had not yet reached the end of the seminary driveway.

"I would rather like to spend a couple of years doing Voluntary Service Overseas, in India," I replied.

"And then what?"

"I don't know...probably work on the farm." (I referred to my father's farm.)

"Then forget about the VSO, you might as well get started with the farming straight away," he directed me. Which is what I did. Although I finally immersed myself in the business to the point of drowning, the thought of helping overseas never left me.

I retired from farming near Southport (UK) in 1997, and we came to live in Spain on the Costa Blanca. I started to enjoy doing a bit of cycling in the spare time I could afford away from the restoration of the run-down property we had bought. A few years later however, I fell ill with septicaemia, followed exactly a year later by bacterial meningitis. I remember nothing of the four weeks I spent in hospital although my wife tells me that I regained semi-consciousness on a few occasions. I left there in a wheelchair, too weak to stand up. A side effect of the illness was that my bladder lost its ability to function; ever since then, I have had to self-catheterise in order to release the urine. I continue to have to do this and I have to be extremely careful about cleanliness in order to avoid infections.

Although my recovery was painfully slow, I learnt to walk properly again and gradually become self-reliant once more, largely due to the help of my wife, Carole. To help regain my

1

strength and fitness, I returned to cycling. The mountains around this area, the Marina Alta, are beautiful and tranquil, a wonderful training ground for cyclists. Over a period of a few years I reached the stage whereby I could be considered a reasonable cyclist.

In September, 2008, I was transfixed by a TV documentary about an orphanage in South Africa where tragedy had been turned into success with outside help. This was just one orphanage amongst many in Africa, but without the outside help it would have had a dire future. Immediately after the programme, I searched the internet and found out about BeMore, a Dutch charity that was sending out volunteers to orphanages in South Africa. I applied that night and was finally accepted as a volunteer after they had thoroughly checked me out.

By the start of November that year, I had begun two months helping out at Thamsanqa orphanage, near Port Elizabeth in South Africa. The experience was to change my way of thinking and my points of reference, in a way that I had not imagined to be possible so late on in life.

During those two months, I learnt more than I taught. I also became aware that any talents I had for care-working were rather limited. On my return home, I could not help thinking that there must be more I could do to help Thamsanqa.

Then I read about the Tour d'Afrique. With cycling now my principal hobby and given my love of adventure I knew in an instant that this was what I was looking for: a platform from which I could raise money to help the orphanage through sponsorship, while cycling the length of Africa.

Thamsanqa

Most people would, I believe, imagine an African orphanage to be an institution where orphans live and receive a rudimentary education, amidst the unspoilt surroundings of the beautiful countryside. I saw myself teaching children in a classroom, playing games and enjoying sport with them on a small field at the side. How wide of the mark that was.

Tia Wessels is a retired, white Afrikaner, quietly assertive with a stubborn determination to do what is right. She had spent her working life helping children as a social worker for Child Welfare becoming the head of that organisation in the Eastern Cape (of which Port Elizabeth, or PE, is the capital). In 2005, already in retirement, she was alerted to the plight of twelve children who had been living together with an older woman in a run-down room. During the night, the landlord, under the influence of drink, turned them out on to the street. Tia was able to obtain some temporary shelter for them through the Salvation Army. With help from the Round Table and two local stores, she fed and clothed the children for one year. With the help of the Department of Housing she acquired three three-bedroomed houses in the black township of Motherwell, near PE. This was the start of Thamsanqa. The name derives from Cheeza Thamsanqa, one of the original twelve children, who sadly died of Aids soon afterwards. The name Thamsanqa means lucky.

When I arrived in 2008, there were these three bungalows, all in Motherwell. Short drives apart, each house provided a home for six children and a house mother. The children went to the local state school where the education was free, but uniforms, books and writing materials had to be bought. Tia had also set up within the local community an organisation of helpers to identify and care for other children found to be at particular risk. With the help of these volunteers, a further 472 orphaned children (at the time of writing) are being cared for.

I stayed, along with a few other volunteers, in a PE suburb some 35 minutes drive from the black township. We lodged with Peter and Daphne, a colourful, coloured couple who also supported Tia in whatever way they could. We were the first volunteers to help out at Thamsanqa, so for Tia as much as for us, there was much to learn. We would help the children with their English or, in the case of those of school age, with their school work, and play games with them. Otherwise, we had work to do preparing a vegetable garden and improving the houses, as well as assisting Tia within the local black community.

It was natural that the children were a little wary of us at first. Why were these white people whom they had never seen before coming into their homes? Normally, white folk kept out of the black township. But once they no longer felt threatened, we were able to gain their trust. The younger ones clearly yearned for the close physical contact normally provided by parents; the older ones were perhaps already too hardened to seek it or be seen to seek it, but nonetheless enjoyed our presence.

As was usual, three of us arrived one morning at one of the homes for about 10am. We were admitted into the tiny space that was the communal area. But the house mother and the children, those who were not at school, stayed in their rooms. It was not clear what they were doing, but we felt very uncomfortable as we were ignored. Should we leave or should we stay? After agreeing amongst ourselves to remain for up to an hour, one of the children, aged about four, popped her head round the bedroom door, first once then twice, until finally she came out. We interested her in a simple jigsaw puzzle we had brought. Soon another youngster joined us. Before long, they had all joined us. No reason was ever given for the cold reception. But when it was time to leave, the house mother and all the children came out and waved to us enthusiastically, which was a little unusual.

On a national level, reconciliation and respect need to replace the mistrust between the various racial groups. These children, and many like them, had not only to cope with that, but also deal with the brutality and abuse they each suffered, very often at the hands of their own kind, before finding a home at Thamsanqa.

For Thamsanqa to merely stand still and provide for the existing children, never mind succeed in expanding to alleviate the ever-growing plight of children orphaned, abused and neglected within a society crumbling as the Aids virus marched through its ranks and many members turned to alcohol to dampen their distress, funds were needed on a regular basis. (This is still the case.)

I might not have been such a good care-worker, but there were other ways to help. I could ride a bike.

Tour d'Afrique

The name Tour d'Afrique (henceforth TDA) refers to the foundation/company and also to the cycle ride through Africa that they organise.

The foundation aims to highlight the part the bike can play in reducing the world's dependence on motor vehicles whilst positively encouraging its use, especially in places like Africa. On the journey through Africa, bikes that have been bought from local small businesses are donated to charities that can put them to good use.

The philosophy of the company is that the riders make their own way through Africa and must be self-reliant; the company provides the framework within which this can be done and gives direction and support. In the TDA's own words, the participants are "responsible for bringing a bike, riding gear, spare parts, tent, sleeping bag, personal funds and medicines as well as the adventurous spirit, physical conditioning and mental stamina" needed.

The cycle ride starts in Cairo and ends four months later in Cape Town, having negotiated about 12,000 km (7,500 miles). The heat of the desert, the loose sand, rock and corrugation of the off-road sections, the long distances on tarmac, all sap the strength and tax the spirit, offering sickness an easy prey. Egypt, Sudan and Ethiopia, Kenya, Tanzania and Malawi, Zambia, Botswana and Namibia all dazzle, drain and delight before the final push through South Africa to Cape Town.

For the sake of those who wish to cycle only a part of Africa, the journey is split into eight sections. Some riders can join at the beginning of a section, and leave at the end of that section or at the end of any ensuing section. In some sections, we were joined by one or more local riders, who added colour and competition.

In all, there were 95 cycling days (called stages) in 2010, interspersed by 23 rest days (non-cycling days) and 2 days on a ferry.

Riders had the choice of being either an expedition rider or a racer. The former were allowed to leave camp as early as they liked. They generally chose to ride at a more leisurely pace so as to take in their surroundings and stop when they felt tired or saw something of interest. The racers were initially given a time at which to start so that their individual finishing times on reaching the site of that night's camp site could be calculated. The fastest rider on the day was a stage winner. The fastest over a whole section, that is with the shortest accumulated time, was a section winner and of course the rider with the least accumulated time over the four months was the overall winner.

The route and daily distances were the same for all riders. Each evening, a riders' meeting was held when a short explanation of the following day's route was given.

The TDA supplied two lorries and two four-wheel drive runabouts. While the riders were cycling, the lorries carried the riders' gear, plus all foodstuffs, cooking equipment and camp furniture. The lunch truck headed quickly after breakfast to the day's halfway point, in order to set up tables on which there would be bread and various fillings, water and hydrating drinks; the dinner truck made for the site of that night's camp to prepare soup and, later, evening dinner.

Fifty-six of us, as well as a few sectional riders and three Egyptian riders, left Cairo on January 16 to push our pedals - and our luck.

My bike

The bike I had been riding here on the Costa Blanca in Spain, was a Dente racing bike that I had had for maybe ten years. When I first bought it, the thought of riding in the mountains around here was a daunting prospect. But there is nowhere in the area that does not require some climbing, so I had to get used to it. Now I seek out the mountains. To watch, from the seat of a bike, the unspoilt scenery gradually unfurl before my eyes, to stop in one of the many quiet villages that adorn the countryside for a coffee... these are pleasures I feel immensely grateful for. (I have written about many of these rides on my blog: www.ericonhisbike.com).

Regular rides averaging around 100 km prepared me well, but for the last two months before leaving for Africa, I wanted my training to be on the bike I would be riding over there, for clearly the Dente would not be sufficiently robust.

A light racing bike would be wonderful for eating up the miles on the good roads in say Egypt and Botswana. But for the rugged off-road sections, a mountain-bike with full suspension would be faster, more comfortable and would best guarantee not ending up with a cracked frame. I looked at what previous riders had used and listened to the advice that the TDA gave us through rider updates and internet forums in the months before the start. I also spoke at length with Dave White in Birkdale (Southport), where my wife Carole and I are based when in the UK. Dave owns a cycle shop there and is an experienced cyclist himself.

A very light bike constructed of carbon fibre would have been worth considering if speed had been so all-important that the chance of it breaking apart under the duress of the roughest terrain seemed worth taking. But if it cracked or broke in Africa, there would be no way of mending it, only the hope of getting spare parts sent over to a capital city, for picking up when we passed through. Aluminium would be light compared to steel. But even so, finding someone in remote Africa to weld aluminium was unlikely.

I decided on a bike made out of steel, for its strength, flexibility and relative ease of repair. It would be heavy, but very strong. Instead of a racing bike or a mountain bike. I chose a trekking bike, or cyclocross. I still find some of the differences hard to work out.

I would have liked suspension, at least on the back wheel, since the part of my lower back where I have had a disc removed sometimes rebels. But this would have increased the weight of an already heavy bike and add to the list of things to go wrong. Instead, I opted for seat suspension; I had read enthusiastic reviews of the Thudbuster and put my faith in one.

For the cycling enthusiast, these are the more technical details of the bike:

Wheelset: 26" hand built by Kore

Shifters: Deore LX Shimano

Brakes: Deore LX

Forks: Reynolds 531 sloping crown

Headset: Cane Creek S3 sealed bearing

Pedals: BBB sealed bearings, single-sided SPD

Seatpost: Cane Creek Thudbuster

Bottom Bracket: Square taper 110 mm sealed bearing

Tyres: 2 sets 23 mm Schwalbe Marathon
   plus 1 set 45 mm Schwalbe Marathon

My other equipment

We were allowed no more than 43 kg of equipment. This weighed heavily on my mind when choosing the tent. I wanted a two man tent, easy to erect and capable of standing all manner of storms. The camping specialist in the shop recommended the

Vaude Ultralight. It came with just three poles, of cord-shocked alloy, and weighed 1.9 kg (just over 4 lb). Reviews were good. I took little convincing, especially since the variety of equipment and items I had so far accumulated already exceeded 43 kg.

That was apart from the 1000 catheters which I would need to take. They also weighed over 40 kg and I delayed speaking to the TDA about it in the hope that I could come up with a solution myself. It seemed unreasonable to ask the TDA to allow me to take twice the weight of anyone else. If all else failed, perhaps I could send some ahead to the Post Office or DHL centre in each capital city that we would pass through. But I would still have to carry enough catheters to last me between capital cities; some "essentials" would have to be left behind in order to keep within the 43 kg weight limit and to be sure of the catheters fitting in the locker. Furthermore, it would mean putting a lot of trust in African reliability - if they fouled up, and my catheters were not where they should be at the time I needed them, I would be on the next flight home. With about a month left before my departure to Africa, I emailed the TDA office and explained my dilemma. Their reply was to tell me not to worry, they would find somewhere to store the catheters other than in the locker. They would not be counted as part of the 43 kg. I cannot over-emphasise my gratitude to the people at TDA for their preparedness to help me in this way.

The choice of sleeping bag was not difficult, but choosing a mattress was a different matter. We would rarely have a flat, thorn and stone-free site on which to set our tents, so the mattress had to be comfortable and tough, but again light, and easy to inflate/erect. I bought a Thermarest ProLite mattress. (I was informed that if the mattress failed for any reason, it could be sent back to Ireland and replaced free of charge at any time....maybe rather complicated when travelling through some deserted part of Africa.) At 1" thick and weighing in at about 700 gm (approx. 1.5 lb), comfortable on the pocket and hopefully the back too, it seemed a sensible choice.

Clothing had to be kept to a minimum. One set of casual clothes was deemed sufficient as we were not planning to go out much! Three sets of cycling shorts and tops were essential. Apart from the infrequent opportunities to wash our clothes, especially in the first two months, we were right to be advised not to wear the same set of clothes two days running if at all possible; this was to reduce the incidence of saddle sores and infections. So three sets should last a week at a push. If any washing could be done during that week, better still. Rarely a week would pass without a rest day, when usually water would be available. At times, we would have access to water in between rest days.

The list of toiletries, medicines and small items was endless and difficult to shorten. Would you, for instance, think of clothes pegs and a clothes line as essential items? In my opinion they were vital in making the most of any chance to dry clothes. On the other hand, some of the bike spares I took, which were heavy, could have been left behind. A head torch was vital to find your way around camp in the dark, to read and write in the tent, to go to the toilet and pack up in the morning, as were spare batteries for it. How about a pillow? No, you can make one with a book and some clothing. A block of soap was essential if only for washing clothes with, but a little washing -powder in a plastic bag went a long way. I took hand-sanitiser which I never used. Whenever we ate in camp, there was always treated water to wash our hands with. I took too much sun-cream; in the southern half of Africa, it became easier to purchase it anyway. Even black Africans have to protect against sunburn.

I needed three tough bags of about 50 litres each, in which everything would be stored in my locker. One would act as the day bag to be taken with me to the tent each night. Another would contain items that I needed infrequently, while the third was something in-between the two.

But right at the top of my list of priorities would be my netbook. (This was my very small, light computer.) Shelter can be found, comfort is a luxury, communication is paramount. Our only communication if not using a phone was through internet. Our access to it was at best intermittent. Even then, the connections were often dreadfully slow and prone to being lost without warning, and usually there would be a queue to use a computer at an internet café. To make the best use of any internet access, we had to be prepared. So I tried to write and store my blog each night on the netbook, no matter how tired I felt. If the batteries were low, I would write in a notebook. While at an internet café, I wanted the need to write up kept to a minimum so as to better ensure that I could successfully send my blogs as an email to our friend Susan Moorhouse for her to then kindly post them onto my blog site. Any time left, I could send an email to Carole and read the wonderful comments that so many friends and family members left on previous blogs to encourage me. It was incredibly helpful in lifting the spirits. With any further remaining time I would look at the soccer news and world news.

My motivation

I was not particularly excited about the trip. That might sound trite, but it is true. It was a physical and mental challenge, one I had no illusions about. Certainly I wanted to prove to myself that I could do it, never for a moment thinking I would not, given decent health and freedom from accidents. Although I do not like camping and I normally avoid any kind of organised group outing like the plague, this was the only way I was ever going to be able to cycle across Africa.

Most importantly, I really wanted to share my experiences as honestly as I could through my blog. Not everyone has the opportunity or desire to do such a trip. I felt privileged to be able to contemplate doing so while relating my adventure to anyone interested.

My ultimate goal was to make enough money for Thamsanqa, such that it would make a difference. I felt donations were more likely if I was seen to be doing my very best, not just taking the easy way out. So the tent was only to be abandoned for very good reasons. No "hello from the Hilton...".

These are the reasons that, as you will see, rest days were consumed in finding internet cafés, trying to post blogs, washing laundry and keeping the tent going, which proved more difficult than keeping the bike going.

Sometimes it is complicated to pinpoint the actual reasons you do something. I had wondered before the trip to what extent I was doing it for the challenge of the extreme bike ride versus helping Thamsanqa. There were times when that challenge seemed overwhelming, but I could never have given up because I felt I was, in my own small way, helping Thamsanqa and drawing attention to the situation in which the children there and many others like them found themselves in.

CHAPTER 2
GOODBYE TO ME AND HELLO
TO PEPE THE POODLE

Sunday, January 3, 2010 was the last day I rode the bike before leaving for Africa. This was a ride with the local Spanish cycling club, Ciclistas Benissa, cycling to Pego for an almuerzo, (late breakfast), comprising a bocadillo (bread roll) of lamb and artichokes, a vegetable grown locally on the Pego marsh, before cycling home via a different route. How I would miss these rides and the food. A lot of my cycling preparation had been with my English friends. How I would miss their company and the tostadas (toasted bread rolls) and coffees that we habitually included in our rides.

The following Thursday, I said cheerio to my wife, Carole. Perhaps I did not realise at the time the extent of the sacrifice she was making. To be left alone for over four months, with time to worry, was not of her choosing, but she rarely showed me less than whole-hearted support. While I was away she was to take in a lodger called Pepe, a poodle puppy to keep her company. I did complain at the imbalance: I would be away for just some four months, but Pepe would be a fixture for many years. Admittedly, I was on shaky ground to think about complaining.

With my bike in its bag, I flew to the UK to our small flat in Birkdale, where most of my equipment was laid out on the bedroom floor. It all had to be finally weighed and configured to meet the requirements of the airline I was flying with, Lufthansa. As far as I could make out, I would be allowed two bags that together weighed no more than 43 kg. These I now carefully packed.

Down the road, in front of a coal fire in the back of his shop, Dave White and I sorted out the spares needed and carefully packed them around the bike in the bike bag. When finished, it was difficult to zip the bag up. These spares, of course, would ultimately count towards the 43 kg allowed by the TDA. (The space released in my other two bags by putting the bike spares in the bike bag, was taken up by items I would carry with me each day on the bike and reading material and food for the flights and stay in Cairo.) Then we emptied 34 boxes, each containing 30 catheters, onto the floor and proceeded to pack them tightly in a bike box. Amazingly, they just fitted - there was room for a spare saddle. If this box was lost in flight, or the contents damaged, my trip was doomed. We tied it up with plastic straps and there was no more we could do. As this box now contained "medical supplies", I would not have to pay Lufthansa to take it. There was ambiguity over whether there would be a charge for the bike bag, something I was unable to settle with Lufthansa over the phone; maybe they would ask for some payment. All told, I was taking about 125 kg of luggage - plus hand baggage!

Those final days were not exciting. I was greatly concerned lest I forgot something and this kept me very focused. Four months is a long time to be without something essential. Any mistakes would be costly. Other than that my main worry was about not being able to see the journey through to the end due to illness or accident. I just wanted to get to Cairo and begin.

The flight on the 13th from Manchester was to take me to Dusseldorf, and from there another flight would take me to Cairo. In Manchester airport, there was so much luggage on my trolley that it kept falling off. It was a bit embarrassing. At the checkout desk, I was told that I would have to pay extra for the bike, something like £200. I felt my face redden. This was not a happy start, though not totally unexpected. When I explained that I was doing this trip to raise money for charity there was some sympathy. The checkout lady called over a supervisor. She spoke to somebody else by phone. Then she told me that she thought I would have to pay something but I would certainly get a reduction when I took the bike bag upstairs. With everything now checked through but the bike, I went upstairs and saw where the outsize packages were being checked through. I thought the lady had said the desk would be on the left; this was on the right, but it depended which way you were facing. When the man took my bag without asking for any money I asked him if I had anything to pay. He shook his head. What a wonderful start.

I proceeded through customs. As I was walking to the departure lounge, I had a terrible feeling that something was not right. I walked back to a group of officials and told them that maybe I had not paid for the bike and should have. They told me that I could not go back and not to worry about it. So I was relieved to get on the plane and take my seat for the journey of a lifetime. There seemed to be a delay. An official entered the plane and spoke to the cabin crew. He then walked down the cabin and stopped right in front of me.

He told me that I had failed to pay for the bike and I could not fly without doing so. I felt a wave of panic and embarrassment. He produced a pay machine and advised me to pay with a card if I wished to continue my journey. I had not even started! He also wanted the full amount. I weakly explained that I had been told there would at least be a discount. I felt like a cheap cad and I am sure that is what he thought I was. He allowed me no discount.

On arrival in Cairo airport, I was sweating lest the bike or some of my luggage had been waylaid in Dusseldorf. Everything but the box containing my catheters appeared on the conveyor belt. I did not panic. I always keep enough catheters in my hand-baggage to last me for 24 hours, in case of a delay when flying. For nearly an hour, I walked up and down while the porters tried to locate the box. When they finally brought it out to me, everything was intact. As I made for the exit, I was stopped by customs officials. They wanted to know what was in the box. I told them, but they did not understand. They wanted me to empty it for them. I cut a corner of the box and extracted one catheter. They still did not understand. I offered to give a demonstration; that did the trick. They let me go.

We were responsible for making our own way to the Cataracts Hotel, some 45 minutes away by taxi on the outskirts of Cairo, nearer to Giza and the Pyramids. The taxi-driver asked me if I wished to go via the scenic route. This would surely have meant through every congested, soukh-lined street he could find before doing a Lufthansa on me. The fastest route, I told him. He nonetheless persisted in giving me a running commentary in English that I found hard to understand and harder to stomach, given that it was only to gain a bigger tip at the end of it. It perhaps may sound mean of me, but I had decided I was not giving tips all the way through Africa for people doing jobs they were being paid for. I was going to live on a shoestring myself and any money I could raise was going to Thamsanqa. He might as well have kept quiet.

Of the numerous cyclists who converged on the hotel, I was one of the last. Some had arrived a couple of days earlier to sample Cairo city. So some friendships were already forming. With the four ensuing months on the road together, I saw no rush to get acquainted. Given my propensity to forget things, I wanted to remain focused.

Within the hotel complex, there were three restaurants, all reasonably-priced. That first night, I had sat down to eat, when an unshaven gentleman, a little younger than myself, asked if he could join me. Jim was an American lawyer who had signed up for the whole trip too. I told him that Lance Armstrong was the only other American rider I knew of; he was not an admirer of Lance, he told me. It struck me as most strange that the conversation did not develop much from there. He later proved to be an interesting person and we had so much ahead of us to talk about, but we did not. Further into the trip, he asked me whether I felt more comfortable with people of my own nationality, as he felt more at ease with Americans. I admired his inoffensive openness and reluctantly realised he had a fair point; when the going got tough, it was natural not to look for challenging relationships. But I believe that age difference can be as great a barrier as cultural difference. On this trip, we had a good spread of ages, weighted of course to the younger end, and representatives of many countries.

There were two riders to a room; I was sharing with one of the youngest riders, Michael. We got on well and were able to help each other with the packing. There was a moment when we were in the room, the whole of the floor and the beds covered with our gear, that I looked out and saw the area outside the hotel disappearing from sight in what seemed a cloud of smoke. Seemingly they were fumigating the area for mosquitoes. I checked again that I had all my malaria tablets with me.

The first morning, the bike had to be reassembled and tested properly while all the gear had to be repacked in a manner that would allow for easy locker access. It was so difficult to decide what should go in what bag. Our main meeting, our induction, was held mid-morning. Only when we were all together, along with the staff, did it sink in what a huge undertaking this was. But Paul, the Tour Director, emphasized a number of times that we were responsible for our own safety. There were disclaimer forms to fill out and copies of our insurance to hand in. Was there something we did not know about?

Great emphasis was also placed on the need for hygiene. Given the difficulty of obtaining water through many parts of Africa, we would have to be resourceful. Drinking water, and water with disinfectant for washing hands, would always be freely available. Hydrating fluids and energy bars would be at hand. A breakfast comprising a cereal and bread with butter and various toppings would be given all days except rest days. The same applied to a lunch of bread, meat or cheeses and fruit, halfway through the daily ride. On reaching camp, a hearty and plentiful soup would be ready, enough to satiate the hungriest rider until dinner was ready at about 6pm. This main meal, although just one course, would provide plenty of rice, pasta or potato, meat or fish and vegetables. Coffee and tea would be available morning and afternoon; I was to be forever grateful for that.

The two lorries and their crew of four were on loan from an African company called Indaba. We were introduced to these valiant individuals, who would stay with us right through to

Nairobi, before being replaced by another Indaba crew. Paul introduced the TDA team to us: Sharita the Assistant Tour Director, James the chef, Chris the mechanic, Caroline and Michelle the medics, and Allison and Kelsey, also full-time team members. Shanny from Head Office in Toronto also started with us, later to be relieved (at different times) by Miles and Michael.

Now a decision had to be made. Those wishing to be racers had to make themselves known. I was not the only one unsure of what to do. My natural inclination was to ride hard, but I did not want to take chances just because I was in a race. Racers would be timed and these times would appear on the TDA website. That clinched it for me. At least the folk back home would be able to see that I was still OK in the event that I could not make personal contact.

As to our cycling the roads of Africa, we were left in no doubt as to where we came on the scale of importance. Bottom. African drivers see cyclists as an unwanted nuisance. They will not give you space, it is up to you to get out of the way. Although this proved not to always be the case, it was an excellent rule of thumb that alerted us to the very real dangers that lorries in particular represented.

Our motto was to be that "in Africa, expect the unexpected". Unfortunately, expecting is easier than avoiding.

The following morning, our final day in Cairo, we were given the opportunity to find our feet, or pedals rather, with a 28 km ride through the traffic of Giza, keeping roughly in convoy. Several TDA staff members on bikes kept the group in shape. Lorries and cars weaved in and out, often hooting their horns in friendly appreciation, children with big smiles yelled out to us, while we made sure that we avoided the donkeys and carts and the potholes in the road. Michael, my room-mate, cycled right into somebody's backside which, given neither was hurt, was quite funny. It was a reminder, though, how careful we needed to be. Later in the trip, Michael was not to be so lucky.

CHAPTER 3
EGYPT

Saturday, Jan 16: Cairo-Ain Sukhna
135 km

We needed to be up at 4.30am to eat some breakfast before hauling our belongings to the front of the hotel. There, lit up in the cool pre-dawn, were two big lorries, henceforward to be referred to as the dinner truck and the lunch truck. They both had storage compartments on both sides, which would hold all the items for cooking, trestle tables and chairs, foodstuffs, medicines and bike maintenance tools. Banks of lockers, separated by a narrow passage, took up most of the space inside the lorries' upper structure. As we queued up, our belongings were weighed. Paul very diplomatically explained to anyone with over 43 kg that they would have to leave something behind. There was no fuss. I had hoped to take my empty bike bag with me for bringing back the bike from South Africa. Paul told me it was really not a good idea, that I would struggle to fit my gear in the locker even without the bag. How right he was. I gave it to one of the hotel staff. One by one, we climbed into a lorry to put our belongings in a locker that each of us had had allocated to us for the whole four months. Most of those who classed themselves as racers, were given lockers in the dinner truck, because this truck would make its way to the day's destination straight after breakfast, to make tents and equipment available to the faster riders on their arrival at the camp, and to prepare soup and dinner.

I was also given a corner in one of the lunch truck's storage compartments in which to put my box of catheters. By cutting a corner off the box, I was able to access the catheters each day, without damaging the box itself. My daily habit would be to

19

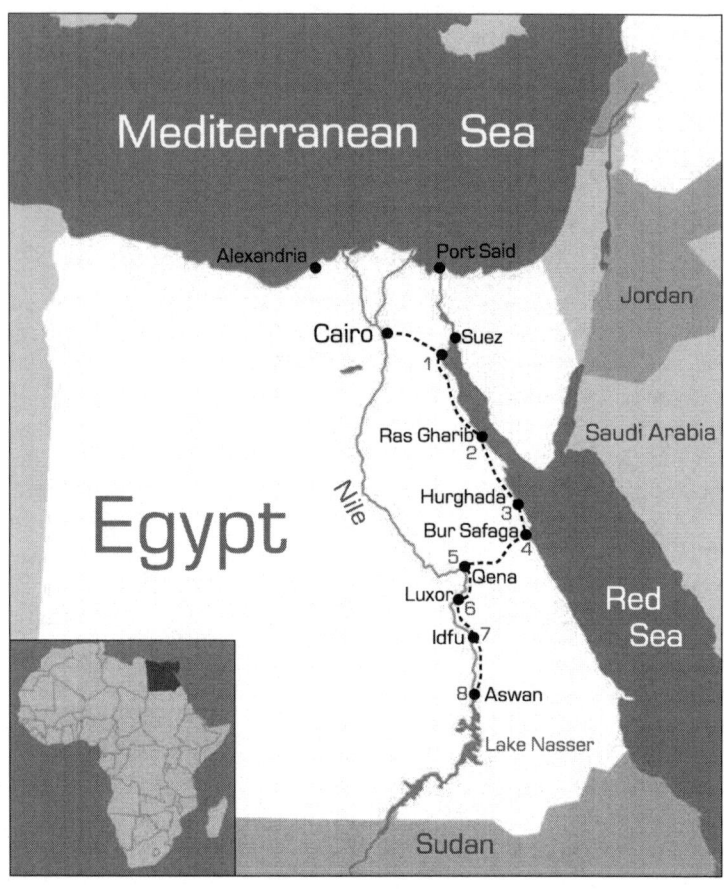

keep enough in my day bag for two days minimum, and enough on the bike for the whole day.

By first light, we were ready with just our bikes and daily necessities, to begin a dawdling 14 km to the pyramids for an opening ceremony. We did not know what to expect, certainly not tables covered by savouries and drinks, a team from Reuters and television cameras; all this alongside one of the Seven Wonders of the Ancient World. Group photos were taken before we meandered down again to the main road as, for a while, we supplanted the Pyramids as the main focus of attention for the early morning tourists.

Now began another 25 km in slow convoy, this time with a heavy police escort, to take us to the very outskirts of the city. Although we were kicking our heels, anxious for our freedom, it would have been impossible to have cycled through that traffic without an escort. But it seemed like the police escort did not want to leave us, even when we were out of the heavy traffic. One police motorcyclist was driving very slowly at the head of the convoy and became angry if a rider overtook him. Some of the riders, Jim in particular, were testing him and urging him to let us go now. The policeman was gesticulating, trying to maintain firm control of the situation. But he eventually gave in, turned round and left us. The restraints were off. The journey had begun, race or no race.

Ahead of us, 110 km of good, flat tarmac would lead us through a hilly, lunar landscape towards Ain Sukhna (camp 1, map Egypt), near the Red Sea. A few fast riders shot off ahead of everybody else The road was perfect for light, racing bikes. Those on mountain bikes would get their turn later. I came in seventh that day, with which I was very pleased. Marcel (Dutch) and young Adrian (Australian) looked very strong on their racing bikes.

Normally, but not always, the lorry which contained your locker would arrive at camp before you. On arrival, you would each retrieve your tent, mattress, sleeping bag and daily bag and set up house before taking soup from the huge cauldron. Then there was the bike to clean. Without proper cleaning the chain would soon wear out in the sandy conditions. After the riders' meeting at about 5.30pm, we all queued up for the nutritious main meal. Soon after that, the desert succumbed to silence once more.

Km covered 135 Yet to go 11,874

Sunday, Jan 17: Ain Sukhna - Ras Gharib
169 km

It was dark outside. But I could hear plenty of voices. It sounded like the staff were preparing for breakfast. No way was I going to be late. It seemed a little strange that no other tent had a light on. Nonetheless, I grabbed a spade, as we had been taught, and walked a little into the desert to dig my one foot square hole. The rocky desert was hard and unyielding. I settled for making a little pyramid over my pile.

Back at the tent, still a little groggy, I went through what would be the regular routine: put on lubricant, (to avoid saddle sores), sun-cream and cycling gear - all to be done within the confines of the tent of course - take down the tent, roll up the mattress and sleeping bag and lug the lot over to the lorry. Still no-one had stirred. The noise had come from a group of travelling Egyptians chatting by a fire they had lit nearby. I set about doing some stretching exercises - boy, was I going to be ready for this lot! Eventually I asked one of the Egyptians the time. It was 3.15am. What an idiot!! I unrolled my Thermarest, snuggled into my sleeping bag and was still asleep two hours later when the first riders were stepping round me to store their gear in the truck.

At 7am the racers were allowed to set off and I left with the leading group...what was I thinking of??? We were bombing along at over 50kph. Marcel was just in front of me. He casually took both hands off the handlebars - something I still can not do, at any speed! - and started to adjust his top. Behind him, I was holding on for grim death.

I did not stay with the group for long. I could not keep up.

A strong headwind soon mustered its strength and became fierce as the day went on. Ras Gharib (camp 2, map Egypt) was 168 km away. I tried cycling with another small group but did not enjoy it, although it would have been the most sensible thing to do. To make the most of drafting behind other riders, you must keep close to the wheel of the rider in front so as to be in his/her slipstream. But this takes concentration. Each time the rider in front changes pace a little, you have to react. If you touch the wheel in front with your wheel, you are almost certainly off the bike. Cycling so close behind another rider, your vision is also very limited; on good roads this is less of a problem, but in Africa you can expect to find just about anything on the road.

Jason was cycling in a group of five. They had stopped; Jason was lying at the roadside, dehydrated. Jennifer gave him a rehydration tablet and soon he was able to carry on. There were three Egyptian riders with us, good riders. I came across one of them by the roadside looking unwell. He did not speak English, but I gathered he was waiting for a lift from a TDA truck. He looked dehydrated. I gave him some of my water for which he was grateful, though I sensed his embarrassment at needing help.

Everyone struggled. I got to camp about 3pm, but it took me till 6pm to clean myself with baby wipes, in the absence of water for washing ourselves, and set my tent up. The ground was too hard to hammer pegs in properly, so I had to find large stones to lie against the pegs and hopefully keep them in place; this applied to the pegs that went through the eye-holes of both the groundsheet and the tent itself, as well as those that held the tensioning strings in place. It was difficult to find stones big enough to hold the tent still in the high wind. All the while, the wind was grabbing at the tent to tear it away before it was secure. Invariably we had to help each other. My mallet was in demand, though the solid rubber head was already shredding.

The riders' meeting was delayed till 6pm to allow a bit more time for those coming in late. Thirteen riders had been picked up as they would not have made it. The latecomers had still to put up their tents in the strong wind and it was now dark. Five minutes into the meeting, the sky was crackling with lightning and before long the rain came.

We all quickly queued up for our rice stew. Some sat in the rain to eat, some under the tarpaulin covering the cooking area. I sat under the lorry.

It had been no consolation to hear that the strong winds at that time of the year are always in the other direction - the previous year, riders were doing 40kph without pedalling! – and it is almost unheard of to have rain there in January.

There was plenty of time to dwell on these finer points as we were all in our tents by 7pm. The wind became a gale that threatened to tear down our exposed tents. With little experience of tenting, certainly none in extreme conditions, I spread my arms and legs to try to help the tent keep its shape. It seemed impossible that it could resist the forces for long. I wondered how the others were faring in their tents. I do not remember falling asleep. I do remember thinking that tomorrow might not be fun.

Km covered 304 Yet to go 11,705

Monday, Jan 18: Ras Gharib - Nr Hurghada
137 km

Allison, one of the TDA staff members, got up for a wee in the night, and came back to find her tent bouncing along the desert floor. Other than that, the storm caused no apparent damage.

After porridge and a peanut-butter pita sandwich, we set off in dribs and drabs for the 133 km to somewhere near the Red Sea resort of Hurghada (camp 3, map Egypt). Only 20 km down the road, a police checkpoint had been set up; the road ahead was flooded. The Egyptian authorities had demonstrated a great solicitude towards our safety and welfare. Now, as our group leaders tried to persuade them to let us through, they agreed that we would be capable of wading through with our bikes, but they would be unable to follow us. That is what concerned them. It took half an hour to obtain their acquiescence.

The winds had lessened and were generally more favourable. The Red Sea was now clearly visible on our left, the Sinai Peninsula shepherding the ships up towards the Suez Canal. For the first time ever, I averaged 30kph on a day's ride. Riders were now getting acquainted and learning to remember each others' names. A lot of riders came from Australia and North

America. I wrote in my blog at the time that "Everything is awesome. The coffee is awesome. What do they say when the see the Victoria Falls?" Never had it entered my head that riders would be reading each other's blogs, until what I had written came up briefly in conversation. I felt that perhaps it was a little resented. Certainly, "awesome" was a word used less and less after that; whether my reference to it was partly the reason or whether it reflected the increasingly difficult nature of the journey I do not know and I did not like to ask.

Time cycling 4hrs 3mins
Average speed 30kph
Km covered 441 Yet to go 11,568

Tuesday, Jan 19: Hurghada – Safaga
103 km

One of the Aussies was named Dan. Referred to as Big Dan, or Aussie Dan, to differentiate him from American Dan Johnson, he was quiet but intelligent, and a very good cyclist. He suggested we ride together, drafting in turns. We averaged 28kph over the day, but it was clear to me that he should be up at the front with the leaders, not with me. I told him so as we came into the little Red Sea port of Safaga. (Camp 4, map Egypt)

Although we had only spent a few days cycling through the desert, now we seemed to be passing through the portals of heaven as we found our camp site, right on the beach, with a beach-bar to boot. What a contrast to the bleak desert.

You might think that all we would have wanted to do was jump in the water, have a few beers and completely chill out. For a few that might have been the case. But the majority of riders set to, cleaning and adjusting their bikes, (with Chris the mechanic there to help), catching up with the washing and posting blogs in the nearby internet café.

Those who chose to take a room whenever possible had a different agenda. With no need to erect a tent, with a shower instead of baby wipes, power points for re-charging batteries and a proper bed to sleep on, they had more time to relax and could start the next day cleaner and more rested. A few riders had decided before the start of the trip that this was to be a holiday for them, availing themselves of whatever facilities they could find. Whenever they felt tired, they would travel in the truck for a morning, an afternoon or a whole day. When a rest day came along, a number chose the best hotel they could find to stay in, even going to the trouble of booking rooms in advance to be sure. At times, illness was responsible for forcing a rider who would otherwise be on the bike to take the truck and maybe book a room.

A select few slept in their tents every single night of the trip, even when not feeling well. A select few could also claim at the end of the journey to have never taken the truck, having cycled every single inch. This was referred to as keeping EFI status (Every Friggin' Inch). For most riders, this was as important, or more so, than the race itself. We would go to impossible lengths to maintain our EFI status.

Time cycling 3hrs 39mins
Average speed 28kph
Km covered 544 Yet to go 11,465

Wednesday, Jan 20: Safaga – Qena
140 km

From Safaga, we gradually ascended into the barren mountains. Over the initial 40 km, we gained 960m of altitude - nothing special, but the headwinds came back to haunt us. I had been experiencing chronic backache, so I had to take it easy. For the first 30 km I chatted with Dave, a smashing lad, who recounted anecdotes about his life in New York as a bike messenger.

The lunch truck was parked up on a flat siding near the top of the mountain pass. I was both hungry and very cold. Patrick, who later became the only rider I fell out with on the whole trip, generously passed me an extra top he had with him.

I cycled the rest of the day on my own. The landscape which in the first hour looked striking, soon became desolate and monotonous. All that had changed was my perception. To take my mind off my aching back and the overpowering monotony, I found myself trying to imagine the Pharaonic armies spilling over the land; but for the last 20 km my thoughts focused entirely on the soup that would be waiting for us in camp, (camp 5, map Egypt).

I creaked in at 3.15pm. Bending and even walking was painful and difficult. Surely this was not to be my undoing? Why was my back stiffer than ever before on the bike? I could not determine what had changed. Ever since having a disc removed from my lower back, just before retiring from farming, back pain could flare up, especially when riding, but nothing like this.

The first priority was soup, three bowls of it – I really needed to get myself a bigger bowl and bigger spoon. Little things that assumed great importance.

Plenty of tents already occupied the area nearest to the lorries. Some riders were sitting nearby, drinking soup, coffee or tea while sat on the camp chairs. James was busy preparing the dinner over his massive gas stoves, set on trestle tables. He always appreciated any help given with preparing vegetables and usually the same few riders, who were amongst the first to arrive in camp normally, would sit in a cluster, chatting together while slowly peeling and chopping.

I was not interested in how fast or slow I had been, or anybody else's time either. I just wanted to loosen up, rehydrate and rest. It annoyed me that I felt positively irritable and touchy. After some soup, I put up the tent, cleaned off and stretched out. When somebody caught one of the ties holding my tents and nearly brought it down, I instinctively shouted out. Oh dear!

About 15 riders had taken the truck at some point during the day, mainly worn out by the headwinds or suffering with knee problems. Of course, they automatically lost their EFI status. Lest you think otherwise, I must stress the fantastic resolve of most riders. Catherine, for example, stuck it out to arrive in camp at 6pm, still to put up her tent. She would show her mettle in Dinder National Park on February 8th. Paddy, who had hardly done any preparation for the trip, kept turning the pedals with badly swollen knees.

Time cycling 5hrs 57mins
Average speed 28.3kph
Km covered 684 Yet to go 11,325

Thursday, Jan 21: Qena – Luxor
96 km

We rose to another very cold morning. I decided to ditch my camelback in order to alleviate the back pain and to do some stretches before setting off. Thus I was one of the last to leave camp, so it was rather exhilarating to speed past some of the slower riders on the descent into Qena. What a joy it was to see trees lining the street, even the odd bougainvillea, and the myriad of transport forms criss-crossing the main avenue. Now we were following a wide canal. Eyes, tense from the desert glare, could relax on the greenery and the orderliness of carefully-tended fields. But it was essential not to be distracted from the road in front. Coming into one intersection, where the traffic appeared to be respecting our right of way, a donkey and 3-wheeled cart suddenly emerged into the cross-section, heading straight for me. If I had braked, we would have collided. I spurted, just enough to pass in front of him, and I moved on with a sigh of relief. Was it really possible to cycle though the whole of Africa without getting wiped out by the locals???

Signs now appeared for Luxor (camp 6, map Egypt). If I had never been there before, I know I would have had to have spent time visiting the ancient buildings on the forthcoming rest day. So I was grateful not to feel impossibly drawn. Interminable groups of kids, often from a long distance away, hollered and waved to us. Most kids on the roadside, held out their hands for us to give them high fives; one youth held out a big stick and hit me on the arm. Other riders had sticks thrown at them. You cannot be popular with everyone!

With little wind, we all made the 90 km to Luxor in good time.

To reach our camp site, we entered a short cul-de-sac which terminated in large, impressive doors. "Rezeiky Camp" read the lettering over the gateway. We passed through into a compound, which was probably once the garden of Mr. Rezeiky's hotel, the back of which faced our compound. Before 35 years of insufficient maintenance had allowed it to gently age and mellow, it was probably a wonderful place. There was room for the lorries to park in the corner of the compound and space for us all to put up our tents. But a surprising number chose to pay 40US$ for a room - and look down on us from their dreary balconies. Others paid top dollar for a stay in one of the international hotels. I preferred to spend a little on laundry and a massage.

A small bar right next to our tents allowed us to relax. I asked Mr. Rezeiky, a perfectly-mannered gentleman, if cooked food was available; he assured me of the finest Egyptian fresh food for the reasonable price of 50 Egyptian pounds, about 10US$, and if I did not really, really like it, I would not need to pay. It was a monster meal, absolutely delicious and different, though he did take the money before bringing the food! Was that a sign that he trusted me less than he did his food?

That evening, after most of us had been beguiled by Mr. Reiziky's charms and paid him for a buffet of not quite as exciting Egyptian fare, we were treated to a show of typical dancing. One dancer, at the same time as continually pirouetting, sometimes at unimaginable speeds, would re-arrange his coloured clothing to create fascinating effects.

Time cycling 3hrs 22mins
Average speed 28.3kph
Km covered 780 Yet to go 11,229

Friday, Jan 22: Rest day in Luxor

The next day was a rest day. For many it presented a once-in-a-lifetime opportunity to visit the truly incredible temples of Karnak and Luxor. A few cycled the short distance to the Karnak temple. But generally it was a time to clean the bike thoroughly, clean the tent and re-arrange the bags before catching up with the blog writing. There were internet cafés which enabled us to post our blogs and in the case of many to go on Facebook.

Saturday, Jan 23: Luxor – Idfu
117km

After the rest day and a few Ibrupofen tablets, my back felt rather better, hurting only on one side. Leaving at 7am, the canal was on our left, while on our right lay fields of intensive horticulture nurtured by the Nile.

A mist lay over the countryside, slowly evaporating in the heat of the rising sun, a veiled beauty slowly revealing her charms. Palm-peppered small fields gave way to softly-rounded, small hills. Roadless villages, of the same clay as the earth with which they blended, clung to the steep hillsides.

I cycled on my own again at a steady 30kph, with no wind and very little gradient. After about 50 km, I came across Gilles, just getting back on his bike after fixing a puncture. Normally he would be with the front riders. To help him get back to them, I stayed with him for about 10 km, alternating at drafting to maintain a steady 34kph. But my back was stiffening and I urged him to go ahead alone. Shortly afterwards, a group of eight riders streamed past me and I tagged on. They were doing a steady 38kph, which required no more effort from me at the back than when I was cycling solo at 30kph.

Our destination, Idfu (camp 7, map Egypt), lay alongside the Nile. Indeed, luxurious Nile barges were tied up opposite the soccer ground where we were camping. We had been told there would be showers and toilets. To our dismay, the toilets and showers were quite disgusting. Water spewed out of cracked pipes and the stained and filthy toilets did not flush. They looked like they had never been cleaned since the time they were installed. There was another building, where a couple of toilets were found that we felt we could use without wanting to retch.

After soup, I wandered into town to look for a hardware shop. I bought a bowl big enough for a St. Bernard dog, and a ladle. Little did I know how much ribbing I would get for the rest of the trip over their size. But the longer the trip lasted, the less I seemed to be able to eat in one go. So they were really a poor investment!

Next, a haircut. The first barber's shop wanted 30 Egyptian pounds but came down to 20. Further along the busy street, another barber quoted me 10. He did a good job, so I asked him to also trim the hairs on my ears. He took a ball of twine in one hand; there were two ends to the ball of twine, one he held with his free hand, the other with his mouth. He thus kept the two strands tight while crossing them to create a scissor movement, skimming expertly over my ear. It was very effective at plucking the hairs out, but painful. Sadly, having had one ear done, I had to let him do the other!

Time cycling 4hrs
Average speed 29kph
Km covered 897 Yet to go 11,112

Sunday, Jan 24: Idfu – Aswan
118 km

This was to be our last full day of cycling in Egypt, taking us into the city of Aswan. (Camp 8, map Egypt) We had all been tested by the headwinds, marvelled at the ancient sights and at the isolated resort hotels embellishing the coastline. The people, where not tarnished by tourism, had shown us great friendliness. The authorities had watched over us diligently during the whole of our passage, without making us feel ill-at-ease. But for me, the strongest images this country left me with were of the productive fields fed by the Nile, tended by generations of families utilising their ancient knowledge, following practices unchanged for centuries.

The following day would see us catch the Wadi-Halfa ferry, to cross Lake Nasser into Sudan. We had been warned not to expect too much from this ferry-boat. The prospect of seventeen hours on what has been called "a cockroach-infested hell-hole" caused some trepidation. I was so happy not to have to do the paperwork and planning needed for this ferry voyage as neither is for the faint-hearted.

At the other end of the lake lay Sudan, whose Nubian civilization pre-dates Egypt under the Pharaohs. It is the country from where wheat originated, where we would encounter tribes unused to seeing white people... and where we would meet our nemesis in Dinder National Park.

Km covered 1,015 Yet to go 10,994

CHAPTER 4
CROSSING LAKE NASSER BY FERRY

Monday, Jan 25

To cross into Sudan from Egypt, we had to take the ferry from Aswan to Wadi Halfa. There was no alternative method of entering Sudan from Egypt other than flying. By 10am, we had arrived at the dockside after an hour-long slow ride in convoy. We were due to be the first allowed on board in order that our bikes could all be stacked together. As we waited on the quayside, I enjoyed an agreeable conversation with Anneke, one of our Dutch riders. Once she had finished the four-month trek she would be going back to Mozambique to continue setting up a charity there with her boyfriend. Their project was to source second-hand bikes from Holland, send them to Mozambique for repair and reconditioning by locals trained by their charity and then offer them to local people at affordable prices, thereby providing much-needed employment as well as a service to the community.

A number of two-berth cabins were available to the TDA group. The alternative was to sleep on deck beneath the stars. Precedence in cabin allocation was to be given to older riders, so I accepted the chance of a cabin which I shared with Paul, a Dutch sectional rider, coincidentally the father of Anneke.

Our little cabin, though stuffy, seemed reasonable in the light of the horror stories we had heard about. Indeed, there was even a bowl of fresh fruit by the side of the lower bunk. I took the top bunk and we took it in turns to open and organize our bags, there being insufficient room for us both to do so at the same time. Other riders however, spoke of having found rat droppings on their beds. Gerald referred to the boat as a "floating rat-hole".

Up on deck, riders who had staked out a spot for themselves, found themselves progressively hemmed in as passengers continued to pile in throughout the day, many with televisions and even washing machines on their backs.

There were only two toilets for our use, the usual hole-in-the-floor type to which we had now become accustomed. Unfortunately, one very quickly became blocked or overloaded. I felt genuinely sorry for the rider who was suffering from diarrhoea. One member of staff had told us beforehand to take Imodium so as to obviate the need to use the loo. She had travelled on the boat the previous year.

The two lorries preceded us on a different ferry boat. With the prospect of the TDA not being able to cook for us for three days, we had been advised to buy sufficient food in Aswan to tide us over. No one was certain if any food would be available on the boat. There had been a baker's shop some 10 minutes walk from our camp site in Aswan. It opened very early in the morning so we had been able to stock up with all sorts of bread and pastries, many date-based and most nutritious, and take a coffee in the local café next door before leaving for the ferry. In fact there was a small café on the boat and we were even entitled to one free meal. The food and service was good, served from a tiny, primitive kitchen from where surprisingly appetising dishes on huge metal plates emanated. This kitchen carried on serving till late in the evening.

I had gone to bed, as had Paul my room-mate, when a message came over the Tannoy from our Tour Director, Paul Macmanus. Everyone had to go down to the cafeteria. To avoid a bottleneck at customs, Paul had issued us with forms to fill out. Along with the copies of our passports which we provided him with, he had preceded us to the boat. Now we were to have our passports returned to us. Down in the café, various members of the TDA staff sat around a table sorting out our papers, while we completely blocked the café and the small passageway outside. Paul, normally very cool and measured, looked a little angry and frustrated. The Sudanese immigration official who was in charge looked intransigent. He seemed to be insisting on something to which Paul took exception.

We were then asked to line up with our passports for a short examination. Our queue blocked the kitchen and the narrow passageway that led past it to the examination room. The kitchen staff had to push through us with their great platters, all the while smiling. The officials checking and stamping our passports were tediously slow. Another official used a thermometer to check the temperature inside the ear of each one of us. By the time I got in there - I was about mid-way in the queue - they were not even looking at the reading, just putting the thermometer in and straight out again, ticking a box and asking for the next in line.

The heat in the cabin made sleep very difficult. Those on deck later spoke of the beautiful, starry sky that smiled on their slumber. In any case, we all wanted to be up at dawn to see the incredible Abu Simbel rock temples. To avoid them being submerged, these massive structures had been relocated in their entirety in 1968 before the Nile River was dammed, forming Lake Nasser in the process. They now lie on the west bank of the lake, some 230 km upstream from Aswan. While waiting excitedly for them to come into view we were distracted by a transport barge that we slowly overtook; there in full view on its deck, were our two TDA lorries.

As the mid-morning sun glistened on the calm waters and lit up the low hills of the surrounding desert, the temples slowly materialised. In the vast, bleak desert their unimaginable size could not be appreciated. Only as we passed at the nearest point, and we were able to make out the diminutive figures of tourists, could we appreciate how immense they were. Even so, I felt strangely unmoved by this detail in the enormity of these lands.

By about midday, we approached Wadi Halfa. I expected to slowly see houses, then a dock. There was nothing at all. The flat-bottomed boat merely came to a standstill in the shallows at the lake's edge, while planks were placed against the boat from a low jetty. At the same time, a few open-backed trucks appeared as if from nowhere and rumbled down the twisting, dusty track towards us. Having been asked to stay on the boat until everyone else had disembarked, we looked on enthralled as huge crates containing refrigerators and other such wonders of the Western world, were man-handled or thrown overboard to be hoisted onto these lorries. People and parcels were simultaneously heaped up together in an unseemly scramble on the rear of the trucks.

In contrast, we embarked dutifully, dusted ourselves off, and cycled away towards the immigration hall, hidden from view a short distance away, there to be moved backwards and forwards through control desks as the officials decided between themselves who had the last say on allowing us through.

Sudan was going to be very different from Egypt. The change was tangible and the drama soon unfolded.

CHAPTER 5
SUDAN

Tuesday, Jan 26: Arrival in Wadi Halfa and camp

Once out of immigration, we cycled as a group for the 5 km to our camp site (camp 9, map Sudan) on the edge of the local soccer ground. Locals were milling around the football pitch where some sort of military parade was taking place. They seemed in high spirits and far more interested in their celebrations than in us. While we set up our tents, a money changer positioned himself nearby with a small table and chair. He was important to us. In each of the countries we visited, we needed to obtain local currency and hopefully change any currency remaining from the previous country, if there was any left. As we had to eat out that night, the money was needed straight away.

Outside the football ground, a cluster of motorised rickshaws, called tuk-tuks, patiently waited, knowing that we would use their services to go to "town". There was no need to barter with the drivers as the price they asked seemed fair and reasonable. The natural warmth of the Sudanese was in contrast to the feigned friendliness of many Egyptians we had met. In fairness, I believe that the difference corresponded to the degree of exposure to Westerners. The more casual approach of the Sudanese, genuinely friendly, was not a ruse to take advantage of every opportunity that came their way.

Wadi Halfa seemed little more than a village. Nothing happened there for six days of the week and then the ferry came in. Tables and chairs suddenly appeared outside the few scattered breeze-block buildings that were littered around a dusty track. Coloured lights offered an inviting appearance.

With alcohol forbidden in Sudan, we were content with soft drinks. Out came fried fish, chewy meat, and potatoes in a tasty sauce. While we waited for the lad waiting on to bring us some

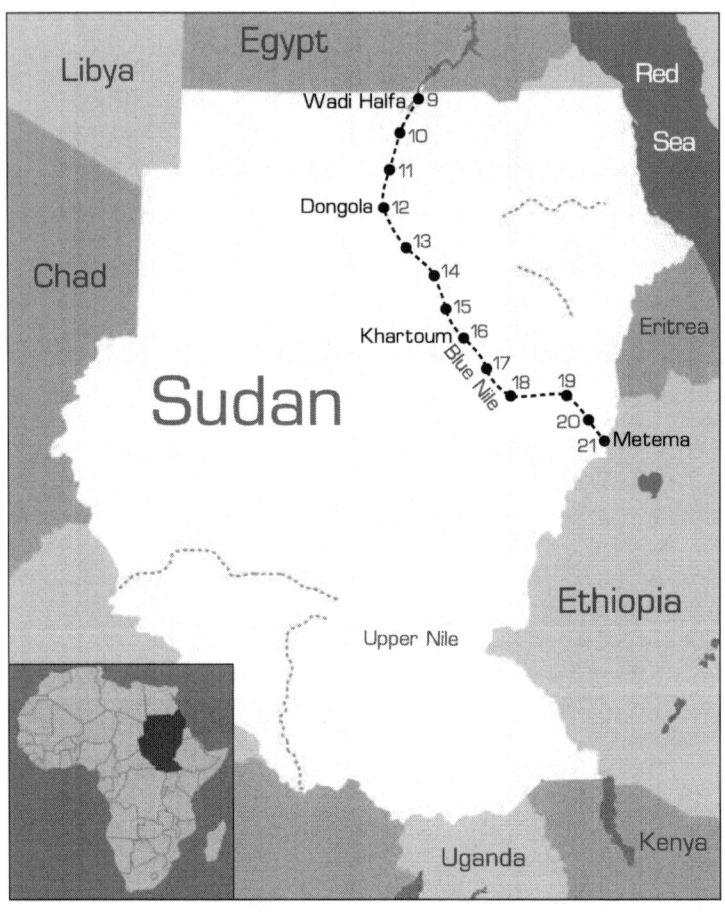

more food, a four-wheel drive vehicle trundled in, followed by two heavily-laden cyclists, tired but also exhilarated at being in Sudan. Meanwhile the lad had forgotten we had ordered more food. His smiles and apologies were profound. He refused all attempts to tip him as we later left.

So much had appeared in the press about fighting and conflict in Sudan. The country is vast, five times the size of Spain. Darfur, where so many atrocities were said to have taken place, lay far to the west of our planned route to Khartoum and through to Ethiopia. There was talk of civil war looming between the Christian south and the Arab north of the country, but for now there was peace.

With the roads to Khartoum recently paved by the Chinese, in exchange for access to the gold mines, the TDA wanted to keep the balance between tarmac and off-road similar to that of previous years. So the first four days in Sudan, which would take us to Dongola, were condensed into three, thus allowing an extra day of off-road cycling after Khartoum. That would be spent cycling through Dinder National Park. We would be the first foreigners to be allowed into the Park. Animals abounded, so we would have to be careful.

Wednesday, Jan 27: Wadi Halfa - desert camp 148 km

This was a most enjoyable day for me personally. There was the relief that my back pain was easing after some adjustments to the seat. The road surface was terrific, there were no pot-holes, no debris on the road and virtually no traffic. We followed the route of the Nile at a distance from it. A green ribbon on the horizon usually indicated where it was, as we passed through the desert. The colours were amazing, ranging from pink pastels to a dense black, each colour distinct from the next. The rocks and hill formations offered such a variety of shape and form as to appear incongruous placed together.

I rode most of the day with Simon, Hardy, Aussie Dan, Tony and Gilles. Sometime after lunch, Dan dropped off for a pee; a little later Gilles stopped, troubled with diarrhoea. In the race, Marcel recovered from having five punctures to finish the day second to Adrian after a final sprint. Amongst the women, Giselda (Gisi) held off Juliana to come first, also after a sprint.

Our camp site (camp 10, map Sudan) was the best yet, just 200 metres from the Nile. Nearby was a village, the houses all similar: single-storey, plastered walls of clay bricks or blocks.

Often with large entrance-doors, their simple design offered a solidity that challenged the general air of isolation. As we set up our tents, a few curious youngsters edged towards us. A girl came through on her little donkey, asking for pencils. Other children were thrilled at being shown how to use a Frisbee for the first time. An older lady with some kids was happy to watch from a distance. Were we seen as intruders or a welcome and unexpected diversion? I think the latter. Any contact we had with local people demonstrated their relaxed openness, wanting to give rather than to take, to accept rather than to criticise the unknown.

Although Nile crocodiles were a threat, most of us at some point in the afternoon picked our way through first the soft sand and then the thin strip of cultivation, to wash off the grime in the cool waters. To relax in the river seemed an impossible luxury, a delight that surpassed all else. For the first time, I felt happy in my own skin and at ease with my surroundings. This was not going to be as horribly difficult as I had begun to imagine. But then, we did not know, nor did the TDA, what lay ahead of us.

Time cycling 4hrs 42mins
Average speed 32.1kph
Km covered 1,163 Yet to go 10,846

Thursday, Jan 28: Desert camp - desert camp 150 km

Each morning was heralded by the muezzin's call to prayer. No matter how isolated we thought we were on any night, the plaintive cry would unfailingly shatter the silence in a piercing crescendo at around 4.30am. Sometimes the voice was punishing and predatory, sometimes musical and inviting. There was no avoiding it, even through the mostly Christian south and Ethiopia.

The cold of the desert morning was no more compelling than the urging of the muezzin to rise and begin the rapid preparation for the day's ride. Yet the heat builds up very quickly in the desert and we had to put as many miles under our belts as possible before being exposed to the merciless sun. I was a few minutes delayed in reaching the road from where our camp was sited, set back some 200 metres over powdery sand. So I had to push hard to reach the group with whom I wanted to ride.

I should explain that it had become usual for there to be three leading riders, behind which would be the first group. A second group followed on, after which came solo riders or twos and threes. I caught up with the second group but after less than half-an-hour somebody wanted to stop for a pee and everybody stopped. Maybe it was considered polite to wait. I thought of the number of times we could be stopping in the heat if members of the group wanted to stop at various times. I decided to keep going. In terms of bonding, it was a mistake I guess.

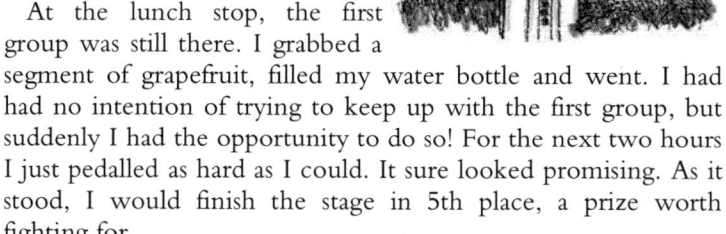

At the lunch stop, the first group was still there. I grabbed a segment of grapefruit, filled my water bottle and went. I had had no intention of trying to keep up with the first group, but suddenly I had the opportunity to do so! For the next two hours I just pedalled as hard as I could. It sure looked promising. As it stood, I would finish the stage in 5th place, a prize worth fighting for.

Only 5 km to go....then they were on me. The first group, in a pace-line, whooshed past, minutes before the finish. As they passed, they congratulated me on staying ahead for so long. I followed them in with a wry smile. (Camp 11, map Sudan)

I made straight for the soup. Starting my second bowl-full, I felt queasy, a bit hot and cold. I crawled under the big truck to lie in the shade. Then I turned over and brought up all the soup. Our two medics brought me over a mattress to lie on and instructed me to keep sipping the hydrating drink they had brought me and to rest. Whenever anybody had a problem, these two young women were brilliant. They gave good advice-and still helped us even when we were suffering after ignoring it.

After a good rest and then dinner, I was fine again.

Km covered 1,313 Yet to go 10,696

Friday, Jan 29: Desert camp – Dongola
110 km

Who would think of visiting a zoo in Africa? Well, our camp site was to be the Dongola Zoo. (Camp 12, map Sudan) A high wall sealed off the small zoo, but the animals inside were all made of stone.

The morning ride to get there was gentle enough. Nonetheless, five riders had piled up and suffered extensive road rash. One of them had made a wrong move as they sped along in a pace line, and they collided, arms, legs and metal tangled in an ugly mess. Generally within the group, there was much talk of sickness and exhaustion, and diarrhoea was now quite common. So a rest day in Dongola was not to be sniffed at.

Crossing the Nile via the new bridge, we had to look for the tape that TDA used to guide us when the route was hard to follow; typically, they would tie the orange tape to various trees, posts or signs. Sometimes local kids would steal the tape and leave us floundering. I would have cycled right past the zoo but for seeing the two big lorries outside.

Passing through the gates of the zoo, it was a surprise to see, in contrast to the sand along the streets, green grass on which to pitch our tents. There was cold water with which to wash ourselves and our clothes, reasonable toilets, a bar and plug points to recharge laptops, cameras and iPods. With a rest day ahead, you might think that there would have been plenty of time. But that was rarely the case.

Always there would be competition for plug points with so many riders all needing to recharge, so it was the first thing I did. It was better to get the washing done straight away also so as to be assured of it drying. That was the next job. Then I put up the tent before washing myself with the hosepipe. By 2pm, most of us had finished all these chores. Heavily-laden washing lines had sprung up all over the zoo, and it was time for food.

Being a Friday, it was a holy day for Muslims; shops were shut till 5pm. A group of us had wandered in what proved to be the wrong direction, finding only a couple of snack-shops. In the searing heat, we turned around and eventually found a café, where we tucked into chicken, vegetables and falafel (fried chickpeas), washed down with cool water.

Along the same street, some of our group had taken over a small internet café, a few waiting outside. On the rest day the following day, we were to find a couple more internet cafés with the help of tuk-tuk drivers, but for now this was our gateway to home and the outside world. The owner said he would open at 6.30 on the following morning. So I got up the next day in time to walk down and be the first in there. But he was still closed, even at 7am. A few people were already going about their business. Several little cafés had opened to serve coffee. Across the street, a man was busy frying doughnuts outside his café. I sat on one of the plastic chairs and ordered coffee and a doughnut. I watched as he mounded the doughnuts on trays; I reckoned there were about 200 and he was still frying.

Once the internet café did open, I spent an hour on the computer writing up my blog, reading comments from family and friends and catching up with the world news. When I came out, a policeman approached me. Sternly, he advised me that he had seen one of our group taking photos. That was not allowed here! I was able to tell him that we had all paid for permission to be able to take photos. (The TDA team had told us that this would be necessary in this part of Sudan and had arranged the permission for any rider who wished to use a camera.) He then became chatty and we sauntered over to a café where I bought him a coffee.

Back at camp, my tent needed a good clean inside and the bike had to be thoroughly washed, oiled and checked over. As we all busied ourselves with these jobs, kids climbed onto the walls to watch us. They were not allowed through the gates. Some started throwing small stones; one struck my elbow. Incensed, I ran outside and found the three kids I thought were responsible. I showed my anger but how do you tell someone off when you do not know their language?

Many of us returned to the same café we had eaten at the previous evening, a short distance from the internet café. Word soon got around the camp when one of us stumbled on somewhere good. The food was tasty and served without delay. A little shop at the side provided us with all manner of treats, from yoghurts to raisins. At least they were treats to us at the time. A tall Arab in impeccable white robes, took our orders and made sure we wanted for nothing. He was, it turned out, on holiday. This was his home town. When there, he helped his friend in the café. We were aware of the many Sudanese who ate out in the little stalls and cafés, so I asked him why this was the case when money appeared scarce. He explained that it was cheaper to eat out; the cafés could buy in bulk and worked on small margins. One of us asked where the toilets were. There were none in the café, he said, but suggested going to the mosque just across the street. That led to some consternation - surely he was not suggesting that we pee against the wall?? He was clearly mystified that we should imagine a mosque to be without a toilet, and by our reluctance to enter. (I thought later of how we should have known a mosque would have a toilet; the muezzin could not chant for so long without eventually feeling the call of nature.)

Km covered 1,423 Yet to go 10,586

Sunday, Jan 31: Dongola - dead camel camp 142kms

I almost took the wrong road out of Dongola. Luckily, some riders were not far behind me and shouted out to me.

The early morning air tried to deceive us with its fleeting freshness. There was a decision to be made. Was it better to go like crazy, suffering the heat for as little time as possible but burning up with the effort, or perhaps stop each time a little shack by the roadside promised some shelter, a cool, soft drink and a chance to cool down and recuperate? I think I had already decided on the latter without admitting it to myself.

By 10am, when I reached the lunch stop, it was already very hot. Later riders arrived there in 40 degrees of heat. The road was very good, passing through flat, sandy desert. Although we were not far from the Nile, very few dwellings were to be seen. I had never expected to find the Nile nourishing no more than a narrow corridor.

The last 18 km were truly awful, like cycling through the mouth of a hair dryer, the body boiling from the inside, crying out for respite from the furnace, with just very warm water and hydrating fluid to slake the thirst. Just back from the roadside lay a camel's carcass, the meat long since stripped away, allowing the sun to burnish the bones. Even in death, the animal proved there was life about. Here was where we were to camp for the night. (Camp 13, map Sudan) As we sat under the tarpaulin that stretched out from the side of the lorry, enjoying the delicious pumpkin soup prepared for us by James, we applauded riders arriving later in 45 degrees of heat. Nearby, a canal fed by the Nile cut across the road. The allure of water proved too much for some, despite the floating piles of what appeared to be turds. Later on, some TDA staff drove to a Coke stop and brought us back some crates of cold, fizzy apple juice. That was so appreciated.

Temperatures soon dropped after dusk, but the tents remained warm for some time longer as the heat rose up from the sand beneath. Lying still, reading or writing, weariness finally took over. But when the calls of nature or those of the muezzin awoke us in the early morning, it was to a contrasting chill.

Time cycling 4hrs 53mins
Average speed 29.8 kph
Km covered 1,565 Yet to go 10,444

Monday, Feb 1: Dead camel - desert camp
144 km

This was the first day on which those who were racing wore scanners. When leaving and arriving in camp, the scanner had to be held against a small device mounted on the back of one of the lorries, in order to record the time. So now racers were allowed to leave camp as early as they wished. Obviously, no-one was about to leave without first taking breakfast. I was the first of the racers - the misnomer that still embarrassingly applied to me - to leave camp, intent on minimising my time in the sun. Eric Defour had set out a few minutes after me and came past before lunch. He usually rode alone, following his agenda of preparing himself for what he considered an even bigger challenge, the Race across America (RAM). While I fuelled up at the lunch truck, the four leading cyclists came and went. They saw Eric as a threat to their race pretensions and determined to pull him in.

I was happy to ride without company. It was bad enough to suffer alone without seeing someone else doing so as well. With no escape from the blistering heat, I could find nothing in any way humorous to write in my blog later that night. The road and the heat seemed to have joined forces in creating an interminable torture. The energy drinks we carried in our bottles were sickly sweet when warm, but totally necessary; it was just so hard to drink enough without wanting to bring it back up. Dehydration would be a constant companion.

When at last I inelegantly made it to camp (14, map Sudan), I could do no more than lie down, keep sipping water and wait to come round. Presumably other riders were the same. I was simply unaware of them, lost in a world of my own. Some, I later found out to my great surprise, had found the ride easier than the previous day. The lucky ones that day were those who stopped at Coke stops, ate cookies, drank cold bottles of Coke and even slept for a while, because a tail-wind gathered strength later and shortened their exposure to the sun.

Right by our camp, there was a shelter of tree branches bound together and covered with thicket. On the floor, old rugs offered a place to lie. Clay pots kept water cool for the passing traveller though we were advised to avoid taking the risk of drinking from them and to refrain from using them for washing or cooling ourselves down due to the scarcity of water. The temperature inside this shelter was a full 10 degrees cooler than outside, registering a mere 37 degrees. As our tents were unusable till after sundown, this was the place to pass the afternoon, venturing out to the lorry for some soup, tea or coffee.

I promised myself that the next day I would carry my camelback and I would stop at every Coke stop I came across.

Time cycling 4hrs 22mins
Average speed 33.3kph
Km covered 1,709 Yet to go 10,300

Tuesday, Feb 2: Desert camp - desert camp
155 km

The desert was pock-marked with thorny trees. The only other indication of life was provided by the occasional donkey pulling a small cart on which would be mounted a metal drum filled with water. Often, the driver would be appear to be a child. From where the water came, and to where it was being taken, was not clear to me.

The first 80 km to lunch passed quickly, aided by a light tail-wind. According to the information given to us at the previous night's talk, we could expect a Coke stop at 108 km. That is to say, there had been one there the previous year. So two water bottles filled up at the lunch-truck would suffice. At 105 km I saw crates outside a shack and stopped. It was a Coke stop and the man even had bottles of Vimto, a favourite of mine. But they were all warm. I decided to carry on a little further. At 108 km, I noticed a red-painted building set back some 100 metres from the road. Strangely, there was no sign of any other rider, but they could be inside. I plodded over through the deep sand to be met by several soldiers in uniform. They seemed as surprised to see me as I was to see them. Stupidly, I asked them whether they had any Coke! Very politely, they told me no, but why did I not take a rest in the shade? Maybe they were thinking my brain was fried. I declined, so they insisted I fill my bottles with water. There in the middle of the desert was a tap and hosepipe. To have refused might have seemed ungracious, so I filled my bottles and said cheerio.

No other Coke stop presented itself until near the finish. It was a shelter in which several local people were drinking. As I threw back two bottles, Patrick appeared. An older gentleman enquired in good English as to where we were going and why. We explained where, and how most riders were raising money for a charity. When we asked to pay, this gentleman quietly, but firmly, insisted on paying for us.

Just before our camp site, we passed through a local checkpoint. There was a mosque and several Coke stops vying gently for our business. After setting up camp, it was pleasant - no, obligatory! - to walk back here a little later and drink in the shade. Some of the riders chose to stay for a few hours before continuing to camp, although it was within view. For some time before reaching there, Jeff had been slumped over his handlebars, struggling to stay conscious as the heat threatened to overcome him. Cycling behind him, his wife Diane was shouting at him to keep him awake. At the first Coke stop he just lay down, immediately fell asleep, and did not wake up for nearly two hours.

A huge finishing flag denoted the end of the day's ride; this was set up by the dinner truck team. But the day's fastest riders, averaging 47kph, beat the truck, saw no flag, and carried on too far before they realized and turned back.

Again there was a shelter beside our camp.(Camp 15, map Sudan) It seemed peculiar to me that we should get the use of this shelter without actually drinking any of the tea that was on offer inside, given that we had our own tea supplied by the TDA staff. I pitched my tent fairly close to this shelter, not knowing that the Sudanese guide who was travelling with us, would chat the evening away inside with the owners of the shelter. Their voices cut through the clear, still air. I could not sleep. I thought of upping tent and moving away. Instead, I loudly asked with as much politeness as I could muster, whether they were thinking of talking for much longer, in which case I would willingly move my tent. They apologised and continued in very low voices. I received the gratitude of other riders the following morning, who found it quite humorous. But I was mortified to learn later that these men had given up any business they may have had from the passing trade in order to let us use their shelter. The Sudanese people invariably appeared generous and warm natured. I felt I had abused their goodwill.

Time cycling 4hrs 20mins
Average speed 34.5kph
Km covered 1,864 Yet to go 10,145

Wednesday, Feb 3: Desert camp – Khartoum
86 km (plus 40 in convoy)

The time taken to cover the 86 km to the lunch truck was what counted towards the overall race standings. But the first 20 km of today's ride were also timed separately as a time trial, a race within a race.

After regrouping at the lunch truck, we continued in convoy with a police escort. For 40 km we wound our way round this concentrated spread of humanity to the outskirts on the southern side of the city.

The time taken in convoy did not count towards the race time, but the rules of the race stated that the same bike had to be used for the whole race, including convoys, except in the case of a total bike write-off due to an accident. If someone got a puncture, as happened to Franz in this convoy, there was no time to mend it so he would have had to get in one of the vehicles. This would have meant losing his EFI status. These worries had been raised during a riders' meeting and it was decided that a rider who encountered a bike problem during a convoy movement would have it immediately replaced by a bike belonging to a TDA member who was not riding that day, without forfeiting EFI status.

For a few minutes our convoy had to wait on the long bridge spanning the Nile, just after the point where the Blue Nile and the White Nile had converged. I tried to pinch myself as to the significance of the moment. Here we were, crossing the longest river in the world, entering the once mighty city of Khartoum, scene of the famous annihilation of General Gordon and his men by the Mahdi forces in 1884. But knowing is different than feeling. I felt in awe, but strangely not particularly moved.

When we did get moving again, we weaved through a long market area where every type of fruit and vegetable seemed to be on display; unfortunately, the healthy smell of fresh produce was swamped by the stench of rot that hung heavily in the still heat. Then the road was lined on one side by an endless line of toilets and sanitary ware for sale. We had not seen toilets like these for a long while and I felt quite envious and deprived. Locals stopped to watch us pass, many shouting "hello", a few throwing stones. This was a poor area, the one-storey buildings looking to be a work in progress, their shambolic roofs a mixture of branches, twigs, plastic and old carpet.

Then suddenly we were there, at the so-called National Camping Ground. It was still only 1.30. A small field at one end of the site was given over to us and we began setting up the tents. (Camp 16, map Sudan) This was the first time I was aware that Jethro, one of the strongest cyclists, and Kelsey, one of the TDA team, were becoming attached. They set up their tents alongside mine and clearly enjoyed each other's company. They never flaunted their relationship though it always raised some laughter when Jethro gave Kelsey the customary kiss on receiving from her, as Race Director, one of the many prizes he won for stage and section wins.

There was a building block where we were delighted to find toilets that were clean by African standards. Another block was used for washing the clothes of the many youngsters who came to stay in the rooms provided. There were taps outside for those of us, most of us I think, who wished to wash our own gear in plastic basins borrowed from the lorries.

In the centre of the site, between the buildings, there was a small football pitch. Sudanese lads were kicking a ball around. Several of our young riders joined in with them, eventually playing a match against them and then showing them how to play rugby. With a rest day the next day, one of the Dutch riders, Martijn, organised for a group of our lads to accompany the Sudanese lads later on in a coach that was taking them to a different part of the city, to take part in a soccer tournament. They did not turn up but the coach did, so our guys went. They played against the under-17s Sudanese national side! Needless to say, our chaps saw little of the ball and some of the older players were feeling the effects for a few days.

The nearest shops and cafés were about a mile away. Cycling there was not really a safe option, so I flagged down a tuk-tuk and asked the price to town. He asked for 2 Sudanese pounds. I asked for a lower price; without a word, he drove off. I was rather miffed that he had not haggled. I looked up the long road and started walking. Just ahead of me, a local bus stopped for a woman to get off. I ran up to it and stepped on. There were no seats free, just rows of sullen faces. I tried to ask the conductor how much I had to pay and would he tell me when we passed somewhere near an internet café. He showed not an ounce of understanding or interest. Then a seated passenger spoke to me in decent English:

"Where do you want to go?"

"The nearest internet café."

"This bus goes to the market; there is an internet café near there."

The term "market" referred to a number of open-air stalls on the wide pavement. Traffic was manic once you stepped off that pavement, a complete free-for-all where you were used for target practice. A couple of times I would certainly have been knocked over if I had not jumped out of the way. One tuk-tuk actually changed direction, not too subtly I might add, in an effort to hit me. Other than that, it was not that the people were unfriendly; they were simply neutral, like they are in most big cities.

I was running the rule over one café when I came across Lani and Andra, two of the Canadian riders. Andra was, I think, the youngest rider of us all. She had a very sweet nature, forever smiling. So we ate together. I cannot remember what we ate, but I do remember the wonderful freshly-squeezed fruit juices. We then went looking for toilet paper - nothing to do with the lunch, by the way - and baby wipes, neither of which we found. When I found the internet café, the computers were occupied mainly by fellow riders. It was to be a continual source of amazement to me how we would frequently find each other in the same places when we hit major cities. I emailed my blog to Susan before walking back to camp to do some cleaning. Oil and cream had leaked from their containers during the desert heat and made a mess inside my bags. The tent needed another good clean.

Just down the road from the camp ground there was a little café. You could walk past it during the day and never notice it. I had noticed it on my way back from town and stopped there for some coffee and incredibly sticky pastries. With a few of the younger lads, I tracked back there in the evening, to find it now lit up with fairy lights. The choice of food was very limited, but we found the fried chicken most appetising.

Km covered 1,990 Yet to go 10,019

Thursday, Feb 4: Rest day in Khartoum

What are rest days for if not a little self-indulgence? I treated myself to breakfast in bed: I still had a banana and half a roll from the previous night. Relaxed after a comfortable night's sleep, I wandered over to the communal taps to finish washing my clothes. Diane and Juliana were already there. A small, poorly stocked shop offered coffee at the entrance to the camp site, so I made my way over there. I explained to the lad jokingly how in Spain a little biscuit usually accompanied the coffee. Smilingly, he reached up to a nearly empty shelf and handed me a little packet of biscuits.

Next to the washing area, an open-sided building faced the football pitch. There were some sockets set in the wall, or rather hanging from the wall. One did not work at all, another seemed to work intermittently, while the third worked fine. While I left my camera and netbook charging, I began cleaning my bike. Our pretty young medic, Michelle, turned up and started to clean her bike. As we worked away, some young lads were kicking a ball around the pitch. Sometimes it found its way into where we were cleaning our bikes. While retrieving the ball, these lads tried to chat with Michelle. She was happy to talk with them until one cheeky laddie pinched her bum, not once but twice. She was very annoyed and told them to clear off.

I returned to town to retrieve a camera cable I had left in the internet café. Once there, I wandered over to an area saturated with little eateries. The main cafés were set back a little from the road with the intervening space, rough packed earth, heaving with small stalls and women selling tea or coffee from tiny tables. The debris was dry underfoot; smoke curled up from the charcoal grills, where sizzling whole chicken, doner kebab, fried perch and sardines cooked invitingly. I stood outside one small café, just watching. On a table at the entrance, a silver-coloured urn, with a neck just wide enough to accommodate a ladle, was revolving slowly. The man attending it would tip the urn slightly, allowing what I presumed to be minced meat to flow out onto a plate. It looked appetising so I asked for some. He grated some cheese, boiled egg and peppers over the top of the minced meat, adding a dash of oil. Two rolls of bread were placed on the plate. After paying 2 Sudanese pounds (about 50 pence) at a desk, I walked inside and sat at a table. I had already started eating before I noticed the two taps and basins at the back of the room for washing your hands before eating. There was no cutlery. It was customary to mop up your food with the delicious bread. Sudan produces some of the best bread in the world. The food was enjoyable.

I had been eating the local food and drinking the water, in Sudan especially, without any problem. Wherever I go, I enjoy mixing with local people and eating what they eat. A number of our riders isolated themselves in hotels, paying up to 150$US for a questionable 3★ standard in order to relax and refresh with some privacy. A night in a room, any room, was indeed a tantalizing prospect, though I felt it was at odds with what I had set out to do.

Leaving the café, the air felt relatively cool and relaxing compared to that in the desert. I decided to drink a tea at one of the small stands, make myself less conspicuous, and just look around me. The woman indicated for me to take a seat; she laughed as I sat down on a stool 6 inches high. She pointed to another which was no more than a few inches higher.

For now, I felt still and at ease, able to take in objectively the lively, local life. For a few minutes, I no longer felt out of place. Absorbing the last of twilight's theatre, I watched the stage set change as many little fires and lights took their turn to shine. I had time to ponder our present position and concluded that, in general, we were strong and healthy. Looking back now, we had become much stronger physically, but so many of us were sick or injured in some way that I can only pressume my assessment was coloured by being intent on keeping a positive attitude. We all knew how important this was. Pivotal to everything was discipline, maintaining as high a level of personal hygiene and healthy practices as conditions permitted.

It was with some reluctance that I decided to head back to camp. I could not afford to miss my sleep. It was to become a valuable commodity.

Friday, Feb 5: Khartoum - desert camp
202 km

After a rest day, a riders' meeting would be held at the end of breakfast. So the routine was to try to have a pee and a poo, pack up the camping gear, put it in the lorry, fill the water bottles and the camelback, load up the bike for the day, snatch some breakfast while listening at the riders' meeting, take a photo of the blackboard to record the day's route details and up and away.

"Remember, in Africa cyclists have no rights!" This was the warning Paul gave us at breakfast. The road out from Khartoum was very busy, with many buses and large lorries. For every driver who stuck his head out and smilingly urged us on, there were many who would unthinkingly drive us off the road. We were told that the road leaving Khartoum was one of the most dangerous in all of Africa. With just one lane in each direction, lorries overtook at the merest hint of a gap in the oncoming traffic. The verge was a mixture of soil and gravel and in places nearly one foot lower than the road surface, which made it impossible to escape without getting off the bike and jumping. This wide verge was occupied by donkeys, tuk-tuks, and vehicles attempting, like ourselves, to dodge oncoming traffic on the road. To survive in this jungle required full attention and defensive riding. It was exhausting and frightening. Time after time, with both lanes of traffic moving quickly towards us as vehicles pulled out wide to overtake, the verge was either too rocky, too busy or too far below the road surface to be a sensible alternative route.

Traffic apart, this should have been a comfortable enough ride. The temperatures had moderated after leaving the desert and the roads were flat, if somewhat bumpy at times. After the 80 km lunch stop, I continued on my own. A further 50 km on, I passed a Coke stop where the riders in the leading group had stopped. There was no point in joining them, I reasoned to myself, as they would be setting off again in a moment. So I kept going and they shouted out encouragement. It meant I would finish in 4th place if I stayed ahead of them. Camp should have been at 162 km. I kept looking but did not see the finishing flag. Paul had told us that the camp site would be in a different spot from in previous years, but as they would try to pick somewhere agreeable, the distance could vary a little from the original estimate. So I kept going, hoping that the lorries had chosen to carry on further than they had initially intended to in their search for a suitable spot.

10, 15 km more. Surely they would not add on so much to the day? With 182 km on my computer, I came to a small town at a crossroads. This could not be right. Pulling into a petrol station for some Cokes, I tried to find out if riders had already passed through. A group of locals tried so hard to help but the language barrier was too much. They had no idea what this thirsty foreigner was trying to impart to them in between throwing cold drinks down his throat. I had to turn back, if only to meet up with later riders. As I left the forecourt, there was Eric D on the other side of the road. He had seen me flash past the finishing flag 20 km back, and had chased after me. I can only presume that lorries passing in the other direction had obscured my view of the flag. After a few km, we met up with Tony Nestor; he also had missed the flag. So, instead of coming in 4th, I was probably 34th! Those 20 km back to camp were into a headwind and I was surprised how difficult I found it to keep up with the two of them. (Camp 17, map Sudan)

Eric D, in the first few weeks, battled it out in the race until he decided that his long-term aim of preparing for the Race across America was better served by building stamina rather than speed. There were days when we would see him cycling back after finishing the day's course in order to put extra miles in. He was quiet and thoughtful, a loner you might say, shaped by the work he did as second-in-command on oil tankers.

We learnt in camp that Laura had been involved in an accident at around the 110 km mark. She was lying in the dirt surrounded by dozens of local Sudanese onlookers when Patrick arrived on the scene. As an Australian paramedic, he was qualified to help. Apparently, riding solo at approximately 38kph, she had collided with a young lad who jumped into her path. She flew over the handlebars and landed on her head. Concussed and in serious shock, she was taken to the local hospital. Dan J and Katja had both been forced off the road and fell awkwardly. Other riders also fell, resulting in five helmets being cracked and rendered useless.

Waiting for the riders' meeting at 5.30, I was chatting to a few others and was most interested to hear Steff's account of her work. She contracted to take problem teenagers, who were either already in jail or heading that way, to camp in Alaska for 50 day stretches. On a few occasions, she would threaten to demonstrate her combative skills when being teased by one of us! She was certainly a tough young woman, though very humorous and always smiling. At the meeting, Tony and I were presented with TDA head-down awards. As if for my penance, I was among the three riders detailed that evening to help after dinner with the washing and cleaning of the huge cooking pots and pans. This was a chore we took turns at. Young Steve had worked up a good little business for himself, offering to take anyone's turn for a few bucks. He was never short of demand; I was surprised how much some riders were prepared to pay just to avoid this task.

Time cycling 6hrs 20mins
Average speed 31.9kph
Km covered 2,192 Yet to go 9,817

Saturday, Feb 6: Desert camp - desert camp
163 km

The day started ominously with heavy traffic. For the first hour, huge potholes lay in wait. Sometimes it was a choice – the pothole or a lorry! I saw Franz by the roadside; he was fine thankfully, it was just that his bag had broken loose. I saw Adam, one of our youngest riders, perform a dramatic leap as he came unexpectedly upon a deep pothole that was a good metre long; he lifted the front of the bike and thrust forward just gaining the other side and correcting his balance magnificently.

The road improved and we could relax again. At the 125 km mark, we drew up to a roundabout where there were cameras, people cheering us and clapping. For the remaining 38 km, hundreds of people lined the road of every village we passed through. We could see them from afar, with yet more running from their huts to see the action. We could have been on a state visit, the reception that we received. I high fived as many of the outstretched hands as I could, but it was tiring.

Naturally, I expected all the riders to be in good spirits after the welcome we had been given. But the later riders had rather a different story to tell in camp. (Camp 18, map Sudan) Rocks had been thrown, some riders were jostled and a seat-post was grabbed hold of. It seemed that the kids became over-excited and if you were not reciprocating, they turned a little nasty. After the previous day's injuries, everyone was nervous to some degree. One of the American lads was so incensed by the rock throwing, he seriously suggested sending a report of the day's incidences to the American Embassy! Obviously no-one had told him yet about Ethiopia.

The following day would see us cycling off-road for the first time. For most of us that meant changing to a wider tyre size. All our spare tyres, fastened down on top of one of the lorries, were thrown down for us by the Indaba staff. Most of us would change our tyres before dinner, but invariably, there were riders arriving late who had to work in the dark. We became accustomed to the sound of a bang on these nights, as someone's inner tube, damaged in the changeover, dramatically burst. Perhaps that was preferable to waking up in the morning only to find a tyre flat. That was also common.

So there had been some emotional talk about the difficulties of the day, and then we had eaten our dinner. Some riders were sitting around having a tea or coffee, others were changing their tyres or servicing their bikes. We appeared to be in the middle of nowhere, though a few men would pass by, and small groups of women carrying firewood trudged past in single file, with nowhere to go in sight. Then suddenly a coach drew up and stopped just beyond our tents. The sight of a coach was in itself enough to turn our heads. Imagine our bemusement when out climbed local women, beautifully dressed in colourful robes, followed by young men in karate outfits. With no introduction that I know of, we were then treated to a magnificent display of gymnastics and karate. The lads and the women stayed a little longer to chat with us, and then left as abruptly as they had come. They were from the nearest village and it was their way of welcoming us.

It was during this impromptu exhibition that one of us noticed Jos looking a little dazed. He had not yet put up his tent. When asked if he was all right, he replied that he felt a little strange. He was then checked out by Caroline and found to be suffering from concussion. Apparently he had been hit by a car some way back, of which he had no recollection, but he had managed to make it to camp. He was immediately transferred to the hospital in Khartoum. Caroline was well-respected for her perspicacious judgement, her willingness to act and her great social skills. She was just as ready to listen to a person's problem as she was to dress a wound. Without any fuss, she got the job done.

Time cycling 5hrs 20mins
Average speed 31.2kph
Km covered 2,355 Yet to go 9,654

Sunday, Feb 7: Desert camp - bush camp
165 km (45 tarmac/120 dirt)

After 45 km on tarmac, we reached a roundabout overrun by a cheering crowd. Here we were to turn left. There was some confusion, as we were in a small village and it was not clear what direction we should take. After a brief stop to chat with Eric D and Canadian Caroline (i.e. not the medic), who were making some bike adjustments in readiness for the dirt tracks ahead, I opted to continue on the same track down which others seemed to have cycled before me.

The rich fertile land now stretched out to the horizon in every direction, isolated thorny acacias breaking up the monotony, but accentuating the feeling of vastness. Some 20 minutes down the track, I came across an old man, some women, children and mules. They were pumping water from a borehole into plastic drums. As I came to a halt, I signalled to the old man that I would like to take a photo. He nodded. By now, the children – and the women – had taken shelter, peering out from behind the donkeys, clearly afraid. Perhaps they had never seen a white person before, though surely other riders must have already passed them by?

I was making good speed and enjoying myself. A while later, I came across Lynn and Gisi, both strong young riders, who had reached there by a route different than the one I had used. They were concerned that they might be heading in the wrong direction. Gisi was mending a puncture. Sure that I was on the right road, I continued till past the 75 km mark where the lunch truck should have been waiting. I now knew something was wrong. Luckily, I had my mobile phone with me; if I could get a signal, I should be able to contact Paul who carried a satellite phone with him. But before I had time to dial, Patrick and Wayne appeared. They still felt they were on the right path and pushed on. Then Gisi and Lynn arrived, followed by Andra. I now rang Paul. It was about noon. He said they knew we were missing and had three vehicles out looking for us. Stay put.

We had stopped where two trails crossed, so there were options. It was tempting to take the left trail. It might bring us back to the correct trail, but would we recognize it? Three trucks passed our way over the next 2 hours, each giving us a different direction to Azaza, our destination. A man appeared on the horizon, walking towards us. He carried an adze on his shoulder. We tried telling him our destination, but he obviously wanted to keep going; perhaps he was on his lunch break. He disappeared towards the opposite horizon. We sipped our drinks, trying to take some shade from a straggly acacia bush.

We were confused and unsure what action to take. Gisi and I in particular did not want to lose the EFI status we still had, and time was running out. Anxiously, we waited.

Finally, in desperation, I rang Paul again to tell him that we were heading back to an intersection where we thought we might have taken the wrong turning. He was not happy but accepted it. Within a few kilometres, however, we met up with one of the vehicles out looking for us. The two Sudanese drivers piled our bikes into the back of the pick-up and filled our bottles with water; they offered us mangoes, oranges and bananas which we scoffed insatiably. By phone, Paul agreed that this vehicle could take us back to where we had left the correct route, we could start cycling, and if we reached camp before dark we would not lose our EFI status. As we rattled along in the truck, we ate bread rolls and cheese spread...gorgeous.

By the time the pick-up had brought us back to the spot where we had erred, it was already 2.45pm. The driver showed us where we should have taken another left outside that last village. A few orange ribbons, hanging from bushes, were quite noticeable as soon as we took the other trail. He also told us that the track we were now going to take was rough and that he did not think we would make it to camp before dark. On the phone, Paul had also doubted we could do it, but was prepared to let us have a go. Andra decided against cycling any more that day and stayed in the pick-up.

The three of us set off and soon understood why our chances of making it were slim. The trail was either very corrugated or rutted with loose sand. We cursed the conditions. The occasional village we passed through certainly had a certain charm. The smell and sight of domestic animals and children running about between thatched huts looked endearingly rustic. But as we tired, they became a distraction we no longer appreciated. Each of us privately had doubts about making it before dark. For the sake of morale, we kept quiet about them.

With 40 km still to go, Lynn was lagging behind. An injury from a previous fall was hampering her. She told us to carry on, but we did not want to leave her alone. She assured us that she would be OK as the driver had told her that there was a TDA vehicle following on behind us. She insisted on waiting for it. (There was a mix-up and she ended up riding in a local truck, very frightened.)

Now there was just Gisi and I, silently pedalling side by side as fast as we could in a race against time, throwing caution to the wind, trying not to do the simple arithmetic that told us there was insufficient time. She produced a tube of paste that she sucked a little of whenever she felt the need for a big boost; apparently, it had many times the "kick" of a Red Bull drink. I tried it, but it did not seem to have any effect, though just keeping up with Gisi was pretty good. (She went on to win the ladies' race to Cape Town, coming second overall.) We seemed to pass through village after village, careering through. We had just passed through one such village; the sun had gone down and there were still 15 km more to camp. Our average speed at that point was about 20kph. I knew I was now holding her back a little, so I urged her to go ahead. I would have a pee. I took off my sodden shirt and began eating an orange. Now I did feel revitalized. A group of maybe twenty children were running out from the village towards me. Guilty though I felt, this was no time for interaction. As quickly as I could, I mounted the bike and pushed for all I was worth. Darkness dropped as fast as a curtain at the end of a show. A TDA vehicle drove up alongside me. Without stopping, I shouted that I was OK and wanted to finish. For the last few km, it followed me, the lights helping me to find my way. The camp (19, map Sudan) was next to a village on a slight rise. Cycling up this short path, I was aware of a loud clattering noise. Then, as the camp came into view, I saw my fellow riders and villagers standing to welcome me in, banging plates and cutlery together. It was a moment to remember. Gisi came over to shake my hand. We still had our EFI status.

Someone brought over the dinner that had been saved for me, while Paddy made me a cup of tea. Then he and Eric D helped me to put up my tent. Their show of support meant a lot to me. What I now would have liked more than anything else was a warm shower. I had to make do with two baby wipes. I had missed the riders' meeting, so I knew nothing about the next day except what we had previously been told, that we would have a fun day cycling through a National Park, teeming with animals, but not yet open to visitors. With an easier day in prospect, I succumbed contentedly to a deep sleep. Perhaps it was just as well that I did not know the truth.

Time cycling 8hrs 8mins.
Average speed 20.8kph
Km covered 2,520 Yet to go 9,489

Monday, February 8: Dinder
128 km

Normally I would be one of the first up, but not this day. There was no hurry. Indeed, I was one of the last to leave camp. A few villagers stood by their huts to watch our departure. What I would have given for their thoughts. Their lives centred on survival; could they understand our willingness to prejudice our own well-being, to challenge the elements instead of harnessing them? I thought not.

The day started with great promise. Leaving the camp site, we immediately had to negotiate the steep banks of the dry riverbed of the Dinder River in order to cross over. There was another village on the other side where the villagers were enjoying having photos taken of themselves, and of themselves and us, and trying to communicate. Camels grazed on the thorn trees. A small train of them was being led along the wide expanse of level silt that was the riverbed. Several times I felt obliged to stop and take a photo from yet a still better vantage point. The setting was idyllic. On taking my camera out of the bike bag, I had carelessly left the bag unzipped. Now looking behind, I saw a trail of items that had popped out as I bumped along. By the time I had picked them all up, I was certainly at the very back.

We had 45 km to cycle before entering the Dinder National Park, home to plenty of wildlife - lions, giraffes, buffalo. What a treat lay ahead. A large embankment marked our route. The gravel on top looked a good bet to cycle on, but frequently we would find it too loose and dropped back down to the earthen path. There were a few falls including one I had myself, but nothing serious resulted. But it was not far off noon by the time I arrived, in close proximity to a few other riders, at the gates to the Park. The fastest riders had been frustrated here by the security police, who had insisted on escorting them through as a group. No doubt they were concerned how dangerous a threat the wild animals posed in the early morning. For how long they had to stay like that, I am not sure. We were told to go ahead in groups of three. With 95 km still to cover, we presumed there had to be good trails through the park. After filling my bottles with the water laid on for us in the entrance lodge, I said I was ready to go and Lani and Lynn decided to join me. Lynn was still out of sorts and kept dropping behind. Lani, a steady but not fast rider, surprised me by setting the pace. I say pace, but we were not exceeding 10kph due to the heavy corrugation and/or thick fine dust. It was plain awful. There were lots of falls as the dust sucked the tires out of control. Would we even make the lunch truck at 70 km? Some decided early on they could not carry on and got in the truck when the chance was there. Anyone with front suspension was faring better, but nevertheless struggling. A TDA 4-wheel drive came towards us, passing along the riders to say that the camp would be at 118, not 140 km, a ray of hope! (Obviously, riders ahead were in difficulty because the route was normally cast in stone.) Furthermore, there would be a borehole at 60 km where we could fill up with water. The heat was oppressive and hung over us like a heavy blanket. When Lani and I reached the borehole, the two TDA 4-wheel drives were parked up alongside. From every seat, a rider looked out dejectedly. The complete stillness was only broken by Miles, the TDA staff member, telling us we could get in if we wanted to. Lani decided to do so. To me, those two vehicles could have been two vultures waiting to pick me off.

I filled up my bottles and wet my head from the borehole, and slumped against a tree. Without warning, my eyes filled up and I fought to hold the tears back. The effort was telling. Shakily, I got back on my bike. Parts of the trail now showed signs of moisture, with palm groves sometimes replacing the thorny thicket. This enabled me to travel a little faster. I do not mind admitting that I was worried about animals now, but I was not going to see one all day. I made it to the lunch stop. Our lorries had taken a route around the outside of the park; even if they could have negotiated a path through, the dry riverbed would have prevented them from getting out. So only the 4-wheel drives were there and I think a vehicle perhaps from the Tourist Ministry. A few desultory buildings harboured primitive toilets and showers. I got the impression that an effort had been made to create a party atmosphere here, which none of us were able to appreciate. A number of riders were still there, mostly those who had decided they could not carry on. The temperature at 12.30 had been 41 and it was now hotter still. I felt totally drained by the heat and the ghastly track. I could not eat for a while, needing to rest. My emotional state embarrassed me; how could 85 km reduce me to this? It took me an hour to rehydrate and feel some strength return. I nibbled away at the food. Michelle asked me how I felt, was I OK? I told her my chest hurt, but I thought it was due to one of the falls I had had during the morning. She immediately checked my blood pressure. I had not the strength to resist. Rick came over to me and just whispered, "Don't kill yourself Eric, too many people love you." It may sound corny now, but at the time it was much appreciated, as much for the fact that he himself, like everyone that day, was way out on a limb, yet he had the generosity to reach out to a fellow rider. He was to show great character in the months to come.

There was always a TDA member with a phone, riding behind the last rider. Each one of them was a keen, experienced cyclist. Theoretically, no-one should get lost. That afternoon, it was the turn of our medic, Caroline, to bring up the rear. She was preparing to go. I asked her to wait for me, as I wanted to attempt to carry on.

To begin with, I was coping, passing Dan J and then Dana and Erin. (I said in my blog at the time that it was Steff and Erin, but I have learned more recently that it was Dana and Erin.) But I could not hold the bike in the loose dirt. I felt weak and a little disorientated. A few times I fell. When I banged my knee in such a fall, about 10 km out from lunch, my resolve broke. I sat under a tree in a small copse, my chin on my chest. I was conscious of dry leaves rustling to the ground around me, falling slowly from the desiccated trees.

Soon, Erin and Dana appeared, determined to go on. Minutes later, a 4-wheel drive arrived. Dan had already got in with the rest. My EFI was lost.

We now crawled behind Erin, Dana and Caroline. There were various pick-ups, some belonging to the Tourism Ministry or security forces, full of riders and bikes. One of the pick-ups got a flat and looked to have a bent axle. Paul had realized the disaster that was unfolding and managed to acquire an open truck from God knows where. This truck stopped to pick up those in the damaged pick-up. Paul advised us to get in as well. Our pick-up could stay behind the last rider while we went ahead. There was already a pile of bikes literally heaped up in the back of the truck. Paul remained on his feet while we the riders sat tightly together. As the truck bumped along, jarring our backs, we had to wear helmets to protect us from the thorny branches that sprung back at us. Twice the truck conked out, but the driver managed to re-start the engine. It was getting dark and each time we reached another rider, Paul asked him or her to get in. There was great unwillingness to do so, fuelled by resentment that the TDA had miscalculated and immense disappointment at losing EFI status. Repeatedly, Dave doggedly refused to get in. Each time Paul, showing great restraint and diplomacy, firmly reiterated that he needed him to get in now, that he would not make it anyway. Eventually he got in. Martijn, normally so gentle natured, was more vehement, threatening to hold Paul fully responsible when the time came. He had to get in. Paul had been a rider himself in a previous year; he knew how important to the riders it was to finish. While it helped in dealing with the issues, it must also have made it more difficult for him in that he empathised with us all but could not afford to let that cloud his judgement.

It was now completely dark. A pair of eyes were spotted in the light of a torch some twenty yards away in the thicket. Paul shouted out, thinking it might be a rider hiding in an attempt to escape being hauled in. He must have decided it was an animal, which might not have appreciated being ordered in. So we rattled on.

On finally reaching the dry riverbed, we walked to the other side where the lunch truck was waiting to take us on to camp. (Camp 20, map Sudan) Our bikes would be brought to us later. It was very late when we ate our dinner. By 11pm, I had my tent up and was determined to put down on paper my impressions of the day. There was no time for me to exchange stories with the other riders, to hear of the falls, the tears and heartaches. I was later to find out that 10-12 riders had made it to the finish. Simon came in first on a mountain bike, followed by Marcel on his racing bike, despite having had two punctures; but Franz narrowly won the stage having left a little later than them. Even they had been out for more than eleven hours.

It was midnight before I lay down to sleep. I forgot to take note of my cycling time; perhaps just as well.

Here is Dana's view of the day:

"We had a special invitation from the government to pass through the park which is supposedly home to lions, baboons, and lots of other wildlife. Apparently, TDA staff has scouted this route previously, but apparently not well. They misinformed us about the riding conditions and "road" surface which meant that most riders, including myself, were using tires not ideal for the type of riding we had to do. Within the first few km, I took the first of many falls that day, straight onto the rocky dirt, and just sat there in a heap of tears wondering how in the world I would get through the day. The roads were nearly impassable and the distance we were expected to cover just seemed completely impossible. I partnered with Erin, a young American woman who is a super-star. Having suffered an early morning fall herself, we were well-matched in terms of our shakiness on this terrain but also with our determination to get through the day with our EFI status intact. Erin, a 26 year old marathoner, has run one on each continent (!) and recently completed her first Ironman triathlon, so she is certainly no stranger to pain. I don't want to overly dramatize this, but I will admit that this day through Dinder, which riders later affectionately renamed The Fucking Dinder National Park of Shit, was the toughest in my life. The terrain was insane, in parts deeply rutted and cracked, in other parts so loose with sand and gravel. It took every ounce of energy and concentration not to come flying off the bike at each pedal stroke. Corny mantras ("Ride Straight, Stay Brave!"), visualizations of ourselves as "intrepid warriors," and stories of our past successes enduring hellish challenges kept us moving forward. Each one of us took turns falling and then pep-talking the other out of tears and back on the bike. It was hot, we were out of water, and the sun was setting. And yes, we acknowledged that we were rare "intrepid warriors who weep" but we continued. Now in the darkness and still in the godforsaken park, twelve hours of riding behind us with more than 18 km to go, we decided we would walk our bikes into camp, even if it took us all night. So we walked, at a snail's pace, imagining the victorious arrival we would make into camp, until the Sudanese police caught us and insisted that our ride was over. We put up a fight but when we saw beady eyes in the distance (which turned out to be reflectors on another cyclist's bike!) we relented and reluctantly boarded the police vehicle with our dreams of EFI shattered. I have to admit, this was pretty devastating. But only moments later, when the police vehicle approached a TDA truck, we saw a majority of our fellow riders dejected, exhausted, injured (and in some cases, very angry with some of the decisions made by the staff) all loaded onto the support vehicle also requiring a ride into camp. Many of these riders had surrendered earlier in the day, some hadn't even attempted the ride, and there were a couple of others, like Erin and myself, who resorted to walking through the Park of Shit until the plug was pulled.

"So we tried to brush off the experience and move on as best we could, but many in the group were completely wrecked. Between the Dinder day and the following one on similarly nightmarish terrain, all but two women lost EFI and a large majority of the men, as well. TWENTY riders decided to forgo the next one or two riding days across the border into Ethiopia by taking a bus to Gondar, where the remaining riders would meet them for our planned rest day. Unbelievable, really, that only three weeks into the ride, twenty folks were either so sick, injured, or exhausted that they bypassed what we knew would be a couple of spectacular (but challenging) days of riding into the Ethiopian highlands."

Km covered 2,648 Yet to go 9,361

Tuesday, Feb 9: Dinder – Metema
135 km (of which 30 on tarmac)

Dinder had been a trauma for us all, staff included. But each day had to be taken on its merits. There had been no time for a riders' meeting so it took place at breakfast. Once told that the day would see us tackling similar conditions to the previous day, many of the riders who had not already decided to catch a lift to Gondar in Ethiopia, opted for the truck.

I set off as quickly as I could after breakfast, with some surprise at feeling resilient. For the first 25 km, the wide track headed straight with a surface that allowed for some speed. Only a few of the top riders were ahead of me. I came across Marcel mending a puncture. How on earth he found time to mend the inordinate number of punctures he got and still remain with the frontrunners I will never know. He soon caught me up and passed with his customary smile. Gilles, Rod and Juliana, all very strong riders, were close by. Our direction turned through ninety degrees as we started to cross an endless plain of harvested sorghum and maize. We completed a kilometre of trail where the earth was dried and fissured, the cracks wide enough to trap a bicycle wheel. Mostly we walked this length. No one complained of the conditions, only of feeling debilitated after Dinder. Sunil joined us; he had had saddle sores so bad in Egypt that he had visited a surgeon who advised him not to ride. So he rode for a day without touching the saddle, then wore three pairs of shorts in the blazing heat of the Nubian desert. Paddy also joined us and, like Sunil, was getting stronger on the bike each day.

I moved ahead a little and was rewarded with one of my favourite moments of the whole four months. Ahead of me, a line of cattle was crossing my path, accompanied by a few tribes people either on foot or on large beasts. One of these riders appeared to be dressed in fine clothes and sat on a cushioned saddle. From the back of the saddle, two huge arches of what looked like elephant tusks but were perhaps tree saplings, reared over the rider and were kept in position by ropes tied to the front of the saddle. I could not get to them quickly enough to obtain a good view, so I am not certain how good my description is. It was such a moving moment to see a nomadic tribe, of which the Sudan boasts so many, on the move. They try to avoid contact with outsiders. Their animals follow the path of the rainfall without guidance, be it through north Sudan or south. They do not recognize borders. Their future existence is in peril as the two halves of Sudan contemplate civil war or separation. As I stopped to witness this scene, I noticed many other small herds in the distance, also on the move. When I asked our Sudanese guide in camp to which tribe they would have belonged, he could only tell me that they were a "very distinct tribe".

Soon afterwards, the trail brought me to a wide track of packed sand. I was able to speed along, creating a wind that mitigated the effects of the fierce sun. Hardly any trees or bushes interrupted the flat landscape, so I was taken a little by surprise when I suddenly found two TDA 4x4s as I rounded a bend. The distance was right for the lunch stop, but there was no lunch truck. Due to the difficulties of the previous night, it was behind schedule but was expected shortly. The fastest racers had not waited around; they had grabbed some energy bars and gone. As we waited, other riders started arriving. There was no shade at all and we were burning up by the time the truck arrived. The riders in the truck helped to set up the trestles and set the food out. Some, deciding that the terrain was not as bad as predicted, lifted down their bikes in preparation for cycling the second half.

Since I no longer had EFI status after the Dinder fiasco, and our vulnerability was laid bare, my objective was now to just try to finish each day without incident. This now seemed to be the adopted policy of all but the keenest racers.

Only 12 km after our lunch stop, we encountered a large village. Narrow streets lined with small shops of wood and thatch crowded the centre into which I cycled and, led there by the throng of youngsters outside, I found three fellow cyclists in a little drinks bar, curtained off from the outside. Cold drinks were available from a fridge. The three of them were soon ready to go. I ordered another Coke, preferring to rest a little longer. When I did leave, a bunch of these youngsters pursued me, trying to outpace me. Some little ones stood, watched and waved. I noticed one little girl cup her hand, kiss it and blow the kiss in my direction. The simple gesture surprised and quite touched me.

The temperature was similar to that in the desert, with only the occasional tree. By each tree I came to, at roughly two km intervals, I stopped and sat down with my back against the trunk to shade me from the sun. Once I felt my temperature had dropped, I set off again until the next tree. On one of these stops, I saw Adam approaching, one of the minority who had completed the course in Dinder the previous day. He stopped and shared a grapefruit with me. He admitted to feeling completely drained. We continued together along what had become a wide, stony road. When it forked, we had no idea which direction to take. For some reason, our hunch was to take the left fork. As we cautiously continued, Gisi and then Reiner, our oldest rider at 69 years old, joined us and agreed with us as to the route. Gisi had a petite frame but she was clearly losing weight as she struggled to hold food down, so her good friend Reiner was helping her as best he could while she cycled on empty. Georgie and Marc, sectional riders who had taken the truck in the morning, came from behind, as did Anneke. By the roadside, a Sudanese rider who had joined us for the section, was sitting down mending a puncture. He spoke no English but was able to convey to us that he had what he needed to patch it.

This stony road headed straight into the distance, giving no indication of the tarmac road which we had been told to expect, cutting across it at a junction where there would be a Coke stop on the corner. Spread out along the road, we pedalled like zombies. All attempts at bonhomie and humour had long since given way to grim reality. Rarely did the TDA get the distances far wrong, so when we had well passed where we should have met the tarmac road, I thought it probable we had all taken the wrong fork. But it was better to stick together – and I could not face turning back. In fact, we met the tarmac road at only about 3 km further on than where we had expected but it seemed an age. Hardy was there, mending a puncture I think. Always a cheering sight, he complained about nothing, accepting everything with a grin. No one else cycled in sandals like he did, with no clips to fasten them to the pedals. He had recently cycled from Germany to Peking with a friend, unsupported, and then on into Russia, covering 19,000 km He was tough to the core.

I made a beeline for some cold bottles of Coke. After the drinks, I struggled to get going again. The tarmac was good and only 30 km of it lay between us and the border town. What energy I had seemed to have vaporised. Anneke saw I was struggling and held back a little to let me draft behind her. Although she generally took her time on the bike, it was not that she could not compete with the best. She enjoyed seeing Africa. But right then, she seemed to be flying and I kept losing her. The lunch truck came past and shouted to me to get in. But I kept on. Another truck with security guards in the back were shadowing us too. With only 10-15 km to go, I shouted to Anneke that I was stopping. I got in the truck.

We made camp (21, map Sudan) in a small walled compound, dominated by a large house used as a centre by some charity organisation. Our lorries were parked outside on waste ground. Catherine lay on a camp bed being attended to by Caroline. She looked terrible. Having completed Dinder the day before, she had tried to continue but had to get lifted after lunch, totally exhausted and dehydrated. (She was later able to look back on this episode as a success because she knew she had taken herself to the limit and beyond.) Marcel told me how he and the other leaders had suffered, with only energy bars to keep them going. He himself had been suffering from cramp and arrived in camp with double vision.

On a more encouraging note, Paul explained that Jos had been examined by a neural surgeon in Khartoum Hospital and although there was no bleeding on the brain, he was severely concussed. He would have a few days of rest there before being moved to Addis Ababa for a few more days of rest. After that it was to be hoped that he would rejoin us. There was a resounding cheer.

After putting up my tent and having a quick dinner, I joined a few others in walking down the road to the immigration office where we had to have our passports stamped with an exit visa.

There was then time to take a shower. The euphemistically-named toilet/shower block had two toilets. One toilet was blocked, leaving the other one in great demand. Of the two showers, one was partially blocked. As three of us waited our turn to shower, Hardy came out of the partially-blocked shower, stepping out of a few inches of dirty water. I asked him how he could use such a dirty shower; with his customary smile and a shrug, he rightly pointed out that at least he was now clean from the ankles up! We waited for the other shower from where Jim was asking how much we would pay him to hurry up. It was a sheer delight to peel away the layers of dirt and grime.

With a little time to spare and having decided not to bother changing my tyres, I walked back down into the village. Scores of parked lorries dominated the centre. The only light was provided by the little shops selling most things except toilet paper and baby wipes, the small cafés offering basic food, and the bars. I stopped at one of these bars. A few mattresses and hammocks, casually spread over the earth pavement, outnumbered chairs. Coffee and tea was made on a little stove, also outside. How relaxing it was to just lounge there awhile with a cardamom tea and a pastry. I could have stretched out and fallen asleep. The mattress was more inviting than my Thermarest.

Hours cycling 7hrs 48mins
Average speed 16.4kph
Km covered 2,783 Yet to go 9,226

The next day we were crossing the border into Ethiopia, leaving us only memories of this immense country. Sudan has nearly six hundred tribes, speaking in over four hundred languages and dialects. So to say we had even had a taste of the Sudanese people and their cultures is an overstatement. But our challenging rides had taught us to respect the harshness of this country, to admire how its people have adapted to it and to be grateful for the friendliness they invariably showed towards us. While this stressed for us the commonality of all human races, it also highlighted the richness of our diversity. I was left with a desire to know more about these peoples and hopefully an opportunity in the future to experience at first-hand their way of life.....without a tent.

CHAPTER 6
EFI

Before arriving in Cairo for the start of the trip, I had given little thought to the idea of EFI. This status was maintained until any part of the course was not adhered to and covered by the bike. Failure to do so meant automatic disqualification from the award. None of us would have been cycling such a daunting distance if we were not up for a challenge. The challenge was lain down to us in Cairo and we could not resist it. But during such a long and difficult journey, where the schedule could not allow for delays to permit riders time to recover, casualties were to be expected. That emphasises the incredible achievement of those twelve who maintained EFI throughout the four months. To do so, each one of them had to cycle when at times they were ill or injured, breaking through one mental barrier after another.

I had lost mine in Sudan. On the two previous days, I had lost my way and expended more energy than I had needed to. But for that, who knows, maybe I might have made it through Dinder. It is still a big maybe. The initial feeling at the time was akin to falling off a cliff and waiting for the effects of the damage to sink in. The truck back to camp could have been an ambulance. I was downright dejected. But the next day, I felt equally driven and determined, perhaps even more so at first. In case the loss affected me more than I had calculated on, I consciously guarded against it until I realised it was not an issue. EFI status was terribly important to us while we had it, but surprisingly, it became irrelevant to us once it was lost. Conversely, in the case of those of us who no longer had the fear of losing our EFI status to motivate us, there still remained the same steely determination to keep going to the very best of our ability. Losing EFI rammed home to us that our motivation had never been dependent on it.

Particularly during and after Dinder, the TDA team were at pains to minimise the importance of EFI, stressing that it was an artificial addition to the trip. They were right and of course were merely attempting to soften the blow for the droves of us who succumbed about that time, while also heading off the anger of many after the Dinder debacle.

Since the day in Dinder National Park was the single most destructive day for EFI status, I would like to make a few comments about it. Certainly, the scouting of the route as to its difficulty had, for whatever reason, reached incorrect conclusions. But when this became apparent on the day, the management did everything they could to limit the damage. Whilst making sure everyone got out of the park before nightfall, Paul in particular had a most difficult job facing down riders whose adrenalin was still pumping; he had to make sure they got in the lorry while agreeing the whole matter could be discussed at a later moment. In fact, the next day everyone was taxed to the limit again and Dinder was conveniently put on the back burner. The TDA had a difficult balance to maintain. They had to admit to having made a mistake and indeed some time later, Paul formally apologised to us on behalf of the company. But at the same time, the ethos of the company is to provide a platform from which participants can fully test their capabilities and draw on hitherto untapped reserves. To denigrate the day or declare it a mistake would to some degree take the shine off the efforts made by the riders. Indeed, although we complained about the day vigorously, I hope I am correct in saying that we all secretly prided ourselves on coming through it.

But by February 15, roughly a week later, only thirteen riders still held their EFI status. There but for Dinder.

CHAPTER 7
ETHIOPIA

Wednesday, Feb 10: Metema - bush camp
100 km

Getting up at 6am, we had to go straight after breakfast to the border control down the road. Each passport had to be checked against a list, three pages long, of undesirables. As these pages were not in alphabetical order, it was taking about fifteen minutes to process each passport. After an hour of waiting, Paul told us to leave our passports with him and continue through the border post, which consisted of a piece of rope stretched between two poles. Hopefully we would not be stopped, and he would present all the passports to be stamped on our behalf.

Cycling over rolling hills on beautiful tarmac, leading ever upwards into the mountainous highlands, this was certainly the sort of riding I would normally relish. The day had been declared a non-race day, in recognition that everyone was just beat up. So no one was rushing. But I could get no pace whatsoever. I was unable to keep up with even the slowest riders. I should have changed the thick tyres back to slicks, but I had not felt up to it. However, that was not the cause. Two nights with insufficient sleep on top of some hard days had not allowed me enough recovery time.

At the lunch truck I got in with Jeff and Diane. They were a lovely couple from Aspen, Colorado. Although they were good company, conversation was somewhat disjointed as I kept dropping off to sleep. The truck stopped halfway to camp to take on water. The clean water that should have been ferried by lorry to meet us did not turn up, so the Indaba crew bought water from locals whose donkeys were carrying water extracted from a not so clean-looking stream. The crew pumped it up through the lorry's purification system and then into the tank behind.

Our camp (22, map Ethiopia) was in a field adjacent to a number of huts. There were not so many of us, as our numbers had been further depleted at lunch when another five riders decided to move ahead to Gondar, by hitching a lift with a lorry. With mountains all around us, the sound of donkeys, cattle and cockerels in our ears, we pitched our tents while children gathered just outside the rope which marked our camp perimeter, watching our every move. We were advised to lock our bikes and remove everything from them that was loose. I retired to bed as quickly as possible and slept for 10 hours.

Km covered 2,883 Yet to go 9,126

Thursday, Feb 11: Bush camp – Gondar 102 km

Unzipping the tent at first light, my first sight was of donkeys cavorting across the field, honking loudly; cows were booming, (they did not "moo"), and village life in the beautiful highlands was already on the go. A few yards from my tent, a young boy was watching over his baby goat. The pastoral scene could easily have lulled you into dropping your guard. Already, kids were on the prowl, looking for the slightest chance to grab something. I was, or so I thought, being very vigilant as I packed away my tent and belongings, but a water bottle went missing. I did not see it happen. A few of the riders caught kids in the act, but I missed the real action: Annelise went tearing across the field, chasing a kid who had taken a bottle. If he thought he was fast, he now knew that foreigners were no slouches either. She managed to bring him down to great cheers, and retrieved her bottle.

Today was another mando day, so called because it was deemed to be one of the most difficult of the trip. (To reflect this, discounted time would be applied to the overall time of the

79

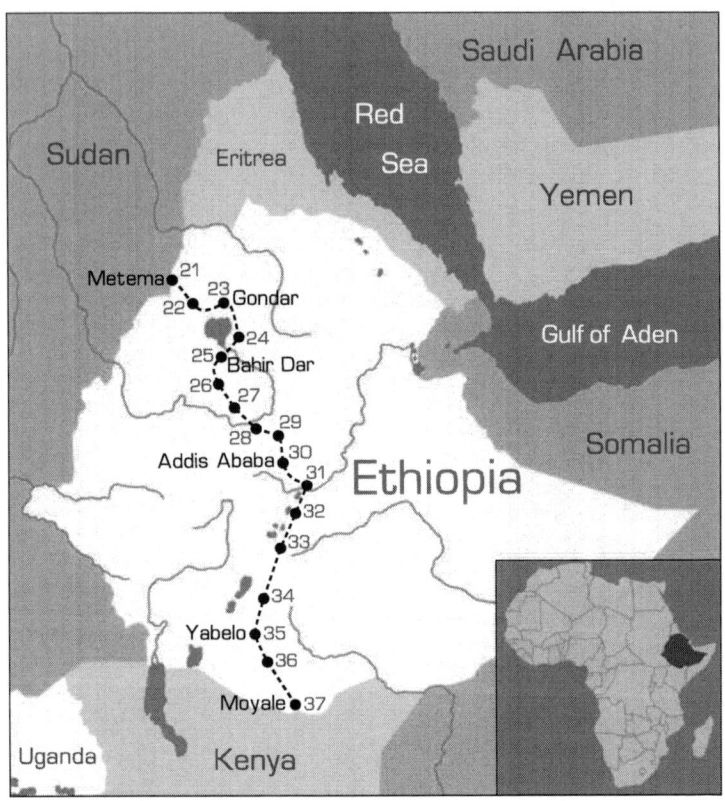

day's winner.) Beginning with a long climb, followed by a steep descent, we would cover hill after hill before attaining an eventual altitude of about 2500m. I felt so much better after a good sleep, but I admit that, after buckling over the previous two days, I was apprehensive of my ability to cope with the day ahead.

The slow ascent gave us the chance to appreciate the subtle, pale hues of the mountain slopes, contrasting with the stronger green of the many trees that mocked the tinder-dry ground. Roofs of thatch or tin ranged over the hillsides denoting the huts and shacks constructed from poles tied together vertically. Vegetables were grown in little allotments; ploughing was with oxen. Everywhere people and animals were on the move, carrying sacks, water, firewood and tef, the staple cereal unique to Ethiopia. It is cut and stacked in clumps, sometimes stored off the ground on the branches of large trees. At some point it is spread on the ground for oxen or cattle to trample on, thus separating the small seed from the straw. Once the straw is removed, the seed is scooped up with large, shallow bowls and thrown up in the air for the wind to blow away the dust and chaff ready for storage. After fermentation, it is made into a nutritious pancake called "injera", as and when required.

40 km into the ride, we reached the end of the long climb, and entered a large village. This was my first experience of the chaotic disregard given to anything faster than a donkey in an Ethiopian village. It was rather unnerving to feel so completely at odds with everything about me, so utterly conspicuous and vulnerable. As we descended from this village, there was a constant stream of people and animals, akin to the evacuation of a war zone. Most were heading up the hill towards the village and kept to one side of the road. Our descent was very fast, through open, even relaxing, countryside. Bignonia flowers, reminding me of home, bloomed by the roadside. Before reaching the bottom of the hill, I came upon the dinner truck, curiously parked up on the roadside, with rocks in front of the wheels. No-one was around. I presumed they had had a puncture or some small problem and I thought no more about it.

The lunch truck was stationed at about 62 km. I arrived with Jason and Jenny close behind me. Soon we were followed in by Eric D and Gilles, both suffering from swollen Achilles tendons. They were followed in by Paddy, who looked all in, and Erin.

Although motor traffic was light to non-existent, we were permanently passing or in sight of somebody on the road or in the fields. Animals grazing in the fields were usually tended by the ubiquitous children. It was most unusual for a child not to shout out "You! You! You! You! You!", (usually spat out 5 times), "money, money, money!", "hello","where you from?", or "where you go?" No matter how you replied, the questions were repeated again and again. A raised hand could be a wave but often held a stone, which was thrown at you just as you had passed. I saw one lad a short distance ahead of me pick up a stone. As I drew nearer, he waved and I waved back with a smile. Once I had passed, I turned round on the seat to look back, and his arm was raised ready to throw. Just giving an admonishing stare or shout was usually sufficient to dissuade the kid from throwing.

I had been wanting for some time to empty my bowels. At the lunch stop, there had been no privacy from the prying kids. Even as I had peed there, they had ignored my rebuffs and made sure they got a good frontal view of me from a little distance away. So now I needed to find somewhere quickly, well away from any kids as they were always so alert. At last, at the top of a short hill, I felt able to stop. Just as I finished, Hardy rode up with Anneke, so the three of us cycled on together. Since the dinner truck had not passed us, there was no rush; our gear would not be at camp. Cycling slowly, we stopped at a thriving village, 35 km from camp, for a cool drink. Quickly we were surrounded by a fascinated crowd. As I was extracting the wallet out of my bike bag, anxious not to be robbed, a mule cart carrying long tree branches turned into the side road alongside me. One of the branches stuck out at an angle to the cart and rammed me up the backside. I realised later, after I had become aware of people laughing as I cycled by, that it had ripped a hole in the seat of my pants.

Laura, now courageously back on her bike after her trauma, joined us as we started to pass through the sizeable town of Gondar and up the steep hill to the Goha Hotel, in whose grounds we would be camping. (Camp 23, map Ethiopia) The hotel boasted a wonderful position overlooking the town and the hills beyond.

Only now did we learn of the day's dramas. Adrian, the 27-year-old Australian vying for pole position, had been speeding through a village at 67kph, and had hit a pedestrian. Adrian was concussed and had a broken collarbone. He faced at least a month off the bike. Also of concern, the dinner truck had been negotiating the fast descent before lunch, when the brakes failed. The driver managed to maintain control by crunching down through the gears, but in so doing blew a hole in the side of the engine. The five riders in the back had feared for their lives so the driver was fêted as a hero for his presence of mind. His immediate reaction was that he never wanted to drive again.

No one knew when the gear from the lockers would be brought up to us. I decided to book into the hotel. I was rather lucky to book the last room available. A clean bed, shower, toilet with soap and towel to myself, private and plentiful space with plugs to charge my electrical items... I suddenly felt elated. I borrowed shorts and a shirt from Michael, my room-mate in Cairo. He was one of the riders who had gone ahead a few days earlier. As it happened, no more than an hour passed before our gear arrived. The TDA team had emptied all the lockers and stashed all the bags into a hastily-rented open truck. This promptly broke down. They transferred them into yet another truck, and finally made it to Gondar.

Paul decided to allow us two rest days instead of one, ostensibly for us to recuperate. This made good sense but the TDA team also needed time, as they had to completely reorganise all the equipment. The dinner truck's replacement was open-backed and could only be used for carrying the gear of those of us who had had lockers in the dinner truck. All the TDA equipment that had been in the dinner truck now had to fit in the lunch truck somehow. This caused logistical headaches for weeks to come, but the TDA team adapted accordingly, minimising the inconvenience to us riders when changes had to be made.

Although we all had cuts and bruises to some degree, saddle sores abounded and a feeling of weariness had set in, the mood continued to be one of resilience, optimism, and gratitude that we were able to endure this experience.

Time cycling 6hrs 18mins
Average speed 16kph
Km covered 2,985 Yet to go 9,024

Friday/Saturday, Feb 12/13: Rest days in Gondar

From the front terrace of the hotel, the view over this city of nearly a quarter of a million people was quite breathtaking. The Royal Enclosure, wherein lie various palaces and castles dating back to the 200 years (1632-1855) when Gondar was the capital of the country, could be seen quite clearly in the centre of town.

I joined Eric D in hiring a tuk-tuk to drive us down to the town. He had been recommended to go to a certain café in the town centre and try their layered fruit drinks. These drinks appeared to be unique to Ethiopia. Sometimes two, but usually three, different fruits were individually blended and then added to a tall glass, one at a time. Visually stunning, tasting of heaven, there was nothing better for a battered cyclist. Eric ordered three to start his breakfast off. I asked where the toilets were, and there was a bit of confusion. There were none, but the staff did not want to let me down. One of them asked me to follow him. While Eric started his second drink, I followed this guy round the corner, up the street a short way and into a little courtyard. He spoke to someone who unlocked a door and showed me the toilet. Although it was the now conventional hole-in-the floor job, there was a flush action. Once I was finished, I pulled the chain, but instead of directing its jet to the appropriate spot, it squirted the water right at me.

The best internet connection, we were told, was to be found in the Post Office building. Before we entered, a uniformed, old gentleman stopped us and pointed at my camera. I thought at first he wanted me to take a picture of him, when in fact he wanted to take the camera from me. I needed to take my camera in with me to download the photos and send them with my blog to Susan. He insisted I put it in this cupboard and sign in the book. Eric told me to take out the memory card as I could use his card reader to download my pictures. Inside, there was a little office with just two spare computers. The connection was good. Unfortunately, when Eric tried to download his photos with the card reader he had just lent me, they all disappeared. He thought my memory card must have contained a virus, but he showed no sign of annoyance, accepting it as just one of those things.

I was in bed in good time. Around midnight I was awoken by voices outside my room. It sounded like a small party was taking place in one of the rooms. It was impossible to sleep through it, so I patiently waited, and waited. Eventually I could not stand it any longer – the first time in a room and I was being prevented from sleeping in it! Opening the door, I immediately saw three of my fellow riders drinking and making merry a few yards away. I asked them if they thought it was reasonable to be making so much noise at gone one in the morning. In fairness, I doubt they realised how much noise they were making; anyway, they agreed to call it a night.

The next morning I was to have the one and only argument that I was involved in during the whole four months. I had gone to the lobby desk and Paddy was there, looking quietly distraught. He had left his bag in the lounge area the night before and it was now missing. It had contained all his money, his passport and other valuables. I have had this experience myself and I really felt for him. Shortly after, I was speaking to another rider about this and he said that Patrick had picked it up for him and taken it to his own room for safekeeping overnight. I soon found Patrick to tell him how Paddy was feeling, but he just carried on walking and said "no problem". This really bugged me. I now went looking for Paddy again to let him know that Patrick had it but bumped into Patrick once more instead. We had strong words which were not pleasant. The bad feeling between us was to carry on for some time.

Normally in a place new to me, I enjoy visiting any old churches and castles in the vicinity, but not this time. I had no desire to do anything remotely strenuous or demanding. All the same, I did have a lot of washing to do and I gave the bike the best cleaning it had had in Africa so far. The staff in the hotel were so friendly and helpful, bringing me out some cloths and offering to help. As I cleaned my bike, a few groups on trekking holidays in the Simien Mountains came and went. I had forgotten how overweight most Westerners were, having had no contact with them for a while, and of course by now we had already lost a lot of weight ourselves. We were to lose a lot more yet though.

Sunday, Feb 14: Gondar – Werota
111 km

This was the day that I was actually hit by a stone for the first time while riding. Many others had missed. It was as if the children could not resist the urge to throw. When the adults wanted children to move, they threw stones at them. When anyone wanted an animal to move, he threw a stone at it. The chance to try hitting a moving target, clad in ridiculous, tight-fitting lycra, was perhaps too good to let pass by. But while many stones found their targets, so many did not that you would wonder sometimes whether or not the throwing was often simply a gesture, like slapping a friend on the back. For a child to wave at you and then throw a stone in your direction would demand a degree of cynicism that I would like to think was not endemic. A majority of the children would wave, would always shout out and seemed delighted to be acknowledged; but answering rarely caused them to stop. For the sake of those who stood in groups to wave, who sprinted across fields in the hope of receiving a wave back and for those little ones, too shy to wave, who looked you in the eye and coyly smiled, you felt compelled to wave until your arm was ready to drop off and answer their calls to the point it became mechanical.

Many of us were by now suffering from fever, vomiting and diarrhoea, the diarrhoea frequently being violent and immediate. Sleepless nights were spent rushing out from the tent without the time to don clothes, and still not making it. Complaints were raised at riders' meetings about some riders not using the spade at night, whereas the truth was they did not have time to. We had been warned this would happen in

Ethiopia, but you imagined you could avoid it with strict hygiene.

For those of us not yet so badly afflicted, this was perhaps the best day's riding so far. There were two tough climbs, but otherwise the cycling in temperate conditions through glorious mountain scenery was superb. Child molestation, ourselves being the injured party, abated temporarily and it was possible to relax, and contemplate a way of life that seemed to have changed little for centuries. It was about five thousand years since oxen were first hitched to a wooden plough in order to till the Nile valleys and here they were, still doing exactly the same. While we used every ounce of our strength in pursuit of a sport, they were expending all their energy just to survive.

At camp (24, map Ethiopia) droves of children came and stood, watching us attentively. Most of them wore a cross, or some other Christian symbol, round the neck. In contrast to the ebullience shown by kids en route, these either kept silent or played quietly amongst themselves. Where possible through Ethiopia, the TDA team arranged for a local to keep them in order while we camped, usually brandishing the big stick that all men carried with them for animal-herding. During the riders' meeting, one young girl was seen leaving a tent. So those of us whose gear was loose in the back of the open truck, took it all with us inside our tents for the night.

Km covered 3,096 Yet to go 8,913

Monday, Feb 15: Werota - Bahir Dar
58 km

Rod, an organised and very competent person, had amused me the previous evening. He confessed that he and Juliana had made a mistake in their choice of tent as it was already beginning to tear. They should have thought twice about buying it, he confessed, when they had noticed the name given to the make of the tent - the Weekender! Now though, the joke was on me. At 5.15am, I had got up to use the toilet before proceeding to take down the tent. One of the two main tent poles snapped, a sickening sound. I passed the one spare sleeve I had with me along the pole until it covered the break and then stuck the two ends of the sleeve to the pole with duct tape.

On the pleasant, hilly ride to Bahir Dar, men and boys were carrying huge bundles of straw on their heads, adopting the hip-moving, short-stepped gait used by walking athletes. We saw a number of small-scale gravel-making operations. Lorries dumped rocks by the roadside for young men to smash into more manageable sizes with sledgehammers. A small army of people, many women, then carried the stones in plastic tubs up a high, wooden ramp, before emptying them into a small engine-driven rock-crusher, which churned them out as gravel. The lorries that came for the gravel were filled entirely by manual labour wielding shovels.

Many trees and shrubs that we pay high prices for in Spain, could be seen growing wild. Palms, hibiscus, oleander and bougainvillea graced the avenue leading into the beautifully located town, bestowing a semi-tropical feel to the place. Bahir Dar looks across Africa's third largest lake, Lake Tana, from where the Blue Nile snakes its way towards the flatlands of Sudan before converging with the White Nile close to the bridge in Khartoum over which we had crossed so long ago, or so it now seemed. (Camp 25, map Ethiopia)

The small area behind the hotel was already fully occupied by tents when I arrived. The alternative was to climb the stairs to the outside terrace on the third floor and join the others starting to pitch their tents there. Some of the riders looked quite ill. Dana had chronic diarrhoea; Hardy was slumped on a chest of drawers looking terribly sick. I offered to help him with his tent, but he insisted he could manage. I started to carefully erect my tent but the pole snapped again, this time breaking on either side of the sleeve. (Lucky for Hardy that I did not give him a hand.) Rick had two spare sleeves and helped me mend the pole yet again and rethread the cord back through the pole.

Once my washing was done, I changed the tyres on my bike back to the thinner size. Now I could go walkabout. I found a small café in one of the side streets, merely a wooden shelter built against a more solid building, with a canvas roof and an earthen floor. I just wanted one of those delightfully refreshing layered fruit drinks. In no time at all, the girl brought me a large glass containing layers of pineapple, avocado and papaya. Being perhaps the most delicious I had yet tasted, I straight away ordered another. Each cost me 6 birre, about 30 pence. Back at the hotel, I headed for the bar. The ornate woodwork and once-luxurious seats gave the bar an air of (very) dated splendour. The barman suggested I try tej, the local wine made from honey. Though supposed to be non-alcoholic, it certainly had a kick. I found an electrical socket, plugged in my netbook and proceeded to update my blogs while enjoying the tej.

In the evening, after searching the town unsuccessfully for water bottles, I popped into a little place recommended by other riders and ordered macaroni. Fifteen minutes passed and I was still waiting, so I ordered a beer. One of the staff brushed against my table, sending the whole glassful of beer down the front of my only set of long trousers. The macaroni arrived at that precise moment. Leaving the food, I headed back to the hotel to change, hoping nobody saw me and concluded that I had wet myself. I settled on paying a bit more to eat in the hotel. I ordered grilled fish and vegetables. Half an hour later, nothing had arrived. Perhaps they thought I had plenty of time with four months to do the trip! I reminded myself I was in Africa, chill out; the waitress smilingly reassured me that they had not forgotten me. They must have forgotten about the food, because when she finally brought it to my table it was stone cold. I sent it back. After five minutes, another plate of food was proffered me; the fish was warm, the vegetables were cold. An insect dashed from the vegetables to the fish, perhaps seeking warmth. But I have to admit that the fish tasted better than any other fish I had EVER had.

Time cycling 2hrs 16mins
Average speed 25kph
Km covered 3,154 Yet to go 8,855

Tuesday, Feb 16: Rest day in Bathir Dar

Leaving my tent at 5am, I went for a walk through the back streets. Small charcoal fires in tiny back yards smouldered in the dim light, allowing me to make out the women who were cooking over them. I presumed they were preparing injera. White-robed figures flitted through the dark streets. Around 6 o'clock, I found a café opening up and I sat down for a coffee. I got talking to a local lad whose English enabled him to field the many questions I wanted to ask. When a UN vehicle passed by, he mentioned that it was a Save the Children vehicle, and then added, "Save the money, kill the children". Shocked, I asked him what he meant. He explained that it was a common phrase in Ethiopia, referring to how so much money that is sent from abroad, remains in the first hands to touch it, without it ever benefiting the children. No matter how true that was, we had been scandalised by the number of buildings and vehicles belonging to various charities that we had witnessed so far in our passage through the country. Begging, or rather demanding, money was commonly encountered, though not as much so in Gondar and Bathir Dar.

Of the thirty seven islands dotted about Tana Lake, twenty were home to Orthodox Christian monasteries. A good number of us had booked a morning boat trip to visit two of these monasteries. As the motor launches pulled away from the little wooden jetty, we were able to appreciate how unspoilt the shoreline of the lake was. Apart from Bathir Dar itself, there appeared next to no development. We soon spotted in the distance a white line on the lake surface, which we assumed to be one of the islands. In fact the islands were much further away, maybe an hour by boat. The white line proved to be a huge colony of pelicans. A boat made of papyrus reeds passed us travelling in the other direction. These are used for fishing and for transport and are similar to those depicted on the tombs of Pharaohs.

The monasteries were different to anything we had expected. After taking our shoes off at the first of them, we passed through the large wooden doors of the polygonal building, to find ourselves in a wide, circular corridor, which allowed us to walk right round the inner, walled-off sanctum, called the Holy of Holies, in which I understood there to be a replica of the Ark of the Covenant. Entry to that area was restricted to only one of the monks. The outer walls of this sanctum were covered by the most amazing murals, colourful, intricate and in very good condition, depicting various Biblical scenes. We were shown ancient manuscripts and tomes, guarded zealously in a separate little building. These island monasteries were used as safe depositories during years of turmoil. Tradition held that the actual Ark of the Covenant was brought to one of these monasteries when Axum was endangered.

Wednesday, Feb 17: Bahir Dar – Bure 163 km

For the whole ride we cycled through captivating, beautiful rolling hills, where agriculture seemed more structured and prosperous. Dense plantations of eucalyptus trees were being cut by hand, graded according to thickness and used extensively for house building. Thinner strips were weaved into works of intricate wicker and lattice, for sale by the roadside.

A two hundred metre track led us from the road, between a few houses and huts, into what could have been a majestic English park. (Camp 26, map Ethiopia) Green grass fields, bounded on one side by a wood, and on the other side by a hill, carried the eye forward to the distant mountains. Mature trees dotted the unfenced meadows, where donkeys, goats and cows were free to roam contentedly. To one side of us, a lad was following five bullocks as, side by side, they walked round in circles, trampling straw to separate it from the grain, which I presumed was tef. Over on the other side of the meadows, men were throwing grain in the air to let the breeze carry away the dust and chaff. I walked over to get a better look at what they were doing. I found the grains that they offered me rather tasty. Then one of them brought me some beans to try. To wash them down, I was offered a cup of cool liquid; I politely refused it. In the face of their friendliness, I felt frustrated at my inability to bridge the divide so easily accomplished by a common language.

With so many of the riders very ill, I felt grateful that so far I had not suffered any fever or vomiting and only a very mild diarrhoea. I had ridden the day at a relaxed pace so as not to put my body under stress. The only blot on the day had occurred during a forty kilometre stretch after lunch, when we were assailed by rocks and stones. Hilda had a dented helmet. Ted had a scarred chest.

Hours cycling 6hrs 36mins
Average speed 23.7kph
Km covered 3,317 Yet to go 8,692

Thursday, Feb 18: Bure - Debre Markos 118 km

We had quite a lot of climbing to do to reach the lunch truck at 2400m. At 96 km, most riders stopped for a Coke or layered fruit drink. Adam was enjoying his drink when he saw an Ethiopian flash past on what he felt sure was Ted's expensive bike. Bewildered as to why this could be, he hopped on his own bike and gave chase. The mystery was soon solved to the accompaniment of some hilarity. Ted had been mixing with some local lads down the road, and had offered one of them the chance to try out his bike. There was no theft involved.

We camped that night (27, map Ethiopia) in a woodland setting. Children clambered into the trees to watch us. When they became too inquisitive, they were chased by a hired local man who sent them scuttling for a while by throwing stones at them. Stones had again been the scourge of the day, with Rick needing stitches in the arm where a rock had gouged a hole.

Apart from a bee sting that was troubling me a little, my only complaints were of saddle sores, most especially on the left sit-bone, and a cut incurred in Dinder that was oozing pus still.

As we sat around the lorry with our soup or beverage, birds of prey circled above, watching for a chance to swoop for some of the meat James was preparing for our evening meal. He started throwing little chunks upwards and with great agility, two of the birds repeatedly dived and usually caught the meat.

Just before turning in for the night, Rick gave me an antihistamine tablet to counter the bee sting. Within an hour, I was feverish. I spent the night tossing and turning as the fever took hold.

Time cycling 5hrs 31mins
Average speed 21.4kph
Km covered 3,435 Yet to go 8,574

Friday, Feb 19: Debre Markos – Blue Nile Gorge 88 km

By morning, the fever had abated but I felt so weak. It was an effort to pack up my tent. I could not have cycled to the corner shop. Unfortunately, this was the day of one of the most awaited rides, that of the Nile Gorge. An 1800m descent to the valley bottom would be immediately followed by an 1800m ascent.

There were only two of us in the truck. I saw very little of the gorge as our transport crawled down the twisting mountain road, content to just lie down. At the bottom, our truck stopped and we emerged for a quick pee. The heat was insufferable. Our guys were now having to climb up the other side in the suffocating, still air. Some would be suffering from diarrhoea and swollen lymph glands. Ted paid a local lad to push his bike while he walked alongside.

When pitching my tent, the other main tent pole snapped in two places. Anneke lent me a sleeve to effect a temporary repair, but I was going to have to get another tent in Addis. We were not even halfway and I had two broken tent poles. If the wind got up, the tent was in no shape to stand up to it. But I was not despondent because, as evening approached, I was feeling better. Maybe I had had a short-term reaction to the antihistamine tablet and nothing more. (Camp 28, map Ethiopia)

Km covered 3,523 Yet to go 8,486

Saturday, Feb 20: Blue Nile Gorge - Debre Libanos 90 km

Having covered barely 13 km, I passed Mickey, an Ethiopian rider who had joined us for the journey through his country. With one hand on his handlebars, the other was carrying a big (say 70 litre) plastic drum. As I passed, I teased him that his water bottles were getting rather big. Only later in camp did I find out what he was up to.

Before the steep climb up to the highest point of our entire continental journey (3140m), we were treated to another 30 km of idyllic, rolling countryside. The farmhouses were more substantial than any we had seen so far in Ethiopia. Their tidy aspect was complemented by perfectly-formed, cone-shaped stacks of straw. The extensive farmland spoke of large holdings, but here and there, areas of about an acre each had been ploughed, creating a patchwork of small fields with no discernible divisions. Animals appeared free to roam. Later that afternoon, Mickey explained the farming system to me. As land was passed down and shared between the children, the holdings became progressively smaller to the point that they were incapable of supporting a family. Sustainable continuity was also disrupted by the rapacity of the country's rulers who could, and did, compulsorily purchase any land they wished, at knock-down prices.

The lunch truck was waiting for us at 3140m, allowing us time to take in the impressive views, before enjoying the fabulous descent.

It was back down on the flat that I was concerned to see Dana by the side of the road, clearly very upset. It was bad enough that her legs had been hit by some stones but it rankled with her that the two boys responsible for throwing them at her then had the audacity to run up to her and shout "Money! Money!" When I stopped, she was trying to explain to two passing Ethiopian adults what had happened. Their vacant expressions gave no indication as to whether they understood or cared. I rode with her for a long while, in case there were any further incidences.

So, back to Mickey. With the ride being relatively short, there was time to relax a little in camp.(Camp 29, map Ethiopia) I started chatting to him, and he told me about the plastic drum. Two teenagers had thrown stones at him as he passed. When he stopped to ask them what they thought they were doing, they smirked and laughed. This so riled him that he chased after them on his bike. Now Mickey was a well-built lad and these kids would not have liked being caught by him. They ran like the wind, crashing their way through the thicket fencing that formed the compound surrounding a house. A big man was sat outside this house and as Mickey stopped at the fence, he heard the man shout at the kids to leave his property. They vanished into the fields beyond.

In their rush to get away, they had left the drum behind. It contained various items of clothing and cutlery. He disseminated them all over a wide area to make it very difficult for the two lads in the event that they came back looking for the goods later. He then went to the nearest police station, knowing that the two lads could well call in there later to see whether a drum had been handed in. If they did, the police would have been forewarned and could arrest them. But the police had all left for breakfast.

So he carried the drum with him for a few kilometres, intending to throw it away. But he came upon an old man sat by the side of the road, and decided to give it to him. This man had a little wheat that he had just roasted and was now eating. He offered some to Mickey. Mickey told the old man how grateful he was to be offered something without being asked for anything in return; so many demanded money and offered nothing. He offered the drum to the old man. At first he declined it, despite its value. He felt it should be taken to the police station. Only when he was told that Mickey had already tried to hand it in to the police did he accept it.

I felt sorry for Mickey. He told me that he felt ashamed of his country. The "give me money" epidemic begs little explanation and is a very sad indictment of the methods used to help these people. As I tried to lift his spirits, I suggested that these two lads had been the exception to the rule. Unfortunately, my words carried no conviction.

Time cycling 4hrs 24mins
Average speed 20.1kph
Km covered 3,613 Yet to go 8,396

Sunday, Feb 21: Debre - Addis Ababa
104 km

Long, slow climbs and fast descents led us through some of the best scenery so far. Bananas and papayas competed within the rampant growth of lush forests, where simple dwellings in the smallest of clearings looked in danger of being swallowed up. Not seen for a while, here again were the round thatched dwellings, grouped together on the hillsides, blending beautifully with the browns and mauves of the surrounding fields. Sometimes travel writers unfairly romanticise the areas they pass through, thus provoking envy in the reader. But it would be difficult to overstate the breathtaking beauty before us and the balance between man and nature that one would like to think prevailed.

At 92 km, the TDA vehicles waited for us all at the top of a hill from where we could see Addis Ababa. We waited for the last riders before starting the hectic convoy into the city. There had been increasing excitement amongst the riders at the prospect of using facilities every city has to offer: apart from internet, there was the promise of a variety of food, ice creams, milkshakes, chocolate and so many other items whose existence we had not forgotten about.

Laura had worked for two years in Addis and gave us many tips on where to eat and shop. Quite a number had pre-booked into hotels, one of them being the opulent Sheraton. The general mood was "I have suffered long enough for now. I am dirty, tired and sick, so I am going to spoil myself as much as I am able." My main priority was to find another tent. Surely that was not asking too much.

The convoy down into the city was faster and less controlled than usual. We cycled in to the grounds of a small hotel where we had permission to pitch our tents on the grass. (Camp 30, map Ethiopia) The hotel had no guests and there were no facilities other than toilets, laundry and showers. Nobody seemed to know whether the hotel was closed or just short of clients. A number of us had stripped off for a shower only to find that there was no water. We came to the conclusion that our crew were filling up the water tanker. Sure enough, within a few minutes the water resumed. There was no hot water, but that no longer bothered us too much.

I engaged a taxi to take me to a mall where I had been told I would find a tent shop. This turned out not to be the case, but I did find the funky Lime Tree café, where they served marvellous fresh food, coffee out of this world, matched by the most divine chocolate cake. Nowhere in Africa did we drink coffee to match that in Ethiopia, for which we might have had the Italians to thank. I spent time fruitlessly looking in other malls before going back to the café for more of the same.

Km covered 3,717 Yet to go 8,292

Monday, Feb 22: Rest day in Addis Ababa

I had to get up at 6am with some urgency, and run to the bathroom. I was to be so grateful that this did not develop into full-blown diarrhoea, as I had a lot to do. The inside of the tent and my Thermarest were minging and had to be cleaned and sanitised. Over at the laundry area, there were several taps and basins, but a little old lady wished to use them herself to wash riders' clothes and charge a modest fee. So I left my laundry with her.

Marcel, Lynn, Anneke and I took a short walk up the busy road for a light breakfast. The café we chose was almost empty, but clean, and close to a Western standard. With no need to rush, the simple pleasure of enjoying omelette, cake and coffee with fellow riders was such that I wanted to laugh out loud.

I left them to go tent-hunting, hoping also to find a small pillow and a thin mattress to supplement my Thermarest. Trying yet another mall, I was again unsuccessful. But there was a barber's shop where for 50 birre, about £5, I had a shave, hair wash and haircut. The well-spoken owner suggested I look for a tent in the mall that he believed to be the biggest in Addis, where I would find all kinds of camping accessories. This mall turned out to be no bigger than a normal Tesco supermarket in the UK, but I did find a tent. The choice was limited to just one Italian manufacturer, with two sizes available. For 800 birre I bought the three man tent size. I was not expecting visitors, but I found my two man tent rather tight for room. It looked the part, but how waterproof it would prove to be was something I could only guess at. I would continue with the

Vaude tent for as long as humanly possible, keeping the new one in reserve.

Several visits to internet cafés had brought me up to date with my blogs and the state of the outside world. Just along from the Friendship Internet café, I found a small supermarket selling goods I was familiar with, like ginger biscuits and fig rolls. It seemed sensible to add these to my diet. Whenever possible after Addis, I would buy biscuits, enough to make sure I could nibble away in camp before dinner and also treat myself to some before sleeping. We had all come to realise that it was virtually impossible to overeat. Of all of us, Sunil was perhaps the most fervent disciple of the confectionery God. Of Kenyan extraction, he was looking forward immensely to our rest day in Nairobi as he still had family there. They would stock him up with all the goodies he craved.

Taking another taxi, I asked the driver did he know where I could find a mattress and pillow. He was sincere and for two hours he drove me around the congested city, pointing out the extravagant mansions of the President, the Prime Minister and the Minister for Foreign Affairs, alongside the clean and tidy hovels of the city's worst slum area nearby, and in between, when he was not stopping to put water in the car's radiator, we dropped into various shops that were either getting a mattress in, had just sold the last one or could order one for me. By the time he dropped me back at the camp, still without the mattress, I felt like I had finished another hard day's riding.

Addis was the end of one of TDA's sections. Marc and Georgie had become a popular couple during the time they cycled with us on that section. The first time I had met them was on the road to Dinder. During the trip, they became engaged. Now they were leaving us. Amongst those joining us in Addis were Viv and Jerry from Manchester. They would stay with us all the way to Windhoek.

Tuesday, Feb 23: Addis Ababa - Koka
99 km

In convoy, we headed for the city outskirts. The roads were crowded with lorries and buses, spurting out great clouds of thick black smoke, like giant aerosols. But we were back on flat roads and soon able to enjoy fast riding once more.

Before lunch, I cycled with Rod and Juliana. They always rode together, an inseparable pair, always near the front. As well-organised, careful and considerate, experienced cyclists, they were great to cycle with if you could keep up with them. Invariably, when I reached camp they would already be sitting around with others, taking soup or drinking coffee or helping James to prepare vegetables. But there was always a smile and a welcome from them for riders coming in after them.

Simon was a different type of rider, very much a mountain biker. Although English, he lived in Johannesburg, where he was happy. We cycled together after lunch. I felt like we were bombing along. I was thrilled to be approaching a region blessed with lakes. The availability of water was already apparent in the number of large-scale horticultural enterprises we were seeing. Fields of strawberries, melons and vegetables, huge complexes of greenhouses for the growing of flowers, all combined to overturn my previous notions of Ethiopia as a completely dry country.

It was still only noon when we reached camp; as we pulled off the road, I just gaped. The most beautiful lake lay before us, its calm waters edged by low hills. Cattle stood knee deep in the shallows; further across, red flamingoes stood like silent sentinels. A hundred meters back from the water's edge, our tents were proliferating on the sandy bank. A flock of marabou storks congregated around two large fig trees nearby. They would strut around like absent-minded professors, as if unsure of their footing, before taking a few quick steps to metamorphose into immense, utterly graceful gliders.

We were now in the Rift Valley. Of the lakes in the region, only one could be said to be free from bilharzia and crocodiles. This, we were told, was not that lake. Unknown to me at the time, the waters had also become severely polluted by chemicals and heavy metals, discharged by small-scale factories producing anything from soap to plastic and by the largely government-owned flower and horticultural enterprises. The thousands of people who depended on the waters of the lake for fishing, for drinking, washing and cooking, were now subject to many illnesses not previously seen. The few local individuals who we saw nearby did not display any sign of health or happiness. I now understand why. (Camp 31, map Ethiopia)

Ignorant of all this I had pitched my tent so that I could lie down and face the view. What a lovely thought that it would still be there in the morning when I unzipped the tent flap.

Time cycling 3hrs 34mins
Average speed 27.8kph
Km covered 3,816 Yet to go 8,193

If you would be interested to learn a little more about the circumstances surrounding the lake's problems, I suggest looking at www.EthiopianReview.com

Wednesday, Feb 24: Lake Koka - Lake Langano 111 km

We breakfasted as the sun climbed from behind the mountains on the far side of the lake. The silent waters slowly changed to an unnatural shade of violet. The sun reached above the mountaintop, its rays skimming over the water's surface. Lines like pencil marks traced the movement of the odd water-fowl and a couple of fishing-boats, daring to scratch the polished surface.

No one was in a hurry, knowing the day ahead was relatively easy and the temperatures, as they had been for a week, perfect for cycling. Already, at 7am, there was an enormous, eye-catching array of fruit and vegetables set up on a stall by the roadside. I wondered who was going to buy it all. All through the day we would see very small stalls, selling either tomatoes or small onions.

We soon left the irrigated area behind us as we passed through open farmland and savannah, the acacia once again the predominant species. Stone-throwing seemed almost a thing of the past.

Two kilometres before our final destination (camp 32, map Ethiopia), orange ribbons were the signal for us to turn left off the road onto a rough track, at the end of which lay the shoreline of Lake Langano. This volcanic lake bore the colour of red clay. The blue-coloured Arsi Mountains, that towered up to 4000 metres, formed an impressive backdrop. The abundance of bird life in the area was a big draw for keen ornithologists. But the lake itself, all three hundred square kilometres of it, was free of bilharzia and presumably of crocodiles too. Riders were soon frolicking in the murky water, made buoyant by the high concentration of soda. I had been so indoctrinated into believing that no freshwater in Africa was safe from disease or parasites, that I could but watch. In any case, if something is coming for me, I like to be able to see it.

Those of us who wished to do so were being given the chance to talk a little to the group about the charity we were riding for. I gave my name in and for a few minutes before dinner, I talked about Thamsanqa. I was surprised that Anneke was the only other person to volunteer. Riders were supporting an amazing mix of important charities and I would have liked to have heard more about them, in detail.

This was the day I decided to hand back my scanner. Remembering to scan in and out each day had become a chore which I sometimes forgot to do anyway. It would be easier to pace myself without any thoughts of competition. The daunting days of North Kenya were approaching and it seemed sensible to prepare. My greatest worry was how to heal the saddle sores before then. They just would not go away, and they made sitting down most uncomfortable.

Time cycling 3hrs 57mins
Average speed 28.1kph
Km covered 3,927   Yet to go 8,082

Thursday, Feb 25: Lake Langano - bush camp 131 km

The ride was more hilly now and saw a return of the kids. The girl riders in particular disliked Ethiopian hill-climbing. Unable to ride fast up the gradients, they were easy prey for any kid with mischief in mind. Normally, a hand on the back, or on the seat, was an offer to help you up the hill. However, as we had been warned, it was also a common excuse to rifle through the bike bag while pushing. Many a kind kid was shouted at for what was probably meant to be a helpful gesture.

A few of us stopped at 100 km for a soft drink (4 birre). A young lad tempted us with a plate of mangoes, beautifully presented on a clean plate. They were irresistible, as was the price of 2 birre each.

Each evening between four and five o'clock, either Caroline or Michele held a clinic for anyone needing attention. The clinic was held in the lunch truck. I went about my saddle sores and Caroline told me that I had an abscess. She asked me not to ride for two days, and if I was lucky, the antibiotics she prescribed me would obviate the need to lance it.

Adrian, we were told, had returned to Australia in order to have his broken collarbone properly pinned. He was hoping to return at a later stage but we never saw him again. Now Marcel joined the list of wounded. He had been involved in a collision and had badly sprained his wrist. No one defined stamina, determination and improvisation, all wrapped up in a misleadingly easy manner, more so than he did. Not to be able to cycle, and to be out of the race he had given his all for, must have been hard to take. But his attitude and manner in no way betrayed his feelings. Eric D, who had pushed himself to the limit in order to win the time trial ascending the Blue Nile Gorge, was finding it difficult to eat; his appetite had vanished. He just kept going. Gilles had not ridden for a week, due to continuing sickness and diarrhoea, compounded by an Achilles' Heel problem. We had left him in Addis Ababa, pondering his future. We never saw him again.

On no other evening had we seen so many people, of all ages, watching us from behind the ropes, ringside if you like. I guessed there to be about three hundred, packed three or four deep. Some of our younger lads engaged with them, trying to show them how to do a Mexican wave. They had no idea what was being expected of them, but both they and ourselves were highly amused at their attempts.

We had seen no rain since Egypt. That was now about to change. (Camp 33, map Ethiopia)

Km covered 4,058   Yet to go 7,951

Friday, Feb 26: Bush camp - bush camp
106 km

The rain started at about 3am and never stopped until late morning. During the night, a couple of riders found their tents were leaking and had to evacuate them. Packing your tent away in wet conditions is not so bad as you might think; the inside should still be dry when you next unfold it. But if you are trying to pack away your tent in the rain with the use of only one arm, then you have a problem. This was the case with Marcel, whose tent was pitched near to mine. He did not ask for help, but was grateful for it.

As the riders pushed off in the rain, I helped the crew, by which I mean both the TDA team and the Indaba staff, to pack away. Everything had its place, and everyone pulled together. No rubbish was ever left. Every night at camp, we had three bins: one was for organic material, which was buried, another for burnables and a third for unburnables. These latter two were disposed of at appropriate locations, although locals found a use for most of what we would consider rubbish. Even as the second lorry began to leave, it was common to see locals start to scour the site for anything we had overlooked. Any leftover food was offered to locals rather than just being thrown away.

This was another mando day, involving 2000 metres of climbing through stunning, lush, green hill country. Cannas, daturas and a few poinsettias brightened the day for us. The mountain bikers were enjoying themselves in the wet conditions. Michael, however, had quite a fall, incurring considerable road rash. Stuart was involved in a nasty incident. Entering one of the villages at speed, he saw two men ahead, talking in the middle of the road. He shouted while keeping to a definite line. Unfortunately, one of the men went the wrong way and Stuart drove straight into him. Although his helmet was broken and he suffered plenty of cuts and bruises, Stuart himself suffered no broken bones. There was no time to gauge the injured man's condition as his companion grabbed the bike, threw it to one side, and started to aim kick-boxing blows at Stuart. Another rider drew up and extricated him. Franz took the stage despite still not having fully recovered from diarrhoea. He also had a nasty, festering scrape on his leg that would not heal despite taking antibiotics. (Back in Luxor, there had been an open man-hole in the pavement, into which he had stumbled.) Gisi took the ladies' first place, beginning to look invincible. (Camp 34, map Ethiopia)

While eating our dinner, two soldiers with semi-automatic weapons, patrolled our rope "border". This was the only time we were given this level of protection. It seemed so utterly over-the-top, ridiculous.... these were just villagers. The absurdity of it all was magnified in comic fashion as a soldier and a youth started fighting. When the second soldier came over to help his partner, the youth broke off to run away; the first soldier started to chase, decided against it but instead picked up and threw a dry piece of dung. I guess it was the next best thing to a stone.

To loud cheers, Paul told us at the riders' meeting that this would likely be the last night a rope would be necessary to cordon us off from our neighbours. With Kenya but a few days away, he was hopeful that we would follow the pattern of previous years and leave sickness and diarrhoea behind us in Ethiopia. Patterns change. Dream on.

Km covered 4,164 Yet to go 7,845

Saturday, Feb 27: Bush camp – Yabelo
120 km

The truck being used as a replacement for the lunch truck had open sides and allowed those of us travelling within to gaze out over the spectacular, forested hillsides. Later, forest gave way to savannah where termite mounds of up to 3 meters and more were more prevalent than vegetation.

60 km down the road, we pulled off for lunch. The five of us riding inside the truck now helped the two Indaba crew to set up the trestles and prepare the food. Buns had to be sliced open, tomatoes and pineapples cut into pieces and avocados de-stoned. But the treat for the day was to be fried eggs. Janet was the member of the Indaba crew who took control of lunches; she had 350 eggs ready to fry. Soon the leading riders raced in, and for a full two hours riders came and went. All the while, Janet was frying these eggs. Riders visibly perked up at being told they were allowed up to four eggs each.

This region was lightly populated, and we saw only a few locals. Five cows followed by two young children appeared as if from nowhere. As the children stopped to watch us, two of the cows reached up to a termite mound, not to eat the insects as we supposed, but to lick the salt produced as a by-product of the termite activity. A grey cockatoo with a white beard settled on the higher branches of the tree we were using for shade; the sun had banished the rain for now. Masked weavers, waxbills and starlings, their feathers a glossy blue, darted about us.

It was clear from his torn shorts that Sunil had taken a bad fall. Cycling at a very high speed, a series of large potholes took him by surprise. He avoided the first few before his bike hit a particularly deep one. He went flying over the handlebars. Though he escaped with no serious injury, both wheels were buckled and the left-hand side crank was bent. Hardy helped him to loosen off the brakes, allowing the wheels to move again. He would have to order new bike parts to be sent to Nairobi, but for now Paul did his best to keep him mobile.

It was the turn of Sharita, the assistant Tour director, to bring up the rear. A few years back, she had ridden solo through

Africa. She was a young woman of great character with a sense of humour and an indefatigable spirit. We were surprised to hear that a lorry had forced her into a ditch. Really, it was impossible to keep up with all the action. Naturally, we were encouraged not to dwell in our blogs about accidents and injuries and frankly, they were so common as no longer to be considered hot news.

The simple motel where we camped (35, map Ethiopia), just outside the town of Yabelo, was one of only a few buildings and shacks near the main track. It offered some very basic rooms for an average of £7, the cheapest costing as little as £4. They were all quickly snapped up as the rain continued. A small garden, which on a nice day might have been attractive given the variety of fruit trees that shaded the small squares of grass, just about allowed those of us who were camping enough room to pitch our tents on the already sodden ground. The motel's one public room had a small desk across one corner. The lady behind it appeared to have control over the orders for food and drink that a few waiters brought from the other side of the garden. They worked hard but it was all a bit confusing as they struggled to keep up with the sudden tourist tsunami. The waiters did not always return with the change from the money you gave them, but I felt that this was largely due to the pressure of the work.

With grey skies, heavier rain forecast, a complete absence of internet and places to eat or to visit, the rest day looked like being exactly that. But Africa can always surprise you. A TV was rigged up and attached to a tree in the garden and suddenly we were reminded that it was Saturday as a Premier League football match between Chelsea and Manchester City lit up the gloom. It no longer mattered quite so much that the waiter seemed to have forgotten my hamburger, which, when it did arrive, proved particularly scrumptious. The football was followed by the England v. Ireland rugby international, which divided the camp; all the non-English rendered their support to Paddy, Ireland's only representative amongst us.

I saw Caroline again that night. She said she had been worried two days earlier when she had seen my abscess, and had been wondering where she could get hold of a surgeon if it became necessary. But the antibiotics must have been working as she was amazed at the improvement. She expected me to be able to get back on the bike after the rest day.

The few shacks that denoted the street, offered a variety of basic items. Simple, sweet biscuits in small packets were obviously popular throughout all central African countries. I replenished my depleted stock. I looked inside one little shack and was taken aback at the sight of a couple of our riders sat down on benches in a tiny room with locals, all chewing leaves of the chat plant, sometimes referred to as khat or gat. These leaves contain an amphetamine-type stimulant, said to cause excitement, loss of appetite and euphoria - all commendable aims while in Yabelo I decided. Judging by the grins, they had been at it for a while. These leaves were big business, increasingly consuming valuable agricultural and water resources. High prices could be obtained for the right quality; the leaves had to be fresh and turgid.

The thunder rolled as I lay in my tent about 10pm, followed by a heavy downpour. I remained dry, cocooned inside. Let the elements do their worst! I opened my last packet of ginger biscuits, bought in Addis, and celebrated, because I had not expected my tent to protect me so well.

Km covered 4,284 Yet to go 7,725

Sunday, Feb 28: Rest day in Yabelo

We all had wet laundry to dry. Those with rooms rigged up washing lines inside, though the humid air prevented the clothes from drying. During the night, one rider was flooded out in his room, while a couple in one of the newer rooms had to pitch their tent in the room itself to insulate themselves from an army of insects. In her room, Dana had to wait for towels to have a shower, but when they arrived, the water stopped running. None of which was worth getting upset about when you were paying a very low price and your mates were out on the lawn! Of greater concern, many riders faced having to put on wet cycling clothes for the last day in Ethiopia, as there was no way of drying the laundry. The forecast was for more rain and thunderstorms over the coming days. I was in the fortunate position of having two sets of clothes that were dry.

The rain had eased by early morning, but never completely stopped all day. The motel had no food available first thing, so I picked my way through the mud and puddles to cross the road. A woman was sweeping clean the soil floor of her lean-to shack, as I sat on a plank supported by three stones and ordered a coffee. From the glowing embers of a small coal fire, she was soon able to pass me a small cup of sweet, strong coffee. There was no milk available, not even in the motel. Three local women came in and took unsweetened doughnuts from a plastic bag that hung from the top of one of the supporting poles. Back in the motel, the kitchen had opened and everyone was trying to order something to eat. There were pancakes, but they immediately ran out. I ordered fried eggs and received scrambled. Did it really matter? You just had to be patient and understanding.

Chris, our bike mechanic, had suggested we could manage the four months without changing our chain rings, so long as we changed the chains a couple of times. Reiner was changing his chain, or at least Mickey was doing it for him, in exchange for taking the old chain. He agreed to do mine on the same basis. Chris' rule of thumb proved absolutely correct, as did other snippets of advice he offered us early on in the trip. With so many riders, many of whom had far more riding ability than bike maintenance experience, he was kept very busy and had to restrict his availability to a two hour window each evening, given that he had other duties also. But he was available to help out whenever there was a problem. Perhaps less so as the trip progressed.

I heard no one express any sadness that in two days time we would be leaving Ethiopia, despite the beauty of the country, the uniqueness of the culture and the friendliness of most of the people. Yabelo had done nothing to change this view unfortunately.

Monday, March 1: Yabelo - bush camp
128 km

Before leaving after breakfast, Paul called the riders' meeting. He reminded us of the tough section that lay ahead of us, and told us to expect tropical storms, unfavourable winds and poor roads. With a smile he added, as I thought I heard him say, that there would be steaks in camp that night. However improbable, I believed him. But he had not said steaks, but snakes!

Despite these dire warnings, the road was good a lot of the day, the winds inconsequential and only a bit of drizzle fell. We climbed up on to a high plateau from where we could see, through a pass ahead of us, the drop down to a plain of startling red, fringed by distant hills with some blue sky now starting to show. Would we be able to dry our laundry after all? Crossing this plain, great banks of clouds were rolling in. But when I arrived at camp, the rain had still held off. (Camp 36, map Ethiopia)

Our first task should have been to put up our wet tents, change into drier gear and put out the washing. But the luggage for most of us was on a truck that was broken down at the lunch stop! As the hours passed, we were all feeling the cold - can you believe it, so near to the equator? We were on a flat, barren plain with no shelter and not enough seats to go round. Drinking tea and coffee helped for a while. I was most interested to look through the book of drawings and doodles that Jason had drawn during the trip. Time passed pleasantly as he described his work as a graphic designer and his aspirations for the future, in his calm and articulate manner.

At 5 o'clock, the two runabouts arrived, having transferred the bags from the lorry. We quickly formed a line to unload all the bags before scrambling to put up our tents. There was nothing to tie a washing line to so I pegged my soggy washing to the top of my tent and popped inside to change. I had my shorts half off when the call went out, "riders' meeting!", at exactly the same moment as I heard the first drops of rain on the tent. As fast as I could, I threw the soggy clothing back into a bag before they became wet.

Dinner followed straight on from the meeting and then everyone dived into their tents. I put a change of clothing in my bike bag for the next day in the hope of taking advantage of any dry conditions while riding, to hang them from my bike, or leave them in the sun while having lunch.

I wrote in my blog what Paul told us at the meeting, namely that "in this area, rather than sink wells straight down, they dig a wide channel at about 45 degrees to the ground until they hit the water table. The water is passed up by a line of women who sing as they work – hence the name 'singing wells' given to the area." Since then I have seen a video showing Samburu tribesmen digging a well while singing, suggesting this as the reason for the term 'singing wells'. I have also come across the following description:

"During the dry season, as the African sun rises, young boys from the Samburu tribe begin to gather around deep wells in the parched riverbed. As they begin to pull water they start singing and from each well there comes a different, simple song. Slowly, small herds of cows and goats appear from the bush, climb the riverbank and make their way down to the riverbed. Each herd recognises the song of 'their well' and comes to drink. Before long, thousands of animals fill the riverbed, called by the crystal clear song of their master. After each animal has drunk its fill, the herds begin to climb back up the banks, led by more young Samburu herdsmen. The singers climb from their wells and disappear into the day."

We would be climbing from our tents in the morning and disappearing into the day, heading for Kenya.

Time cycling 5hrs 24mins
Average speed 24kph
Km covered 4,412 Yet to go 7,597

Tuesday, March 2: Bush camp – Moyale
102 km

For two days now, I had noticed that the women wore more colourful garments, unlike the dingy clothing seen during most of our three weeks in Ethiopia. Often they inelegantly chewed on a stick of sugar cane.

The morning ride took us down quiet roads, through mainly savannah, with birdsong replacing the "You! You! You!" of the kids. There were some spectacular birds that I did not know the names of, apart from a type of hornbill seen in the trees at camp. South African Steve was well clued-up on African birdlife and was always ready to share his knowledge. At times during the trip, he would draw my attention to colourful birds that I had not noticed.

The border was on the road leading into the very small town of Moyale. There was no difficulty or delay in passing through, first going to the Ethiopian control for an exit visa, then the Kenyan side for an entry visa. Our camp was on the edge of town, in a gated area owned by the Kenyan Wildlife Service. (Camp 37, maps Ethiopia/Kenya) Maybe an acre in size, a few low buildings provided office and living accommodation for personnel. There was nowhere suitable for us to be digging holes, but a small hut housed two showers and two toilets. Women were frantically filling a tank on the rooftop by passing up buckets of water as fast as we were emptying it by using the facilities.

All of us hung up washing before walking to the village, either to get new sim cards or to try the only internet café. For some reason, riders were having problems with the sim cards they bought. The internet café was useless, the signal so bad that it was taking twenty minutes for each change on the screen.

All the same, it felt great to be in Kenya, it felt different in ways I could not pinpoint. The pressure of overcrowding and poverty seemed to have eased. I actually imagined we were entering a bright new world. For three weeks we had suffered a relentless barrage of child chant and stone-throwing that had traumatised us. Ethiopia had drained us physically and mentally.

Ahead of us lay reputedly the hardest week of the four months, but we were in relatively good spirits, sufficiently battle–hardened to take it on. We prepared for the rough tracks by changing to our fattest tyres.

Km covered 4,494 Yet to go 7,515

CHAPTER 8
KENYA

Wednesday, March 3: Moyale - Sosolo bush camp
79 km

(I should warn you to gloss over the first paragraph if you are at all squeamish!)

With nowhere to dig holes, a small queue for the two toilets quickly formed. They had been clean hole-in-the-floor basins the night before. It was easy enough to work out what had changed. The local ladies must have left the header tank with insufficient water and the toilets did not flush. The further back in the queue you were, the greater the pile that confronted you when your turn came round. It just was not a bright start to the day.

The dirt road was not nearly as rough as we had expected. I had found that by moving my bike seat forwards slightly and sitting down more on my upper legs than my bottom, I was able to maintain a modicum of comfort without affecting the abscess. Over the roughest sections, I just stood up on the pedals. There were no climbs, no spectacular scenery, mainly thorny scrub for as far as the eye could see towards the distant mountains. But we all had this accentuated sense of being in Africa, more so than ever before. Leaving the hostile environment of Ethiopia behind, our tensions disappeared. English was more widely spoken, parents seemed to have more control over their children and people looked healthier.

A very small village of huts lay secluded behind where we camped. (Camp 38, map Kenya) At the sight of large groups of high-spirited juveniles swarming towards us, I was suddenly apprehensive. As we pitched our tents, they moved amongst us.

There were no ropes to impede them, but nor were they needed. Some young girls were incredibly excited to see Dana's red-painted toenails when she changed from cycling shoes to flip-flops; they rubbed the varnish to see if it would come off on their fingers. They were fascinated to watch how the tents were put up. I was unable to give a good demonstration myself as a pole broke once more. With yet another sleeve, this time given me by Kelsey, I made another repair.

A couple of the riders had, I believe, washed their faces or stood in the shallows of a nearby pond. This was the only water supply for the villagers. Two elders ventured into our camp to ask that we refrain from using the water for cleaning; they were very polite. As it was, we were parked on the trail leading into their village. In the failing light, camels, donkeys, cows and their herdsmen passed by us en route to the village. Children filled jugs with water from the pond and carried them back to the village on their backs.

The zip on the entry flap of my tent just would not fasten properly when I went to bed. I had not experienced that problem before. I knew that some riders used chain lubricant to keep all their zips running smoothly, so I made a mental note to apply some the following evening. After bringing my blog up to date on my netbook and backing it up on a memory stick, I settled to finish reading a book I had brought with me, "Amazing Tales for Making Men out of Boys", by Neil Oliver, the presenter of the hugely successful TV programme "Coast". I do enjoy reading books that have a relevance to what I am doing or where I am. I had sort of hoped that this collection of heroic tales might encourage me; in fact, I found them enthralling. The author looks for a common trait in his real-life heroes, one that might explain their ability to rise above human mediocrity. He seems to have concluded that each one of them had a strong, supportive mother. That made me think about all the orphans in the world, and especially those I was trying to help at Thamsanqa in South Africa: if a mother is capable of

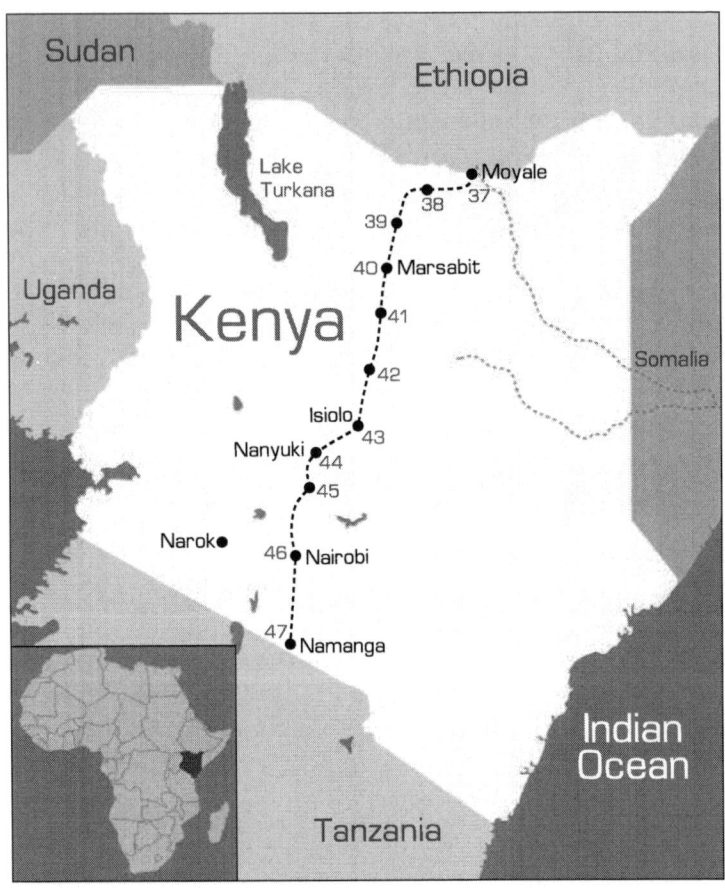

making such a difference to a child as to enable it to become almost superhuman, what an incredible difference the lack of one must make.

Time cycling 4hrs 10mins
Average speed 18.5kph
Km covered 4,573 Yet to go 7,436

Thursday, March 4: Sosolo - Lava rock camp
85 km

Taking down my tent, it was soon clear that no amount of lubricant was going to fix my tent – a pole had broken yet again. That had been the reason the zip would not fasten correctly. The tent was beyond repair now. All the same, I crammed it back into my locker, unsure whether I had become attached to it, which seemed unlikely, or whether a sixth sense told me I would later have a use for it.

The first 45 km were tough, very bumpy and rocky, interspersed with some short, smoother sections of gravel. By 8am, the temperature had risen to 100F. Within the first fifteen minutes, a dik dik crossed the road in front of me and shortly afterwards I noticed a porcupine scurrying for cover. There were baboons about, but I never saw them. You really had to keep fully focussed on the track in front of you, forever changing tack in search of the least difficult surface.

The lunch truck was awaiting us on a small rise from where you could see a line twisting through the barren terrain to the horizon, a thin inexorable ribbon. Some riders chose not to ride after lunch, joining the sick and injured in the truck. Erin in particular was quite ill, suffering from kidney and gall bladder infections. We had been warned that conditions would get progressively harder during the day, and that was certainly the case. No sign of life, no traffic reassured us that we were not alone in this world.

I stopped to tighten my seat and was totally surprised to see a car slowly pass by, with Spanish number plates no less. The two girls inside waved. It was not hard to catch them up as one of them was now employed removing large stones from the car's path. They were from San Sebastian in the north of Spain; their final destination was also Cape Town. They had seen us a few times, they said, starting in Ethiopia. It was an unexpected pleasure to be able to exchange a few words in Spanish. This was not to be the last time we met.

Our camp site (39, map Kenya) had no defining features. We were still on this wide plain. Lava rocks and boulders were sprinkled all over the ground. On the horizon, storm clouds were brewing, while a dust cloud rolled towards us. As I ate my soup, the dust storm arrived, but thankfully only lasted a few minutes.

This was to be the first night in my new tent. Identifying how the different parts of the tent fitted together was not instantly apparent, so I was grateful for Rod and Juliana helping me. Worryingly, Rod confirmed it was identical to their Weekender. Well, it seemed fine to me and the extra space was most welcome.

Tomorrow, we were told, we would be challenged by 85 km of the hardest conditions so far. This was not music to the ears. I had started the day with my back as supple as a bread board; with the help of paracetamol and plenty of slow stretches, it had eased up considerably. But I had reached camp feeling very tired and dehydrated. It was proving to be so hard to replace the perspiration each day, principally because the fluids were warm to very warm, and most unappetising. I had tried pretending I was drinking weak tea, but I had failed to convince myself. This was, and continued to be, a major problem for me.

We could look forward to a long day in the saddle, in temperatures that would rise above forty degrees. It would not be fun - neither interesting, stimulating nor physically beneficial. But for now, I could stretch out in my voluminous new tent.

Time cycling 5hrs 35mins
Average speed 15kph
Km covered 4,658 Yet to go 7,351

Friday, March 5: Lava rock camp – Marsabit 85 km

I rose at 5am to clean and oil my chain by the light of my head torch and generally get prepared. We were not allowed to start breakfast before 7am, however much we would have liked to. Our TDA staff knew far better than we did the dangers of cycling these tracks in poor light. Our enthusiasm, though I think the word does not accurately describe our mood, had to be curbed.

Within the first few kilometres, three riders jacked it in and joined the others already in the truck. It was very hard to push through the loose stones and maintain balance. When the size of the stones forced you to cross from one groove to another, great care had to be exercised in surmounting the ridge of stones in between, particularly those of us without wheel suspension. Very few riders did not come off at some point. Jerry was an early casualty. He was a very good cyclist with lots of experience. As I approached, he stood by the track, holding his arm as he waited to be picked up. I asked him if I could help him at all but he understated his condition and told me he was fine. In fact, he had skinned his elbow to the bone and had to be taken to hospital.

Our lunch truck was parked under the wide-spreading branches of a solitary large tree, not far from where a hill announced the end of the plain. But just before the truck there was a low building with crates outside. It was a Coke stop, the only one we would see all day. Like vultures we descended on the place and stripped them clean of all their cold drinks. The poor guys struggled to keep control, excited perhaps at this sudden upturn in business, but anxious not to miss getting paid. Arriving parched, tired and impatient, we must have seemed aggressive, pushy and perhaps not to be trusted. They had very little change and offered chipatis instead of money. With our lunch truck next door, they met some resistance. As soon as the cold drinks ran out, the voracious mob moved on to the lunch truck.

A few kilometres after lunch, the combination of heat and tiredness was making me feel unsafe on the bike and I joined the group on the truck. Half the riders ended up in the truck that day. Up at the front, there were about six riders who were battling it out each day for the stage win. Franz won this one. Simon missed seeing the finishing line and ended up doing 110 instead of 85 km.

We were camping that night and the following day, a rest day, in the grounds of a Catholic school, run by Sisters. (Camp 40, map Kenya) There were no children about, presumably because it was the start of the weekend. The simple brick buildings were arranged around grassy areas and were clearly cared for. The head Sister had a store where she kept cold drinks and packets of biscuits. She was a delightful person, but no pushover and not about to charge minimal prices. Who could blame her? Town was a couple of km down the road so most of us were happy to pay 300 Kenyan shillings, about £4, for a meal which the Sisters cooked for us. They were surprised to find that they had not cooked enough to satisfy our hunger. I told the head Sister that we really missed cakes and puddings and suggested that she could do good business if she had them available. She took notice.

Km covered 4,743 Yet to go 7,266

Saturday, March 6: Rest day in Marsabit

At 4.30am, the rain came down in true tropical fashion. I was so happy to find that my tent did not leak that I gave no thought at all to my washing on the line. The astute ones were those like Rod and Juliana who rushed out at the first hint of rain and brought all their washing in before it became thoroughly soaked.

The Sisters of Nazareth had agreed to prepare us a breakfast for 7.30. They must have been mildly surprised to find us queueing up well beforehand, standing under the eaves of the buildings out of the rain. For 200 shillings, about £2.60, they provided us with a boiled egg each, bread, margarine and jam, with coffee and tea.

I had asked Sister if there was any way of getting transport into town, as it was still raining steadily. She told me I was in luck, two of the Sisters were about to drive down. I was welcome to go with them if I cared to wait just a few moments.

Time passed and several times I was told, just to keep my spirits up I believe, that they would soon be leaving. Eventually, I realised that they could not bring themselves to say that there had been a change of mind.

There was no other way to get to town other than by walking. Just as I started out in the rain, the TDA 4-wheel drive pulled up with two riders already inside, on its way to town. Was I delighted to get a lift! But no sooner had we left the gravelled school driveway than the vehicle began skidding, the wheels spinning. The tracks had become a quagmire through which even our bikes would not have negotiated a passage. We tried pushing to help it round a bend. It was going nowhere, neither forwards nor backwards. So we got out to walk, joining others of our group, most of them in flip-flops. Although we were not at all cold, our trousers were like drainpipes well before setting foot in town. Ironically, while we walked in totally unsuitable clothing with no protection, a fair number of the locals held umbrellas. The occasional vehicle we saw on our way veered from side to side in the thick mud, with nothing to grip on to.

At the little internet café, I explained that I would like to buy a pair of trousers and asked where I might be able to do so. A young man, who turned out to be the owner of the internet café, led me down the narrow, muddy street to a clothing stall. The seller did not measure me. He just handed me a pair which fitted me perfectly. I still have them.

There was something I liked about Marsabit. The corrugated shacks from which the shops did business could not be described as charming; the little "hotel" where we ate a full dish of pasta for £1.50 and freshly-pressed mango juice for 20p, made no pretensions with its sawdust floor; the goats, huddled outside the bank like patient customers sheltering from the rain, did not suggest a financial hotspot. But I was impressed by the relaxed, friendly manner in which people would obligingly go out of their way to take you somewhere to which you had asked only for the directions, by the strength of the broadband signal in the internet café, by being able to buy a sim card, and also a pair of sunglasses after the last ones just broke in two, and especially by being able to end the huge inconvenience of having weak batteries in my head torch with the purchase of good quality new batteries.

The setting was quite pleasant, especially after the harshness of the surrounding plain. The 1700m high mountain on which Marsabit flourishes, is the result of volcanic activity. The thickly-forested higher slopes are nurtured by condensation, caused by the upward movement of warm air from the surrounding desert floor. Birds and animals abound in this veritable oasis.

The afternoon sun soon dispelled the rain and mist, even drying out most of our washing. For the evening meal, the Sisters had laid out simple food in buffet style. Repeatedly they refilled the plates but eventually replaced them with a selection of baked cakes, each bearing a price tag. Their coffers were being well-filled, but so were our bellies! Freshly-baked sponge cake, can you imagine. I thought Sister's suggestion that the cakes would be good to carry with us the next day as there would be nowhere to buy anything was hilarious. My cakes never even got through the door of the canteen.

As I settled to sleep, my mind drifted over all the names we had been called on this trip so far. Farang, or farangi, (meaning stranger), had been very common, but I had also been called father and papa as well as, less respectfully, motherf——r. But right from the start, our tough, dry-humoured main driver, Erril, had called me "old man". In fact I was not the oldest, Reiner was, but I kind of became used to it and certainly did not resent it. It was sad that he, and the other Indaba crew members, were soon to leave us in Nairobi, to be replaced by a fresh crew.

Sunday, March 7: Marsabit – Laisamis
97 km

The wind got up during the night. Opening my tent flap at 6am, the hill-tops were concealed by the swirling mist. A storm seemed imminent. But at least the previous afternoon's sun and the night's winds had returned the tracks to a passable state.

Our first 55 km were not expected to be difficult, as we would be heading generally downhill. In fact the first few km were steeply downhill, but the track was very rough and in places muddy. Picking my way down carefully, I could not believe my eyes as Simon passed me like a bullet, in a straight line. At first I thought he must have been out of control, but he had front suspension and was a very experienced mountain-bike rider. He and those others who had suspension were, generally speaking, enjoying the rough dirt. In one way, I was happy not to be speeding so that I could breathe in the lushness of the vibrant greenery and the deep red earth that sustained it. Soon, a jackal crossed the track some 30m ahead of me, a bigger animal than I had thought. Others were to see gazelles, baboons and elephants.

As we dropped down to a lower altitude, the vegetation gradually changed into rather dry bush country that benefited from the excess waters shed by the slopes of Mount Marsabit. One particularly boggy stretch demanded that each of us dismount and carry our bikes through. I walked into the bush to use the toilet. Returning to my bike, who should I see but the two Spanish girls again. This time they were in trouble, marooned in the mud. Several of our riders had been pushing their car backwards and forwards and were on the point of returning it to firmer ground though not on the side the girls would have wished to be. They would simply have to wait for a truck to pull them through. Meanwhile, they were very concerned lest they had burnt out the clutch. As we ate at the lunch truck later on, they breezed past us. One of them shouted jubilantly to us, "Who says you need four-wheel drive to get through Africa?" Only five kilometres later, we passed them again; one of the girls was inspecting underneath the engine.

Three riders had stopped to engage with a group of tribeswomen in very colourful apparel. It appeared that the riders were taking photos and the women were demanding money. They were carrying machetes and seemed to be agitated. I chose not to stop. Frequently during the morning we encountered individuals or groups of this tribe, who we assumed were members of the semi-nomadic Samburu. They were normally very friendly and inquisitive. Brightly-coloured, beaded necklaces, earrings and bracelets adorned their bodies. Sometimes exotic arrangements of feathers and flowers were worn as head wear. Some had painted their faces in striking patterns. The men bore scars on their chests, perhaps self-inflicted.

After leaving the lunch truck we started into a two mile stretch where a steady expanse of floodwater was pouring into the bush around us. The contrast between the swirling inundation and the withered bush appeared contradictory. Just

where the track reached its marginally lowest point, it was covered in deep water and severely churned up. In the middle of this, a lorry sat immobilised at an awkward angle, barring the path of an oncoming lorry and our two lorries. I would very much have enjoyed watching the unfolding spectacle to see how the drivers tackled the problem. I was reminded of extricating impossibly bogged down tractors and machinery during my time as a farmer.

Hereafter, the track became extremely corrugated, but our efforts were helped by partial cloud cover and a light breeze. It was enough to do to finish, but not atrocious.

Our camp site (41, map Ethiopia) lay in the fold of a dry river bed. Children came running out of a secondary school on the other side to greet us and help or hinder. I must admit to intolerance as I struggled to remove stones and thorny plants from a patch of ground; a couple of kids wanted to get involved and would not accept that I wanted to do it myself. I was just too tired at that moment in time. Tents were going up on the

124

dry river bed where the firm flat surface of sand and gravel was perfect for pitching. I felt less vulnerable on the higher ground. A man was filling the water drums that children were bringing to him by working the pump of a well by the side of the dry river bed. He was happy for us to wash our faces in the water he pumped out.

It was exciting to think that soon we would be seeing Mount Kenya. Only two more days of these very rough tracks. But a lot can happen in two days.

Time cycling 6hrs 40mins
Average speed 14.6kph
Km covered 4,840 Yet to go 7,169

Monday, March 8: Laisamis - bush camp 89 km

I heard the thunder, saw flashes of lightning through the dark, and the light tapping of rain on the tent began. It was time to be up anyway. I was fortunate in being able to take my tent down and, along with the Thermarest and my very full holdall, carry it over to the lorry before the skies opened. The heavy drops got bigger and the intensity rose to a crescendo. Half the tents were still standing. The dry river bed was already a fast flowing torrent that would have swept away the tents in their path, but everyone had managed to move in time. There was just one tent on the other side, rapidly becoming isolated. I pointed it out to Paul and he charged over the river to alert the rider inside. The dry balmy evening we had enjoyed had given no warning of this torrential rain, so the tarpaulins had not been pulled out from the lorries and there was no protection for the breakfast. Baked beans were rapidly diluted to soup, leaving hard boiled eggs or soggy Weetabix the only options. One or two riders delayed getting up in the hope that the storm would quickly pass; they finally had to surface and take down their tents in the sheeting rain. I was torn between breakfast or taking the mudguards off my bike. The muddy conditions would clog up the small clearance between the thick tyres and the mudguards, and I had to store the mudguards in the lorry before it left. Both lorries wanted to move out straight away before they became bogged down.

The rain eased but never left us all morning. The heavily corrugated track was covered by either a few inches of water or by fine wet sand, so although it was a little less bumpy, the effort of pushing through the sand was strength-sapping and reduced our speed to as low as 5kph. Riders later compared it to cycling through a river, upstream. But I was rather enjoying it! There was no sun to berate us, but neither were we cold, despite being drenched. Many times we crossed rivers that were dry the day before and were now gushing. We saw no wildlife yet I sensed it all about me. The only sounds were those of birdsong and the loud croaking of frogs.

With 10 km yet to go before the lunch truck at the 55 km mark, we were blessed with some good fortune. Road making was in progress. The method employed was to create a perfectly level, earthen base, firm and compacted, onto which tarmac would later be laid. While this work was in progress, traffic was diverted along a temporary, usually rough track. Through middle Africa we would encounter a tremendous amount of road making and whenever we could, we would ride on the prepared surface of the new road.

This seemed too good to be true. Viv, who turned out to be such a wonderful cyclist, was not accustomed to off-road and she said to me: "I was just about to give up. It is all right for you, you have your charity to keep you going. I was just thinking about how much I would rather have been back at work!" In places, there was deep flooding, but this just made it more fun. For 10 km we cycled like the wind.

For lunch, I ate 14 rounds of bread with a mixture of either tuna and tomato or peanut butter and syrup, followed by a banana. I could have eaten more.

The road making continued to supply us with a great surface for riding. Arriving in camp about 3.30, I had just enough time to pitch the tent, clean myself and the bike with water taken from puddles in the road, clean and oil the chain, put out some laundry and attend the riders' meeting. The upshot of the meeting was that there would be no more than another 25 km of dirt before we hit the tarmac on our way to Isiolo.

Looking around and hearing riders talk, it was apparent that everybody had lost weight. For a long time now, Caroline our medic had been telling me that I was losing too much weight, but others were losing a lot more than I was. Rick was one of those losing a lot. He said to me that evening that "each night I tell myself I will not ride tomorrow, but each day I get up and put on my cycling shoes".

By 8pm, someone in a tent near me had started to snore. Suddenly, a loud bang pierced the night; someone's tyre had burst. The snoring stopped. (Camp 42, map Kenya)

Time cycling 6hrs 16mins
Average speed 14.2kph
Km covered 4,929 Yet to go 7,080

Tuesday, March 9: Bush camp – Isiolo
81 km

The day started brightly but never became too hot thanks to plenty of cloud cover. The cycling was no longer very bumpy and the traffic was minimal – what more could we ask for? Small groups of tribes people were the only folk we saw. The men usually carried spears. Several times we passed Samburu sitting by the roadside selling large sacks of charcoal. Each bag cost about 700 shillings (about £7).

Some of the day's journey saw a return to tarmac, but this ended for a while as we came into Archers Point. It was here, a few days previously, that floodwaters had swept through taking several huts with them. Six people had been drowned. As we crossed the bridge, the river was still a raging, red torrent. The track was treacherous, causing several riders to fall.

On reaching Isiolo, we carried on for a few more kilometres to a motel/camp site called Rangelands. (Camp 43, map Kenya) The smell of newly-cut wet grass welcomed us to the paddocks where we could pitch our tents. The toilet and shower block were without water, but we eventually got somebody to solve that problem. Some traditional superior-looking huts were available for about $20, and again, a number of riders booked in.

Most of us changed our tyres in the afternoon. For the dirt roads, I had been using 2" tyres, running them at 2.5 bar. But as we now expected to be back on tarmac right through to Tanzania, I replaced the mudguards and put on 1" tyres inflated to 6.5 bar. All my tyres were made by Schwalbe. So many riders had had punctures, often repeatedly, due mainly to the long, tough thorns dropped by many of the trees and bushes, yet I was still to have a puncture.

Many of us spent some time drinking beers and eating chips in the small bar. Patrick became very merry. Gerald, who was normally bubbly, sat very quietly by the bar. He had a prostate infection and was feeling quite ill.

Jerry, who had come off his bike on leaving Lava Rock Camp, was still receiving treatment for his arm. The wound had turned septic and despite the use of antibiotics was not healing properly. Michelle was treating him in the truck so I was waiting outside for my bum sores to be looked at. When the rain started again, I asked if I could wait inside. As I entered, Jerry passed out. (I had not bared my bum at this point, I might add!!) I slapped his face to bring him round, which alarmed Michelle, and then I ran for Caroline. Jerry soon came round and claimed to feel fine, but he certainly gave us a shock.

Time cycling 3hrs 21mins
Average speed 22.9kph
Km covered 5,010 Yet to go 6,999

Wednesday, March 10: Isiolo – Nanyuki
70 km

I was just about to get out of my tent at 6 in the morning when a sudden downpour dissuaded me. You do not mind getting wet, but it seemed rather more civilised to have breakfast first. It lasted only 15 minutes.

We climbed for 30 km in temperatures perfectly suited to our needs. Green pastures gave way to golden fields of wheat and barley, stretching up the steep slopes of the many small hills dotted about. As we rode ever upwards - we had 1400m to climb in this stretch - the fields grew ever larger. The landscape spoke of colonial influence and control, where the black population helped and benefited the dominant white population in a symbiotic relationship. It is not my intention to draw judgement on that situation, as my knowledge is inadequate, merely to observe.

A further observation was (almost) forced on me. As I was enjoying the ever widening views at my own pace, I met up with one of the female riders. We stopped to take some photographs. Without any warning, she walked away no more than ten paces. Facing me, she shouted that she could wait no longer, at the same time dropping her shorts and crouching. I was quick enough to turn away to save my blushes, because clearly she would have had none. No comment was passed by either of us as if it was the most natural thing in the world.

The lunch truck was waiting for us at 40 km with what should have been a view straight over to Mount Kenya. Alas, it was enveloped in cloud. My appetite had been whetted by the long climb and we were treated to one of the best lunch stops of the trip. Janet was cooking french toast for us, as many slices as we could eat. As we devoured the delicious egg-bread the sun came out, the clouds broke and we were allowed a glimpse of snow on the mountain. Then, for just a few minutes, we were treated to a full view of the snowy peak.

Across the road, a high wire fence was spoiling the fantastic photo opportunity, so I crossed over to hold my camera through the fence. I was literally shocked into realising it was an electric fence. The many greenhouse complexes, like the one this fence protected, were clearly profitable enterprises. In the main, as I understand, flowers were being grown for export to Europe. Everywhere was manicured, cared for and protected.

From there, it was downhill with a tailwind, very fast, and most of us made the 70 km total to the Sportsman's Arms Hotel before midday. We were camping on their grass, with rooms available to us for taking a hot shower – my first, I think, since Luxor. I was very pleased to find out that Viv, who had thought about throwing in the towel on the dirt two days earlier, won the ladies' section of that day's stage and the previous day's stage outright. (Camp 44, map Kenya)

Km covered 5,080   Yet to go 6,929

Thursday, March 11: Nanyuki – Rafting camp 104 km

At a point 2 km south of Nanyuki. a large sign indicated that we were about to cross the equator. After cycling there for a photo shoot, we headed off into the glorious hilly countryside, passing school after school.

Jerry was back riding again. He was still not well, but promised to take it easy.

Our destination today was the Mike Savage White Water Rafting Camp. (Camp 45, map Kenya) Leaving the main road, a rough track led us down to a large grassy bank, alongside which the Tana River raced in full spate. At the top of the bank, stone buildings with thatched roofs complemented the idyllic setting. As usual, our first chore was to get our gear out and pitch the tents. As I was pulling mine out of my locker, in came Patrick. We had not spoken since Gondar, when we had had that row. We had just ignored each other, which was both unpleasant and awkward. I turned to him now and suggested we put behind us what had happened and shake hands, which we did. That was an end to it at last.

I knew my clothes were full of sandy dust, but no matter how long I washed them under the taps, each time I wrung them out, the water was brown again. Once I filled a bowl of water I realised why - the water itself was brown, obviously being extracted directly from the river.

The camp offered a $60 option of a four hour furious rafting experience. The opportunity proved irresistible to eight riders who thoroughly enjoyed their hair-raising adventure and repeated dunking. The sound of the rapids just downriver carried to where we had pitched our tents. A footbridge spanned the river. I started to cross it, but my attention was immediately drawn to a colony of masked weavers on an overhanging tree. Their nests were roughly conical with a short spout through which to enter; they hung rather like lanterns from the tree. Their mainly bright yellow feathers with olive-green streaking contrasted with their black heads. As they busied themselves about their nests, I could have watched for hours.

Before dinner, everyone congregated for the weird riders' auction. Any items left lying around whether in camp or in the lorries, were tidied up by the Indaba crew or TDA staff. Understandably, this was not a chore they relished The Indaba crew slept in the lorries and were not happy to have to tidy up after the riders. To encourage us not to leave anything around, once in a while all items were auctioned off. One of the Indaba crew acted as auctioneer and stated what the starting bid would be. The currency was in cans of beer or some other drink, to be given to the crew or TDA staff. Anything from sunglasses to sleeping bags would go under the hammer and it always surprised me how much riders would offer. If the item meant enough to the rider who had lost it, he/she would have to bid to get it back. Although the auction was conducted with great humour and seemingly enjoyed in general, I personally thought it distasteful, especially when an item of particular personal value to a rider went for a bid beyond his/her means. I assume that some arrangement must have later been agreed.

I was fascinated to be told that the British army used this camp to acclimatise some of their battalions before leaving for

Afghanistan. A battalion was due the following day, just as we left for Nairobi.

Time cycling 4hrs 3mins
Average speed 25.9kph
Km covered 5,184 Yet to go 6,825

Friday, March 12: Savage rafting camp – Nairobi 137 km

The TDA staff organised so well what could have been a perilous parade through the centre of the city in full convoy. We all cycled at our own pace for the first 65 km to the lunch truck. From there, three groups of riders set off at intervals. Each group was led by a TDA staff member and one of the Kenyan riders. (There were four Kenyan riders with us. One of them had only one leg, but he was very fast; he had represented his country at the Para Olympics. Around Nanyuki he was fêted as a hero. Another was a national rider.) Each group was led through some heavy traffic for about 30 km, up to a point out to the west of the city. From there, we followed the directions we had been given for the remaining 40 km. The riding was arduous, in part due to the traffic. Vehicles allowed very little room for cyclists which was stressful. Gerald had one close call: "At one stage, one of those minibuses almost hit me, he was so close, just because he wanted to pick up a passenger 50 meters ahead of me. I got so upset that I stopped next to him as he was busy boarding that passenger. I told him in very rude English what I thought of his driving skills. Mistake.... Big mistake... Mini bus drivers are notoriously aggressive and stupid, so imagine now, me a white guy lecturing one of them in his own country... As I finished telling him what an arse-hole he was, he pulled a big metal pipe out of his door and screamed at me "I kill you!"... This was the end of my 30 seconds of glory... I came back to some sense of survival as fast as I had lost it by going after this guy, jumped on my bike and pedalled as fast as I could. He chased me with his taxi and tried to hit me, but I was expecting that so I jumped into the ditch next to the road as he came at full speed from behind me."

I rather enjoyed seeing the fruit and vegetable market we passed by, though the stench reminded me of Ethiopian toilets, the beautiful residences and landscaping of the gardens behind high security gates in the embassy area, and the market gardening amongst the hills of the city's western extremity, as we skirted the notorious slum area of Kibera, just 5 km from the city centre.

Approaching the Karen shopping mall, I was cycling with Paddy, Reuben and Erin. Instinctively, we all pulled in and more or less ordered identically: 2 milkshakes, a blueberry muffin and a chocolate brownie. They never tasted so good. An interesting situation was also developing between them. The three of them were becoming good friends, while Reuben and Paddy were also competing for the affections of Erin leading to much banter and fun in the weeks to come as their relationships took shape.

Karen was the suburb where we were to camp at the headquarters of Indaba, the company contracted by the TDA to supply the lorries and their drivers. As we entered the gated enclosure, one of the lorries was already being stripped and serviced.

Warm showers and good toilets welcomed us. The simple facilities and the chance to order plates of food contributed to a "home from home" feeling. (Camp 46, map Kenya)

Time cycling 5hrs 55mins
Average speed 23.2kph
Km covered 5,321 Yet to go 6,688

Saturday, March 13: Rest day in Nairobi

Late at night, sleep was a little difficult as a few riders drank themselves silly at the bar. One rider became so incensed with the racket that he left his tent and confronted them. A few heated exchanges took place but common sense prevailed and the noise abated.

It had become commonplace to see riders walking around camp wearing the earplugs of their iPods, vacant expressions on their faces. During long days of cycling, music became their companion, while in camp, they were able to enter their own, more private world. I made up my mind to buy an iPod if I could while in Nairobi. Like most riders, I caught a taxi to a large shopping mall where the two bike shops that we found held a disappointingly narrow range of stock, but a few of us bought iPods and we all indulged our calorie-demanding appetites.

Having bought an iPod without knowing anything about them, I now had to learn how to load it with music. I did have some music on my netbook and Franz very kindly transferred this to my iPod. He also offered to download for me the music from his own iPod though he warned me that the music might not be to my taste. There was so much of it that I felt sure of finding enough that I would like.

Of the 300 bikes that the TDA foundation donated to various needy groups as we passed through the continent, sixty bikes were donated to three different organizations at a ceremony in camp. Fifteen bikes were donated to Mazi Majuri, an organisation that the TDA had supported for the past four years. Their representatives were accompanied by Masai children who entertained us with traditional singing and dancing. Fifteen bikes were donated to representatives of the Arrow-Webb hospital, a facility helping local people in the city of Nairobi. Finally, thirty bikes were given to the Great Rift Valley Development Organization to be distributed to individuals in the western and eastern regions of the country. One woman stood up in front of us and in a very shy voice related to us how the three bikes they had received the previous year had helped her community of HIV infected women to raise money. They used their bikes to carry the milk and vegetables that they produced to sell in the nearest town. With this small income, they were able to look after themselves and their children. These women had been rejected by society, as is unfortunately often the case in Africa once HIV status is made public. With no other source of income or support, they had decided to join forces and fight back by becoming a small, independent farming unit. Those three bikes had helped these women to survive and to look forward to a better day.

Sunil had a wonderful time with his family and came back with a pleasant surprise for the rest of us. His uncle had kindly sent him back with two big boxes of biscuits for our general consumption. For about a month, we would have the luxury of taking biscuits with our evening tea and coffee.

Sunday, March 14: Nairobi – Namanga 164 km

Some riders, their section finished, prepared to say their goodbyes, others awaited a taxi to take them to the airport for a flight to Zanzibar, while a new group of sectional riders joined us. Bags were going in or out of lockers, queues forming, everyone snatching some breakfast while listening to Paul hold the riders' meeting. There was real excitement in the air with the enticing prospect of three rest days in Arusha not far away now. Many riders dreamt of the safaris they had planned, some left now to spend a week climbing Mount Kilimanjaro.

We soon left Nairobi behind, passed through a busy village preparing for its Sunday market, and into open, hilly pasture land. The seriously-potholed road was deserted, apart from a few guys filling potholes with soil taken from the roadside.

Occasionally we would pass a church from where the singing gradually rose in volume and then faded away as we pushed on. In truth, I felt like singing myself; perhaps it was because, increasingly, I felt like I really was in Africa. I had never expected crowds, or menace; more a sense of space and timelessness.

Fifty km of this rough road led us to a super-smooth highway. The cycling was easy and fast. But at 100 km, everything changed.

Where the recently laid road ended, traffic was diverted on to a track. But as always, we ignored the signs, preferring to utilise the surface prepared for the new road. The operators of the road machinery, despite it being a Sunday, were actually on site and signalled for us to go through. I say "us"; in fact, at this point we were fairly spread out and I was alone.

A kilometre further on, I could see the surface ahead glistening. Clearly, tar had recently been laid, though supposedly not on a Sunday. Perhaps it would be a little tacky. As I sped on to the new surface, tar splashed up like water after a heavy downpour. I could not direct the bike to the side. It started planing. The bike slid from under me, and the momentum carried us both forward, sliding over the glutinous, tarred surface. It happened so quickly, I needed a minute to recover my senses. Incredibly, my only injury was a slight abrasion to the elbow, but I did not know this because that side of my body was covered in thick tar, as was my camelback which also had a broken strap. The bike looked like it might not function. Unsure of what to do, I trudged to the side of the road. Across the other side of the road, a local woman expressed her sorrow at my predicament. I indicated that I was fine and began pushing my bike towards the rough track on the other side.

A number of us fell foul of the tar that day. Stuart had extensive road rash. Reiner could not get up and walk. Two riders behind him alerted the TDA vehicle and the three of them cleaned him up using petrol. They carried him on a makeshift stretcher to the 4-wheel drive for the transfer to Nairobi hospital. Although no bones were broken, he had incurred severe ligament damage.

With another 69 km yet to cycle, twenty of it on dirt, the incident took the shine off what would have been a great day's cycling. The seat was pasted to my shorts which in turn were pasted to my buttocks, reducing friction. Perhaps therein lay the cure for saddle sores?! My fingers were difficult to separate, but the bike worked.

Arriving in camp (47, map Kenya), hungry and thirsty, priority had to be given to cleaning myself and the bike before dark. I used petrol to clean the worst off myself, and then spent a good hour and a half cleaning the bike lest the tar hardened on it overnight, paying particular attention to the chain. Now I knew how I would be spending a lot of my spare time in Arusha. Getting myself reasonably clean posed a great problem too. I had used petrol to remove the thickest of the tar but still a coating remained, even after a hot shower. By the time I no longer looked like a stick of licorice, it was time for the riders' meeting and dinner.

I believe we were all accustomed to mishaps by now. No longer did they surprise us, we just dealt with them and moved on. There was no point in looking for sympathy as everyone had their own problems. Without a positive attitude we were finished. One effect was to draw us together somewhat, acknowledging that we were in this together. There was no blaming. We just needed to prepare for the next day.

Coming to a sticky end on our last full day in Kenya did not tarnish our fond memories of its people and varied landscape. We had seen a side of the country not witnessed by the tourists on the safari trail, a side of it shorn of the glamour.

Having finally put up my tent, I crawled inside and turned on the iPod. The tar was forgotten. Having come through the day without injury, I felt I had conquered the day and been invigorated in the process.

Time cycling 6hrs 11mins
Average speed 25.7kph
Km covered 5,485 Yet to go 6,524

CHAPTER 9
TANZANIA

Monday, March 15: Namanga – Arusha
121 km

This stage encapsulated all the different road conditions we had travelled on up until now, from the very best to the very worst. The lush countryside thrived on both sides of the sprawling, untidy border post of Namanga, where our passage through customs was easily effected, the persistence of the money-changing touts being the only hassle. The continuing presence of Masai people made it difficult to forget that we had actually left Kenya and were now in Tanzania.

En route to Arusha, the massive bulk of Mount Meru dominated the landscape. With a height of over 4500m, it formed the centrepiece of the Arusha National Park, one of many parks in the region. Its densely wooded slopes supported over 400 species of birds and many animals, including leopards and monkeys.

Arusha marked the halfway point of our trip, time-wise. Three rest days awaited us. Our camp site (48, map Tanzania) was the Masai Camp, a small camping and backpacking lodge on the edge of this bustling town. The traditionally-styled main building offered a shady retreat to sit, read or write in comfort near the drink and food bars.

Apart from those who had already taken off to Zanzibar or Mount Kilimanjaro, another twenty-four riders had booked safaris, principally to the Ngorongoro Crater, leaving a pleasantly quiet camp.

Time cycling 5hrs 30mins
Average speed 21.9kph
Km covered 5,606 Yet to go 6,403

March 16/17/18: Three rest days in Arusha

The twenty-four who were setting off on safari needed an early breakfast, so the kitchen was fully extended. Paul Porter and I decided to take breakfast in the town centre, 3 km up the road. Paul had cycled the first half of the TDA the previous year before breaking his arm badly and was now back, to finish the second half of the journey. He was a Professor of Agronomy at a US university. Given my farming background, we held a common interest.

We squeezed into a daladala, (one of the ubiquitous and cheap mini-buses), like contestants in a game of Twister. There was no room for the "conductor"; he hung out of the side-door. The usual response to the question of how many people can fit in a daladala was "two more". Some of these vehicles bore the colours of Manchester United, Liverpool or Chelsea football clubs. They seemed an easy if frenetic way to get around. Adam, Simon and Andra did have a bad experience on one of these buses however, on the first rest day. They were coming back from town, with not many other passengers in the daladala. Suddenly, it shot up a side street and the locals were quickly pushed out. When our guys tried to leave, the conductor blocked their way and demanded a sum of money. Apparently he was menacing and they were frightened, but they managed to push past him and escape.

Paul and I had no such problem. After a hearty breakfast, we separated as we had different agendas. I met Frank in the bank. He had just finished college in Arusha and was intent on entering university to study tourism. I asked him where I might find a bike shop and we set off on a whirlwind tour of the town. Worse than in Nairobi, bike shops were very, very basic, but I did finally get hold of a multi-tool. I had no success in acquiring some new shorts and cycling gloves. Our route took us through the outdoor market. My eyes were drawn less to the bulging stalls selling every type of fruit and vegetable imaginable, but to the many women sat on the floor each with nothing more than a plate of carrots or tomatoes to sell. Avoiding the huge water gulleys, only partially covered by

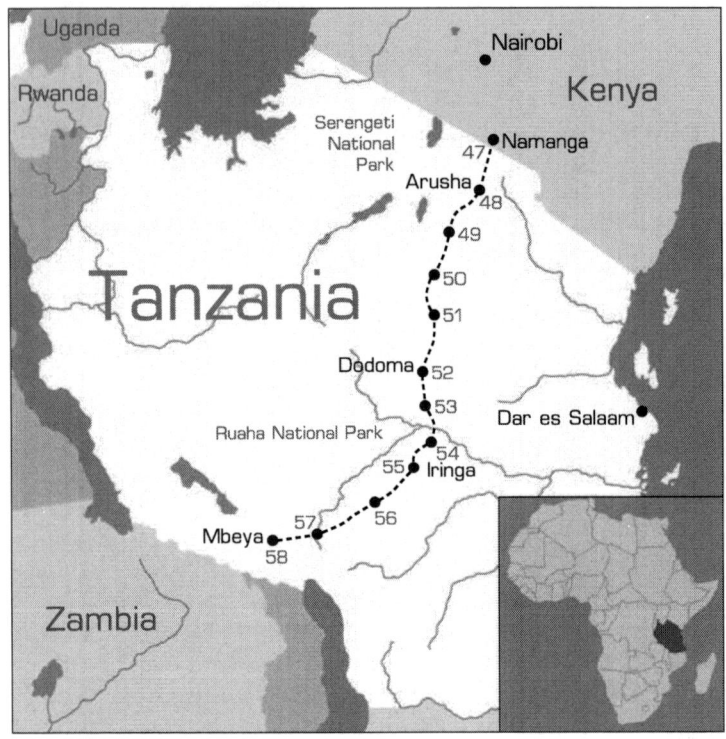

concrete slabs, and hanging on to my bag tightly, I struggled to keep up with Frank. I was no longer used to walking.

I bought turpentine, a brush and liquid detergent - all necessary ingredients for the afternoon's labour of removing the tar still stuck to my bike. A man was selling coconuts from a wheel barrow. I bought us one each, 1000 shillings a coconut (about 50p). The man chopped the top off the coconuts for us to drink the milk inside. Then he deftly cut up the flesh inside for our later use. I gave him 5000 shillings and he went off to find change. Ten minutes passed. Frank insisted it made no sense for the man to run off with the change as his barrow was too valuable to him. But he agreed that we should take the barrow if he did not reappear soon. A few minutes more and he was back. I was very glad about that because I do not know what I would have done with a wheelbarrow.

Frank illuminated my ignorance about tanzanite, reportedly the most precious of all gemstones. Found only in Tanzania, the first stones came to light not far from Arusha in 1967. Interested by Frank's assertion that they can exhibit fire like an opal stone, I agreed to be shown some. I followed him down a little alleyway, up some steps, through a narrow corridor, and into a tiny room. Mr Big was sat behind a small desk that took up half the space in the room. The desk was completely clear apart from a small set of scales. Three other thick-set men were present, each with a big smile exhibiting badly-stained teeth, and fancy bracelets. For fear of getting in too deep, I explained more than once that my interest lay only in looking, not buying. I am not very good at assessing whether malice is present or not, but I certainly felt the four big guys in the tiny room a little intimidating. Big boy showed me some tanzanite stones, very beautiful, but without fire. Then he produced uncut tanzanite, which did have fire. He explained that the fire is lost during the process of grinding and polishing. He tried to interest me in a stone for US$240. Perhaps it was my generally rough appearance, my tar-stained skin maybe, but he correctly sensed a lost cause. I thanked them for their time and left with Frank. Outside, a man sidled up to us, surreptitiously opening some tissue paper to display a few stones. They really looked good, a stronger blue than the ones we had just seen. Frank dismissed him abruptly and confided in me that they were glass.

It was time for me to get back to camp. Whether Frank was hoping for a tip or just enjoyed practising his English, I do not know. The fact he asked for nothing encouraged me to make sure that he realised how grateful I was for his time by paying him.

The afternoon passed quickly as I absorbed myself back at the camp site in stripping the tar away and revealing the original yellow of my bike. By 7.30, I had given it a final wash and I celebrated with a pizza.

Over the three days, I ventured in to town a few times, to use the internet and have a look round. Outside the gates of our camp, there were a couple of women by the roadside, roasting corn cobs. They sold them very cheaply. It was my intention to try one on the third day, but they were no longer there. We were all conscious of our weight by now, and the need to eat as much as possible, whenever possible. I had lost about 5 kilos, which was average for the men, though one lad had lost 12 kilos. Strangely, the women were not recording much weight loss at all; this apparently was usually the case, but I do not know why. I know that the women felt it was very unfair. I was just happy to be able to demolish a giant portion of chocolate cake after breakfast without feeling the slightest twinge of guilt.

A local man who worked at the camp was able to organise any sewing we needed doing. Ever since Gondar, I had had to wear my ripped shorts. He arranged to have them repaired and the strap, that was ripped off the camelback when I fell on the wet tarmac, sewn back on.

With 7 days of dirt tracks ahead of us, I changed back to fat tyres. But I found that the front tyre rubbed on the frame, no matter how I tried to adjust it. Chris assured me that the rim was still true but the tyre had become warped and there was nothing that could be done about it other than wait for sufficient rubber to be worn away. The idea of the tyre acting as a brake in the week ahead did not thrill me, but there seemed nothing I could do about it. I renewed all the rubber tubing on the handlebars, which by now was badly damaged, and brought all my laundry up to date. My feeling of getting on top of all my chores was rather dashed on the second night when two of the poles of my new tent snapped. With sleeves taken from the first tent and plenty of duct tape, I casually presumed all would be well again.

During the course of the afternoon of the third day, riders arrived back from their adventures. I was surprised that their return left me feeling resentful. All together we made up a big group, too big a group in my opinion. Apart from the greater difficulty in accessing our lockers or even finding a seat at breakfast or dinner, it allowed for small groups to operate within the whole, thereby precluding the camaraderie of a tightly knit group.

Several were not yet finished with their jaunts, preferring to now fly to Zanzibar for a rest rather than get back on their bikes. Those who had returned from safari could be split into two categories; the ones who had stayed in a safari lodge looked relaxed while those who had stayed in tents looked worn out.

Friday, March 19: Arusha - lakeview camp
107 km

Once we reached Arusha town centre in the early morning light, there was a stretch of road jammed with traffic, no one giving way and especially not to cyclists. But then we were away, passing carefully-managed coffee plantations protected by mature trees, out past the small airfield and once more into the copious countryside.

Not far out of town, a cyclist casually drew alongside me, one I did not recognise. I did have some trouble hearing his very soft voice, especially given that he spoke with a Danish accent. Trying desperately to accept this intrusion into my private space, as I am never one for talking much when I am cycling, I got his name completely wrong. He explained how he had ridden the Tour d'Afrique in 2008, and gave his name as Bent. Now this rang a bell; I had read blogs of riders from previous years and I thought I remembered a rider called Alan Bent. So the whole time I was calling him Alan. His name, I have only recently found out, was Bent Nielsen. His wife had died in 2007 after a long illness. Rather than brood over what was a terrible loss to him, he signed up for the 2008 TDA. That was the year in which there were troubles in Kenya. The riders had had to fly from Ethiopia to leapfrog Kenya and spend the two weeks which they should have been cycling twiddling their thumbs in Tanzania. During this time, Bent met a young native woman. Once he had finished the TDA in Cape Town, he returned to Tanzania and settled down with his new love in Arusha. As a former professional cyclist and trainer he now spent his time training local riders and organising bike tours in the region.

He had put up a sign in one of our lorries, inviting any riders during their time in Arusha to visit his home, where he rented out apartments, and to sample how local people lived. I had not seen this sign, much to my chagrin because he had also offered tents and tent accessories of leading German manufacturers. My first tent was German made. I felt sure he would have been able to sort out my pole problems. He stayed with me till the lunch stop before returning home. He must have been experiencing a strong sense of nostalgia - he had come fourth overall in 2008, despite being 60 years old, but the effort had left him with a permanent heart problem. The memories were perhaps both sweet and sour.

After lunch, I walked over to my bike and heard a hissing sound. I looked round thinking there must be a snake. But it was my tyre going down. A thorn had given me my first puncture. I put a new tube in and got rolling not without a real feel-good factor.

Like many of the names given to our camp sites, the name Lakeview Camp Site was not a truly apt description. (Camp 49, map Tamzania) The lake, Lake Manyara, had to be pointed out to me, as it appeared as little more than a thin line in the distance. The long grass of the field cushioned our tents. There was a shower house which was clean. Outside it, a bucket was left to take water from a large drum for use inside. Personally, I was very happy with the arrangement, as the alternative would have been baby wipes again.

Not far from us, a very small Masai village was presumably the source of the many flies that bothered us. They would disappear by dusk as other insects took centre stage. The villagers had set up a primitive bar to sell us drinks that they kept cool in a cold box. A few of their children mingled amongst us as we sat around chatting. I got into a good conversation with Lani. She was a Canadian resident of Asian origin. Though not a fast rider, she was relentless, rarely missing a day. While most of us would stop for a Coke whenever possible, she steadily continued with a smile; sugary drinks did not agree with her and she stuck to water. I was fascinated to hear the reasons for her doing the ride and why she would finish in Cape Town and then start another similar type of ride across Asia. However, at this point in the journey she admitted to wanting to just get it over with. She was finding herself a little bored I think after each day's ride, or maybe the tedium and unremitting daily routine was getting to her. She would not have been on her own in that respect. I suggested she might enjoy talking to all the riders individually, hearing their reasons for doing this trip and logging it all down. She thought that would be really interesting and started straight away.

After dinner, some of the villagers came back and put on a little show, playing the drums and play-acting. Riders were happy to put a few coins in the hat that was passed round afterwards.

Time cycling 4hrs 11mins
Average speed 25.5kph
Km covered 5,713 Yet to go 6,296

Saturday, March 20: Lakeview - Lembe school 120 km

We knew there was a hard day in front of us, the whole of it on dirt, with 1200 metres of climbing. The road took us through small villages and along an idyllic lake where the gentle movements of the fishermen, plying their nets from shallow canoes, suggested a reluctance to disturb the tranquil waters. Everywhere, the luxuriant growth spoke of nature's ability to provide.

But already, huge bulldozers and excavators had begun to widen this small road. Large waterholes had been dug, perhaps for the future storage of water, and the spoils levelled over the road's surface to build it up. At regular intervals, deep canals had been cut across the road, with huge pipes waiting to be installed; diversions constantly slowed our progress. As lorries sped up and down the road, moving soil, clouds of dust enveloped us. For a few kilometres along the roadside, lines of men with pick-axes were digging a small trench in preparation for laying a long plastic pipe to either move water to, or effluent from, the many huts that lined the road. I was very surprised during this stretch at twice being the target for stone-throwing.

We left all this behind after about 50 km as we started climbing. Each slope of the land was thickly forested while all flatter land was given over to small fields growing mainly maize in between clumps of banana trees. The heat was building quickly as we climbed to where the lunch truck was parked at 60 km. I thought at this stage that we had finished a lot of the climbing for the day, but I was soon told that the real climbing still lay ahead of us. There was a strange air of resignation at this juncture, a tiredness of spirit seemed to have overcome us. The normally bullish or jocular comments were not forthcoming. It was as strange as it was unusual, especially since we were surrounded by some of the most magnificent countryside you could wish to see.

Sure enough, after lunch we soon started a long tough climb, up and up through dense tropical forest. I surprised myself by letting the few riders I was cycling with go ahead while I walked a little. I would never normally get off my bike to walk, no matter how slow I had to go, unless the surface was too bad to cycle on. But the surface of the track was OK. I soon stopped altogether to cool down and have a pee. No one was around, perfect stillness. Just as I was about to relieve myself, a local man on an old bike appeared on the track. He stopped and just stared at me. Then a few children, casting furtive but not unfriendly glances at me, sat down on some rocks a few metres away from me. Clearly, I would have to wait for a pee. I ate one of my energy bars, listening to the children chuckling. Here was a good opportunity to interact with the locals, but because I was tired, I could not be bothered to make the effort. I hated myself for feeling that way.

At the top of the climb, there on the left was a little shack selling cold drinks. I wondered whether it had been placed there in the knowledge that many riders would be passing through on this one day. There was no other traffic. Several local men were sat down outside and were curious to know how old I was.

Now we began a roller coaster ride through these unspoilt mountains. Sometimes long vistas opened up for us of endless, rolling hills, carpeted in forest and cultivated tracts, bananas and papayas thriving alongside sunflowers that grew to a height of twenty feet. Then we were descending again along a gravelly track with loose stones ready to upturn the unwary.

The villages we passed were very small, usually consisting of no more than a few brick-built, tiny buildings with tin roofs, sometimes with a little store selling soda drinks, biscuits and basic necessities. Pumpkins, maize and a few other vegetables were often cultivated in small patches adjacent to the houses. As we passed by, villagers would come to the roadside and clap, smile or offer encouraging cheers. Frequently we heard the words "pole, pole", swahili for "slowly, slowly", which at times, given our tedious progress over the treacherous track, could have been taken as an urge to go faster!

As always, the first job after pitching the tent, was to get inside and clean at least essential parts of the body with baby wipes. But the temperature, which had been hovering above 100 degrees Fahrenheit, had barely dropped. Inside the tent the heat was magnified. So while cleaning off the day's sweat and grime, new sweat was pouring from the pores. (Camp 50, map Tanzania)

Having seen and felt the warmth of the local people, it was always saddening to hear of anything other than kindness. A case in point was what happened to Knut, one of our Norwegian riders. He had stopped for a Coke along the way, and came out to find his bike computer missing. By chance, the dinner truck was passing, driven by Gert, who spoke Swahili. He stopped and addressed all the villagers there and then.

Remarkably, the computer reappeared. We had not felt the need to be too careful in Tanzania. But during the night, a number of water bottles went missing from the bikes, which surprised us.

Before I fell asleep, I heard the villagers, just down the road, singing for about half an hour. Not for the first time, I was aware how close I was to village life in central Africa, but without the energy, time or opportunity to immerse myself in it.

Time cycling 7hrs 25mins
Average speed 16.3kph
Km covered 5,833 Yet to go 6,176

Sunday, March 21: Lembe school - bush camp 99 km

We had camped at an altitude of 1500m. The mist, woken from its slumber by the first light, drifted above the tops of the forested mountains and followed their slopes down to take refuge in the valleys below. It seemed that all the villagers were lining the road to wave us off as we sped along the bumpy track, keen to make as much progress as possible before the heat assailed us. During the first few kilometres, we encountered a number of men, sometimes in small groups, opening earth gulleys from the roadside and into the land to act as drains; did they know something we did not?

Although descending, the track was rocky with pockets of loose sand. At the bottom of one particularly scary descent which ended with a sharp bend hiding a hollow of soft sand, Sharita had carefully positioned herself with a big camera, ready to capture the many falls that she anticipated would occur. Sharita was a tough cookie, one we came to very much like and admire.

Villages must have been set back a little from the road, as we saw few huts, but rarely did much time pass without seeing someone, whether it be children shouting greetings, men with adzes over their backs or women carrying firewood on their heads. Cattle and goats often crossed the track without warning. You could but keep your line and leave it to them to get out of the way, just as the occasional bus, hurtling along, expected us to do.

Lunch at 61 km was so welcome. The constant jarring and vibration was taking its toll, especially on our hands, wrists and arms. After lunch, the now wide track became less corrugated but more of a continuous sand pit of deep loose sand. It was impossible to maintain any speed at all. Away from the road, there were many, narrow, packed-earth paths used by the villagers, that made for more comfortable riding. Some riders, it turned out later, had made good use of them. Jeff in particular was most elated as, for a long stretch, a local cyclist led him through the labyrinth. Not all were so lucky. Dave got six flats, and managed to lose his way. He ended up biking through a cornfield and yelling "JAMBO" (Swahili for hello) at the top of his voice until a local found him amidst the corn and set him back on course.

There was one Coke stop at about 80 km, where I stopped with Adam, (Canadian) Eric and Pete. Now, tall Pete was as affable and easy-going a character as you could wish to meet. But he was getting a bit hot under the collar as the woman behind the counter could not understand that he wanted two Cokes not one. A simple enough thing, but with the heat and stress of the day, his patience momentarily deserted him. We were all surprised how tough the conditions were. Most riders found the previous day, a mando day, to have been easier.

Dana had this to say about the day in her blog: "I was completely exhausted when I woke up in the morning. There simply isn't enough time to recover sometimes when the riding is tough and long and you go to bed only a couple of hours after the ride ends only to wake up and have to get on the bike again. In any event, I got on the bike and suffered through the first 30 km, taking a pretty big fall very early on, around 7 km. Erin, riding directly behind me, saw the mess unfold in slow motion. We were riding on loose and rocky terrain and I hit a patch of deep sand. Erin says I flipped upwards and backwards and I jammed my right knee in the fall. Covered in dirt and sand, I pathetically shouted "self-pity, self-pity, self-pity" because saying it versus just feeling it can somehow make the whole situation seem absurdly funny. Once Erin made sure nothing was broken, she did what a good friend would do which is to continue to ride and leave me in the dirt with an opportunity to regain my composure and dignity. 'Take a moment', she said and rode off."

Arriving in camp (51, map Tanzania), in my case about 4pm, but considerably earlier for the racers, the dinner truck was still to arrive. The rack above the cab which carried the bikes, had broken and needed welding. For those of us with lockers on that truck, that meant we had nothing to clean ourselves with, no tent to put up, not even a cup and cutlery. All we could do was sit around and wait. When it finally arrived an hour later, it got well and truly stuck at the entrance to the field. Eventually, we were allowed to go over and take our stuff out while they continued to try to free the truck.

So there was little time for anything after that, just a late dinner and bed.

Km covered 5,932 Yet to go 6,077

Monday, March 22: Bush camp – Dodoma 113 km

The rule was that you were not allowed into the lorries to put away your baggage in your locker more than half an hour before breakfast. This was to give the Indaba crew, who slept inside, ample time to get out and about. In practice, they were out well before then and several of us would increasingly enter a little earlier in order to conjure up for ourselves a few precious minutes with a coffee before breakfast. Coffee was always the first thing the staff made in a morning. The fresh brew in a big pot was preferred to the instant coffee.

Now however, we were to be allowed to access our lockers half an hour earlier, at 6.15, with breakfast brought forward accordingly to 6.45. This was a most welcome move as the sooner we started out on our bikes in a morning, the less exposure we had to the sun.

Everyone took off in their own time. I left about 7.10. A few riders had decided to hitch hike and were immediately in luck. A Presbyterian minister was on his way to Dodoma in his air-conditioned vehicle. He picked them up and had them in town for 9.30. So they were the few that had the time to visit the centre of Dodoma, Tanzania's administrative capital.

Kelsey was using the local paths and making better progress than I was on the straight, gravelly track. I decided to try it. Certainly the surface was much easier and more interesting. Intending to catch Kelsey, I rounded a bend and there she was, stood with her bike on the ground, looking quite shaken. On the floor lay a local man, his bike beside him, his mouth area bleeding. He was complaining bitterly. He had come from a side track, perhaps in the same manner he had done hundreds of times before, only this time he collided with a foreigner who he probably believed had no right to be there. I tried to console him, but there was nothing to do but move on.

For the rest of us, it was a delight to once more ride on tarmac as we approached the capital after another day of slogging through sand with continual thirst. Our destination was a small motel on the outskirts, where we would be able to pitch our tents on the grass. (Camp 52, map Tanzania) I arrived soon after 2pm, desperate to wash my laundry and charge up my camera and netbook. I went straight to the dinner truck and started extricating my tent and baggage from the locker, when Jeff came in to get something. "We got a room," he said. "They are only charging 25 dollars for a double." I thought for a moment. By the time I had pitched my tent and done the washing, how much time would there be for drying? On principle, I was there to camp. But let's be practical, I thought. I stuffed my tent back in the locker and went to reception. Just one room left. I asked her to show me it. The toilet did not flush, there were no towels and the basin needed a strong knee against it to hold it in place while using it. "I'll take it!" I said. It cost me £10. But I soon had the washing out to dry, days of grime removed in the shower and I felt justified in treating myself to the most wonderful ice-cream that a vendor was selling in the street. Then my soup, a coffee, and a beer in the bar with Steff, Reuben and Leah. Leah had joined us only a few days earlier as a sectional rider. As a reporter for a large Canadian newspaper, she would have plenty to write about.

By 10pm my washing was dry, my electrical items all charged up and I slept contentedly.

Hours cycling 5hrs 42mins
Average speed 19.7kph
Km covered 6,045 Yet to go 5,964

Tuesday, March 23: Dodoma - bush camp
93 km

Finding the correct way out of Dodoma proved more difficult than coming in. To help us, staff had been out early in one of the vehicles, tying pink ribbons at important turnings. Unfortunately, a mistake had been made and most of us were heading the wrong way. Paul came shooting after us all to redirect us. I was fortunate not to have gone too far up the wrong road, but those who were racing had cycled quite a way further; in a sense, the better the rider, the more time he/she lost as a result.

The ride was actually very pleasant, but the surface was again bumpy and very sandy in parts. After lunch, there was a tiny Coke stop. We drank warm Coke in an octagonal shelter, with benches for about eight of us. Just behind us, a lady was cooking meat in a pot over a charcoal fire. She was running a "hotel" we were told. Two young men were unloading huge sacks of seeds to store them in a little room behind us. Nearer the road, two young men sat under a shelter studiously playing bao. The word "bao" means "board" in the local Kiswahili language and the game consists of a wooden board which has rows of holes carved into it and each player has his own stones (or seeds) which he must "sow" into the holes of his row. It is popular in many parts of Africa but seemed particularly so in Tanzania.

As we approached camp (53, map Tanzania), heavy clouds closed in on us. While pitching my tent, a shower came and went. That brief shower produced the most memorable full rainbow I have ever seen. It was remarkable that the colour densities above and below the rainbow bore no comparison to each other. Meanwhile, local children used our camp area as a playground, fascinated by our presence.

I welcomed Hardy's comment at the end of the day that he had felt tired all day as the effort of five consecutive days began to show. If he was tired, why should I be surprised at feeling worn out? As it turned out, I should not have been too encouraged, he was in fact going down with an infection.

For a couple of weeks now, I had noticed a lot of the locals shouting out what sounded to me like "baboon" when I passed, often accompanied by a laugh or chuckle. Had I deteriorated so much? As it seemed not to be happening to anyone else in the group, I decided to ask Ali, a native Kenyan who was one of our drivers, what he thought. He explained that African men normally do nothing at all once they reach fifty; they just sit around until eventually becoming ill and then die. What they were shouting was the Swahili word "Baboo", (sometimes spelt "Babu"), a greeting expressing love, affection and respect to a grandfather figure. Groups of children had also been shouting out to us "Good morning, Teacher," to which some of the girl riders had got in the habit of replying with "Good morning, students". It was beautiful to hear.

Time cycling 5hrs 20mins
Average speed 17.6kph
Km covered 6,138 Yet to go 5,871

Wednesday, March 24: Bush camp - bush camp 99 km

Shortly after leaving camp, we passed through a village where already there were animals and lorries scattered about the large open area and children were playing football. It looked like a market day and sure enough, for fully fifteen kilometres, we were to witness small groups of goats or cattle being driven along the track in that direction.

We incessantly searched for the smoothest part of the track, so we were constantly changing our tack on the dirt. Turning into heaped loose gravel in order to cross onto a better surface is when most often a fall resulted. A motorcyclist in a grey suit was coming my way. I was on the wrong side of the road, but I was not about to risk moving over just at that point. For him, it would be much easier. But he did not realise until too late that I was determined to keep my line. When he did try to take action, he was travelling too slowly, lost all momentum and came off. He was agitated and angry. You might think badly of me, but I did, quietly, find it rather amusing.

As we topped a small rise, the wonderful view of Mtera reservoir opened up below us. The descent was fast. We crossed the dam wall and on to lunch at 54 km. Food had become a little more varied recently especially with the increased availability of fruit. We were now eating fresh mangoes, pineapples, guavas, passion fruit, and the biggest, most ripe avocados imaginable.

The track had not been too bad and yet we all felt tired. Then Jenny mentioned that the temperatures were getting up to 39 degrees during the day. Tony added that he recorded the temperature in his tent the previous night as 32 degrees. I thought I had had a fever, but it was actually just the ambient temperature.

After lunch, clouds rolled in and kept the temperature down somewhat. Our camp (54, map Tanzania) lay on a remote, lightly wooded hillside, from where we could look back over the flat expanse that we had crossed since lunch and beyond that to the reservoir, now looking like a silver thread edging the dark mountains behind.

Eric D offered me some water to wash myself with. By packing all his gear in square boxes, he maximised on the amount of space in his locker, creating enough room for a small drum of water. Although I only used 2-3 pints, I felt like a new man. We had cycled six days in a row on rough tracks, without a rest. The only tarmac had been in Dodoma itself. We badly needed a rest day. We expected the following day to be relatively short, enabling us to cycle into bustling Iringa very early.

Hours cycling 6hrs 47mins
Average speed 14.4kph
Km covered 6,237 Yet to go 5,772

Thursday, March 25: Bush camp – Iringa 74 km

During the night, it threw it down. It was still raining at 5am. So I decided to give it a little longer, and fell asleep again. When I awoke at 6am, the rain had practically stopped. I did not waste any time taking down my tent, for fear of missing breakfast, but I did notice that another tent pole section had splintered.

The chances of getting to Iringa very early were dashed by the news that we would be climbing for the first 20 km and for the last 20 km also.

As we set off, the mountains were covered in mist which turned to light rain at the top. But I loved the freshness in the air and the cooler temperatures. Frequently we saw men cutting the high grass along the roadside with large knives, something so often neglected at home despite the availability of machinery.

Sunflowers and maize were still the predominant crops, all the work being done manually. The few houses and villages that we encountered were, like all others in Tanzania, clean and orderly, no matter how simple and basic.

We arrived in the bustling town of Iringa to stay in the grounds of a girls' secondary school about 3 km out of town. (Camp 55, map Tanzania) Most of the shops were of the small shack style. I did not hold out much hope of finding a new tent pole.

We would have a day's rest or rather a day not cycling there, before heading off out to the main road for three days of cycling to the Malawi border.

Km covered 6,311 Yet to go 5,698

Friday, March 26: Rest day in Iringa

James had the job of not only cooking for us, but also of buying in all the ingredients. So at each town we came to, he would make for the market and buy in enough for the days until the next town. Now, with about 11 sectional riders joining us, and other full-time riders coming back from their breaks, he would have about 85 mouths to satisfy. He took a genuine interest in African cooking, both in the ingredients used and in the method of preparing them. After cooking for the previous year's TDA, he had a very good idea of what was available and where to find it as we passed through Africa. We were never allowed to go hungry and given the restrictions of availability, he varied our meals as best he could.

I intended going down to the market with him at about 10am. At 6am, a number of us were looking for a toilet that worked and a tap that had water. Neither was easy to find. I washed my laundry and cleaned my bike. With no food there at the school, and feeling too hungry to wait for James, I joined a number of others and went into town to the Hasty Tasty Too café. The third generation Indian owner had a remarkable menu and the name of his establishment told it all. But even his resources were stretched by our demanding appetites.

Paul Porter and I wandered down to the market, where James was negotiating for his bulk purchases. Lorries were unloading at one end of the market. I noticed huge sacks of avocados that a fit man was struggling to unload from a small lorry. Each sackful was valued at £25. They had been grown near the Malawian border. At the other end of the market, a bus with a full load of passengers, drove right up to the entrance of the market to unload round, cane baskets containing tomatoes and eggs. These baskets came in various sizes and were in some instances lined. The bus also had a lot of these baskets in the luggage compartment. A basket on the roof contained hens.

Staples like millet, rice and potatoes were piled high on small stalls. As I stood admiring the perfectly arranged grain on one stand, the grain suddenly started quivering, until very briefly a head appeared, that of a rat. He looked very quickly in both directions before dropping back down. You would of course expect there to be rats in a market environment, but to see one so obviously at home amongst the food rather  offended my sensibilities. Determined not to be so squeamish, we bought a smallish pineapple for 50p. Passion fruits, about 30 in a bag, cost us a further 50p.

I returned on my own to camp as I had had a few things still to buy. I flagged down a daladala. But when it pulled up, I thought "No way!" It was already jam full. There was a woman in the doorway with a hen under her arm. Doubled up behind her, was a very large lady. I did not get chance to reconsider – I was bundled in, literally. My arm was unavoidably resting on the large lady's buttocks, while only a quick reach out for the side of the van with my other arm, prevented me from butting a man between the legs. The "conductor" was fiddling with my feet. I thought he was trying to upend me completely, but he was trying to push my feet inside so he could close the door.

Back at camp, my washing was dry, lots of riders were already working on their bikes. I joined them in changing back from fat tyres to skinnies in readiness for the following day's return to tarmac.

For dinner, it was back to the Hasty Tasty Too for chicken curry and a milkshake..... to start with anyway.

Saturday, March 27: Iringa - forest camp
105 km

"Single file! No iPods! These next three days will be the most dangerous days of the Tour. If you ride side by side, the lorries will run you over like a piece of shit, and will not stop to look back at the mess!" Thus Sharita left us in no doubt at the morning riders' meeting that we had to be on our guard.

Being back on tarmac felt great. The traffic never materialised, perhaps due to it being a Saturday, though those lorries that did pass us, clearly saw us as a nuisance that should not be on the road. We continued through the verdant hills of Southern Tanzania, seeing the simple houses, usually with windows and doorways but no glass or doors, with sunflowers and maize grown patchwork fashion, according to the folds of the ground.

For mile after mile, the planted forests of the Sao Forest Reserve were being harvested and replanted, part of an initiative between government and private enterprise. Our camp for the night (56, map Tanzania) lay alongside a track through one of these forests.

Km covered 6,416 Yet to go 5,593

Sunday, March 28: Forest - bush camp
128 km

From an altitude of 1850m, we followed what must have been the spine of the mountain ridge, always looking out over vast expanses of pristine greenery with no sign of other roads, fences or villages, just wilderness. With moderate temperatures, a good road surface and little traffic, this was one of the best cycling days so far. (Camp 57, map Tanzania)

Time cycling 4hrs 43mins
Average speed 27.9kph
Km covered 6,544 Yet to go 5,465

Monday, March 29: Bush camp – Mbeya
95 km

Our last full day in Tanzania brought us to Mbeya. (Camp 58, map Tanzania) Again, we were using the grounds of a small hotel. There was no hot water and the water was brown, but at least we could wash our cycling gear. After doing that, I walked 200m into the melee of shops and street vendors, a cacophony of music, shouting and horns blaring. I entered a small café to order food. I was taken through the back into a small courtyard. Spartan rooms formed two sides of what was clearly a hostel, while on the third side there was a tiny kiosk for preparing food. Availability was restricted to chips, fried beef and fried banana. A chair was brought to the only table where a man was already seated. His name was Bawela. He was a long distance lorry driver, currently taking clothes and haberdashery down to Angola. He received no holidays and often drove up to 20 hours a day. He once drove the 1800 km from Dar es Salaam to Lilongwe leaving one day and arriving the next. (I was thinking at that moment to get off the road each time a lorry approached in future.) He was paid US$75 a week, out of which he had to pay all his own expenses. Yet he managed to find $1500 a year to send his only child to an international school, because he knew that there was no alternative if she was ever to rise out of the poverty he found himself saddled with. His whole demeanour spoke of decency, his face betrayed a man growing old before his time.

Lining up for dinner that evening, I found myself next to Franz. A time or two he had helped me with small computer problems, something he was well qualified to do as a specialist computer consultant. I mentioned a small problem I had and in a stern manner he said he would look at it but that would then be the last time he wanted to see my computer. As I asked him whether I had upset him in anyway, I touched his arm and he warned sharply, "Do not touch my arm!" "What is wrong with your arm, Franz?" I asked. He explained that it was festering and he was not feeling well. I told him to forget about the computer, it was not important, and proceeded to ask him if he was taking any vitamin pills, which he was not. Given that he had suffered for weeks with first his leg and now his arm, I suggested he started to take vitamin supplements. I had a stock of cod liver oil capsules as well as vitamin C and multivitamin tablets from which I made up a 20 day supply for him. This would last him until his girlfriend joined him in Livingstone, from where she would ride with him to Cape Town.

After dinner, I walked down to the same area as earlier. There were no street lights but the place was buzzing. In the back streets, I stopped to take it all in. On one side of the street, visible through an open window, I saw a large room packed with people sat on benches beside long tables, drinking a white liquid out of large beakers. On the other side of the street, folk were suspiciously coming and going through a small doorway. What were they doing? A man saw my curiosity and signalled for me to go in. Naturally, I resisted. His English was very limited, but he was talking about bamboo juice. He led me through the doorway and down a dark passageway, leading us past various small rooms, each containing a few people, all seemingly drinking. The passage opened on to a small courtyard with access to half a dozen more rooms. In one, a man was up dancing, another had a TV blaring out. I wondered what I was doing here, receiving funny looks, one hand on my wallet, the other on the custard creams I had bought. The small room we entered was filled by a dozen men sat around a table. On the table was the same white liquid I had seen through the window – bamboo juice, served in 1 litre plastic jugs, at a cost of 300 shillings per litre, about 15p.The atmosphere was friendly. As I did not want bamboo juice – it smelt like silage – I was served a Coke. A man who spoke some English, explained to me that people drank as often as they could afford to. If you bought 5 litres of the juice, the price halved. He would usually drink 5 – 10 litres in one sitting. Nobody seemed drunk, a bit spaced out perhaps. But it was only about 8pm and drinking normally continued till about 10pm. Home-brewed beer (pombe) is common in Tanzania; when it is made from fermented bamboo juice, it is called ulanzi. It is alcoholic, but is not generally dangerous. This of course, I only learnt later.

My curiosity sated, I now just wanted to get back to my bed, so I politely said farewell. My guide, Matthias, led me out. Back on the street, he wanted to show me inside the room on the other side. It was much the same except for a much higher percentage of women, and also led into a courtyard with small rooms leading off. In one room, a man stood out from the rest, appearing educated and prosperous. He wanted me to stay and talk. But his forthright manner led me to believe he had already drunk quite enough and I passed on the opportunity to converse with him. This trip seemed to be making an unsocial animal of me.

Matthias insisted on walking me back to the hotel. He warned me to be careful at night as there was always a bit of danger for foreigners. I was very grateful for his kindness in looking after me, and it seemed fitting to give a short embrace. Unfortunately, we both moved our heads in the same direction and embarrassingly bumped our heads together.

Tanzania had proved to us that no country was going to be easy on this trip. The TDA's well thought out schedule made quite sure of that. But this country had provided us with scenery that had, in my opinion, surpassed even that of Ethiopia. The lush growth and the gentle, relaxed nature of its people would have been hard to leave but for the prospect of even more beauty in the next country, Malawi.

Back home, my wife Carole had to celebrate yet another of her birthdays in my absence. She had chosen to organise a coffee morning and sale of our home-grown freesias to raise some extra cash for Thamsanqa. She made a tidy sum through her efforts.

Time cycling 4hrs 7mins
Average speed 27.9kph
Km covered 6,639 Yet to go 5,370

CHAPTER 10
MALAWI

Tuesday, March 30: Mbeya - bush camp
120 km

While having our breakfast, mist suddenly descended and obliterated the magnificent views of the surrounding mountains. From our altitude of 1600m, a 20 km climb to 2450m lay ahead of us, taking us over the mountains and then down to Malawi.

Quickly cycling up through the mist to reach the sunny heights, we looked back on the thick layer of trapped cloud below us. There was no flat land, just unending hills in every shade of green, small fields growing all manner of crops, resembling a tartan tapestry. Children were on their way to school, men and women walked purposefully, usually with an adze over the shoulder. The dwellings were very simple, of mud or bricks, roofed with tin. But with such a highly fertile soil and a wonderful climate, why were they so poor? We were witnessing their countryside at its most lush and productive. But the rainy season at this altitude had almost passed and from May to November, the hills would turn the colour of lightly browned toast. I was amazed to see poinsettias, daturas and rhododendrons flowering profusely at over 2200m. Bananas were particularly prominent, cabbages could be seen, but we also cycled past large tea plantations. The scenery was captivating. On both sides of us, in the mid-distance, flat-topped mountain ranges signposted our passage. Tiny shops sold the beautiful coloured cloths used by most women to wrap themselves in. Women walked along the road carrying huge loads of bananas. But we catapulted up and down those mountain slopes, in what was the most exhilarating ride so far, at speeds too fast to allow us time to take in the richness of sight and sound about us. Rather than savour these moments, the

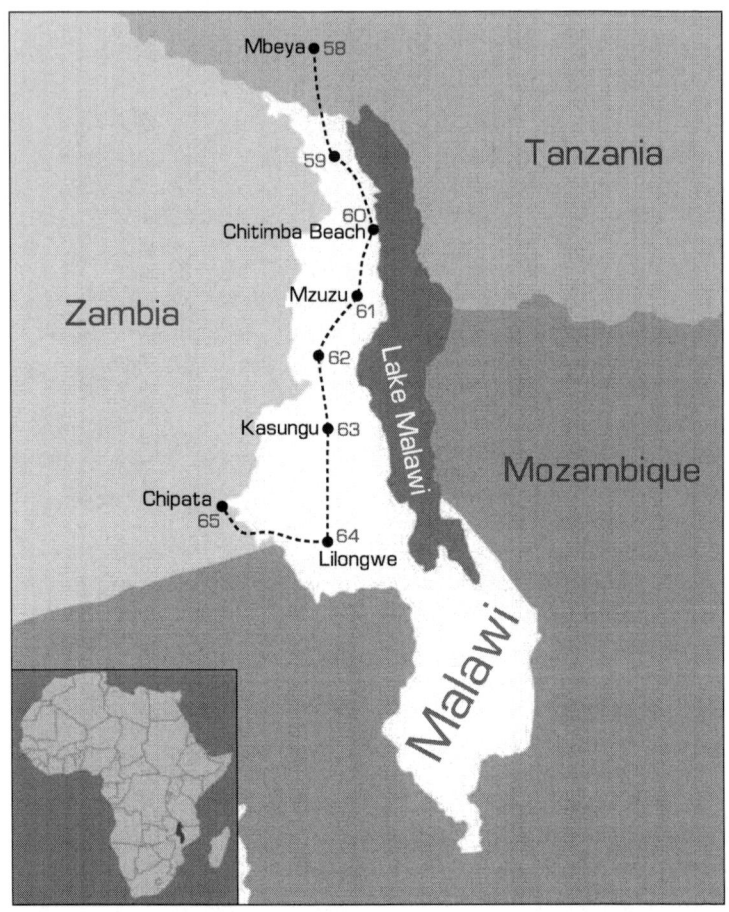

fresh mountain air and nature's opulence led us forward at a frenetic pace to voraciously devour the miles.

After 106 km, we approached the scruffy border crossing. Sometimes we had crossed borders without noticing any difference in the place or its people. But as we crossed into Malawi, the distended bellies of so many of the children, their ragged clothing and tendency to insist on being given money suggested to me a country not unlike a luscious fruit rotting in the heat and humidity. Begging for money is not a trait inherent in the person, but one often borne out of so-called aid; but of course it is understandable in a wretchedly poor person. Although humour is hard to imagine in such surroundings, I do smile at the thought of the man, not badly-dressed, who shouted to Rod "give me your bike!" He was perplexed by Rod's reply, "give me cow".

Just 10 km further on we arrived at our bush camp (59, map Malawi), where a perimeter rope had to be used once again, reminding us of Ethiopia, as hundreds of children surrounded us. They watched us eat our soup, then our evening meal and were back again at dawn to watch us take breakfast. Perhaps we should have been understanding that a number of our bike computers and various small items like sunglasses were lifted.

Time cycling 4hrs 50mins
Average speed 24.9kph
Km covered 6,759 Yet to go 5,250

Wednesday, March 31: Bush camp - Chitimba 122 km

As I was taking down my tent at 5am, the soothing sound of Africans singing floated out from the little brick building adjacent to our camp, which the villagers used as a church. It lasted perhaps five minutes.

We were all looking forward to riding to the camp site (60, map Malawi) at Chitimba Beach on Lake Malawi. Firstly though, we had to cycle 3 km to the nearest town. Instead of being swindled by the money-changers at the border, we had been advised to take out money from a bank. In a little store selling a few basics, our queue filled the narrow aisle as we waited for the sole cashier to take our newly-gained Malawian currency.

Heading south, rounding the northern end of Lake Malawi and down its western side, the flat terrain was initially devoted almost entirely to the production of rice in small paddy fields. Oxen provided the power. There were many people about on the road, on foot or cycling, but no motor vehicles. Although near the lake, we could not see it.

Our first good view occurred after about 70 km. The rice fields had long since disappeared and there were fewer people. Cycling up a rise, the lake appeared on our left, dark blue through the sunglasses, with the ridge of mountains behind it. There were no more views till about 90 km when we dropped down to a small, fishing village, where thatched, mud huts huddled together by the lakeside. The villagers' diet depended on fish which they dried on long racks, made from reeds. There was absolutely no modern development to be seen. The reason I supposed, was the incidence of disease. We were told that Malawi was the easiest country in the world in which to catch malaria. One of our riders was soon to fall very ill with the disease and needed hospitalising. Then there was the bilharzia in the water. Snails, which are common to the reeds on the lakeside, are hosts to bilharzia, whose larvae can pass through our skin. Once inside our bodies, they constantly copulate and produce eggs, infecting our major organs. There is effective treatment and indeed there were no reeds at Chitimba beach. Mark, one of the sectional riders, who had spent a lot of time working in Malawi, also informed us about the putsi fly which can lay its eggs on clothes drying on the line. The larvae burrow into your skin, creating boils, out of which emerge the adult flies. There were many other tropical creatures waiting to use us as tropical fare. Furthermore, all our cuts and bites putrefied rather than healed in the heavy, humid heat. Sores that had seemed to be drying up, now reopened and wept.

That said, after 125 km of cycling, much of it into a headwind, these thoughts in no way diminished our delight on arriving at the camp site. The thatched huts that housed the bar, toilets and showers, sat on the edge of the wide sandy beach, looking across the lake to the mountains beyond. Just before dark, a few of us walked to the water's edge. Listening to the lapping of the water, driven by a stiff breeze across the lake, we watched an electrical storm playing out over the Tanzanian mountains on the far side, some 50 km away.

The storm did not reach us, but we got a terrific downpour during the night. It woke me up and only then was I aware that there was an almighty racket coming from the bar, where a group of overlanders were letting their hair down. That was about 2.30am. Although sweaty, neither that nor the noise prevented me from having a magnificent sleep.

Km covered 6,881 Yet to go 5,128

Thursday, April 1: Rest day at Chitimba beach

Dawn brought with it a light rain shower, but through the tent flap I could still see the lake. After washing my dirty clothes and putting them out to dry, I shaved before inspecting my tent. The poles had snapped so many times that I no longer had any sleeves with which to repair them. Knowing other riders also had tent pole problems in no way at all helped me. But by taking a good pole from my first tent, I was able to stave off the day of complete tent failure.

High in a large shade tree near my tent, two disassembled bikes had been wedged between the branches. This was after all April Fools' Day. Poor Steff was feeling quite ill that morning and felt incapable of enjoying the joke or retrieving her bike. Jennifer, perhaps the owner of the other bike, brought it down for her.

The setting at Chitimba Beach was relaxing. In front of us lay the third largest freshwater lake in Africa, from which half of the world's aquatic fish originate. A few of us had been dithering over whether or not to swim in the lake. But when you think that our showers were probably pulling water from the lake, there seemed no sense in depriving ourselves of our last chance to swim for a long while. The water was tepid but refreshing. A few local children were already playing in the water. Their huts could not be seen through the trees, but dugout canoes, drawn up on the beach some hundred yards away, gave some indication of their location.

Although a rest day, the TDA provided us with breakfast and dinner because the camp site kitchen could not cater for so many mouths. Local villagers sold us three pigs, and by mid-morning had begun roasting them over spits. Accompanied by rice and vegetables, the pork was delicious. Some riders apparently complained about the amount of fat on the meat, which I thought extraordinary. For once, I felt no compunction about eating all the fat.

Tiny waxbills and other types of finches flitted about. The wind was getting up, though not enough to drown the castanet-like clicking of the frogs. Lightning flickered over the water. To put my mind at rest, fearing a storm, I checked my tent again before settling in for the night, and yet another section of a pole was starting to splinter. I decided that if the tent was around my ankles in the morning, it would be time to come up with Plan C. I was thinking in terms of canes. Something easily renewable.

Friday, April 2: Chitimba beach – Mzuzu
136 km

A bridge forming part of the lakeside road had been partially washed away, forcing us to follow a route a little further inland. After following the lake for 16 km, our detour entailed an 8% climb over 10 km that presented us with incredible views. Below, we could see the Chitimba river discharging its muddy waters into the lake. The twisting road followed the cliff faces, down which waterfalls bounded at speed. Halfway up this climb, sweaty in the early morning heat, we stopped - at least, those of us not racing did - by a 30ft waterfall right alongside the road. The cool, pulsating water provided the best shower so far.

Once over the top of the mountain, we enjoyed an exciting descent to the rushing river, which we followed upstream through a very long winding valley. Crossing the river at one point, there was a little store where we stopped for a drink. (I am saying "we", though we were cycling mostly singly or in couples, changing positions quite often.) On the verandah, two men were taking tobacco leaves out of a sack, grading them for length and bunching them. A man looking on was the farmer, who spoke decent English. He told me that he grew a variety of crops, which included 3 acres of tobacco. These bunches were going to the auction in Mzuzu. He smiled when I asked him about price; maybe he preferred the two workers not to know how much money he received. But he then told me that the price normally started at about 1-2US$ per kilo, and could reach as high as 4.50.

A lot of tobacco was grown down this valley. Tobacco leaves hung to dry under numerous thatched shelters. For us passing by, they presented a pretty sight. Unfortunately, this major Malawi industry had been controlled by international companies who had connived to keep low the prices they paid. Growers and workers, including at least 80,000 children (in 2008), had been forced to live in poverty as a result. Wheat, cassava, millet and maize were also being grown, but on a lesser scale.

I would not normally be aware of the day or the date, but it still came as a surprise that it was Good Friday and I had not realised. It was brought home to me when we passed a procession of people on the road, mostly dressed in purple robes, praying behind a large cross being carried at the head of the procession. They took up one full side of the road as presumably they followed the fourteen Stations of the Cross.

Our overnight stay in Mzuzu (camp 61, map Malawi) was once again in the grounds of a small hotel. My first job on arrival was to go hunting for canes to see if I could use them as tent poles. I found plenty of cane round the back of the hotel and cut myself some lengths. But they were not flexible enough to work with; it was a complete waste of time. Franz advised me to have a word with the three Dutch sectional riders who would be leaving us when we reached Lilongwe in three days time. One of them did agree to sell me his tent at a reasonable price. As a number of riders were having problems with their tents, I was indeed lucky to have asked early enough.

Back now at 1500m, the air was very noticeably fresher. Instead of sweating in our tents, we were able to sleep comfortably.

Time cycling 6hrs 19mins
Average speed 21.8kph
Km covered 7,017 Yet to go 4,992

Saturday, April 3: Mzuzu - Luviri school
126 km

Thick grey mist had descended on Mzuzu, bringing with it a creeping cold. As we climbed out of the town between walls of forest, the mist turned to light rain. Along the roadside, stacks of tree trunks in a raw state or already shaped into beams and battens, awaited collection. The heavy machinery worked at a distance from the road, hidden from our view, the wood brought to the roadside by tractor and trailer. Flat deck and container lorries parked patiently just off the shoulder of the road, waiting to be loaded manually. I was quite surprised to see a number of lorries from the UK, whose names I was familiar with.

Cycling into camp (62, map Malawi), set amongst various low buildings scattered around a field, we could have been forgiven for thinking there was a party under way. This was Easter Saturday, and Malawians clearly took their Christianity seriously. A queue of people carried bowls with them into one of the buildings and came out with them full. Kids were kicking a deflated football about. Some of our lads blew it up and had a game with them. I was told that the locals thrashed us. Later on, women and older girls came swaying between our tents, singing religious hymns. Their singing continued late on into the night from somewhere nearby. Despite being wrapped up tightly in our sleeping bags in the cool night air, everyone could recall the renewal of singing at 4am.

Time cycling 6hrs 5mins
Average speed 20.7kph
Km covered 7,143 Yet to go 4,866

Sunday, April 4: Luviri school – Kasungu
112 km

As we were finishing our breakfast at about 6.45, a group of the women sang and danced nearby with great joy, almost deliriously. It was Easter Sunday after all. I envied their energy and blissful rapture as I pulled on my jacket to cycle off into the initial cold.

Even at such an early hour, women sat by the roadside with bowls of vegetables or fruit. Who they hoped to sell them to I do not know – we saw less than twenty vehicles all day. Many people were walking however, often dressed appropriately to go to church. Groups of children would sometimes await our coming, screaming hello and goodbye to us in the same breath and literally jumping up and down with delight.

At the lunch stop, Simon was hunched over on a chair. He was desperate not to lose his yet intact EFI status. But the staff were worried that his symptoms resembled those of malaria. He was taken into the truck for a quick test, which proved that thank God he did not have malaria. So he got back on his bike and struggled on.

(Camp 63, map Malawi)

Time cycling 4hrs
Average speed 28kph
Km covered 7,255 Yet to go 4,754

Monday, April 5: Kasungu – Lilongwe
131 km

I was having difficulty finding a spot by the road where there were no people or houses. It was post-lunch, and I needed the toilet. But most of the ground was planted up with small plots of maize, with the huts just out of sight behind. I did not want to contaminate someone's working area, and even less did I want to be caught doing so. Eventually providence provided, not a soul in sight. I did what I needed to do, came back to my bike and, for the first time while cycling, took out the iPod I had bought in Nairobi. I put the plugs in my ears with a bandana to cover them - otherwise they just dropped out - and then became aware of a woman and two children standing beside me. The mother was carrying a hen under her arm. She said hello and I said hello. Then the awaited words, "give me my money!" Said with such a smile, you would have thought she was just politely calling in a debt. "Nice hen", I said stupidly, and cycled off.

We discussed at such length between ourselves as to why it should be that so many felt no indignity in begging. Clearly, these people were very poor. They were also, perhaps, the most genuinely friendly and good-natured people that we had yet met. This culture of expectation, of something for nothing, had to have been super-imposed, by the large donor organisations, and travellers that pass through irresponsibly throwing out sweets or money for the children to fight over.

In Lilongwe, our camp site for the night (64, map Malawi) and for the following rest day, had hot water, a pool and a bar/restaurant. Mature trees gave plenty of shade for us to pitch our tents and relax on green grass. I immediately knocked back two glasses of cold milk, which I had craved for weeks, a beer, two coffees, a club sandwich, rice salad and a Mars bar.

With the so-called Malawi Gin section of the trip now finished, eleven sectional riders would be saying their goodbyes.

Mark was one of them who had integrated with the group very quickly. He had a way with words, and a wit to match, that had been like a breath of fresh air. He had brought a depth of knowledge about Malawi with him from his time working in Malawi for the DIFD (formerly the British Dep't for Overseas Development). I was very sad to see him go.

Another sectional rider, Jos, had agreed to sell me his tent for US$50. Bought especially for the trip, he had only used it for the week. He explained that while most riders were threading poles through tent seams and pegging down, he merely took out the tent from its outer sleeve and it opened out for immediate use. Folding it away was almost as quick, once the technique was mastered. This tent was now to be my back-up, to be used only when I could not squeeze another night out of tent number two.

Time cycling 5hrs 11mins
Average speed 25.3kph
Km covered 7,386 Yet to go 4,623

Tuesday, April 6: Rest day in Lilongwe

No book could have been more relevant at this time than one I now borrowed from another rider. Its title was "The boy who harnessed the wind", written by William Kamkwamba. He recalls his childhood in Kasungu in simple, unexaggerated terms. The majority of people lived on the land, barely sustaining themselves or their families, prey to the vagaries of nature. They never had enough cash to chemically treat their staple crop of maize so that they could store it. So they had to sell it to the government and later buy it back at exhorbitant prices. As the reader is taken through the horrific famine of 2001 and its far-reaching consequences, the heartbreaking circumstances are balanced by the hope and inspiration he gave his people through his own ingenuity and determination.

I now knew that some of the people who I had been passing on my bike would have lived through those harrowing times. The smiles they wore would be what caught the tourist's eye; the scars they bore would be less obvious. The lady with the hen would surely have been one of them.

Although not as high as in S. Africa, the HIV percentage of the population was very high here. We had all noticed how many coffin shops there were strung out along the roadside.

It came as a surprise to me then, that this small city, in such a poor country, appeared to offer most of what you would expect in a non-third world country, with the exception of fast internet. After washing my laundry, I walked down to town for about 6am. Some young men were picking through a refuse skip while little stalls were being erected. All pretty quiet. I found a small hotel for breakfast, then used the internet to post the blog. When I came out, it was into very busy crowds.

Reiner, you might remember, had suffered a bad fall on the tar, some time back. He had been waiting for us in Lilongwe. His hope, to start cycling again from there, was not to be realised. But he started to sleep once more in his tent at night, ride the truck, and as soon as his mobility allowed, would resume cycling.

Laura, who had fallen ill after recovering from her fall in Sudan, had then been knocked to the ground by the side-mirror of a bus travelling at 40kph while she was walking in Nairobi. Apart from a severe gash to the head and other abrasions, she had again suffered concussion. Throughout all of this, she would always, incredibly, have a smile. But she had had no option other than to return to Belgium. She had been gone perhaps two weeks. The word now was that she was coming back.

Wednesday, April 7: Lilongwe - Mama Rula's camp 154 km

We were fascinated to see the many uses that the locals found for their bikes. Leaving the outskirts of Lilongwe, we saw many cyclists, all heading towards the city, with two vertical spars directly behind their back, to which they had lashed a carefully stacked pile of firewood, up to 6 feet high.

At 122 km we arrived at the Zambian border. At every border up till now, I had carried my yellow fever vaccination card with me. Today I had forgotten it, and the customs official would not let me through. I desperately needed a wee and was directed to a small kiosk some twenty metres away. A man stood outside, taking some small payment. I had used up all my change and was embarrassed at having to plead poverty to gain entrance. Worse still, in my rush to get to the toilet, I had forgotten to take a catheter with me and did not realise until inside the cubicle. I had to go back to my bike, get a

catheter and walk past the man a second time, trying not to be fazed by his withering look.

The customs official was uninterested in my excuse that my yellow fever vaccination card was by now in a locker, in a truck, some 30 km over the border in Zambia. We could not obtain a phone signal to contact someone at camp. I tried four times to persuade the official and on the fourth occasion, he finally relented, or got fed up, and let me through, warning me to remember next time. I was not actually thinking of returning.

Arriving in camp quite late (65, map Malawi), by the time I had finished my chores and had dinner, it was straight to bed. The following day, our first in Zambia, was going to be tough. Instead of the programmed 174 km, we would be cycling 197.

175

We had been offered the opportunity to spend our first night in Zambia staying overnight in a village. I had been the first to put my name down. Irrespective of the condition I would arrive in, and without any idea of the status of the families involved, I sensed a unique opportunity. In that, I was correct.

Time cycling 5hrs 58mins
Average speed 26.2kph
Km covered 7,540 Yet to go 4,469

CHAPTER 11
ZAMBIA

Thursday, April 8: Mama Rula's - school camp
197 km

After lunch, there was a marked change, as we exchanged the tropical plethora of plants for firstly pasture land and then bush, where isolated herdsmen tended their small groups of cattle. Villages of mud huts with conical thatched roofs, again became the norm.

As perhaps for now, you have had a bellyful of me bemoaning our bruised, beat-up and bedraggled state, I shall fast forward to the point where, in such a state, I arrived at camp (66, map Zambia). Normally, I would leave my bike where I intended to pitch my tent and extract my gear from the locker in the lorry to begin the tedious process of pitching and cleaning. But I knew I was going to spend the night in a village and did not expect to be using my tent. However, senior members of the TDA staff were not about. Riders who had arrived earlier or who had ridden the truck, sat about drinking the huge amount of beverages Tony had bought back in Lilongwe to celebrate his fiftieth birthday, with everyone invited to join in - unless of course, they had somewhere else they had to go! The reason for the absence of staff soon became clear. Michael, with whom I had shared a room in Cairo, had collided with a local man on a bike, 5 km after lunch.

Zambian riders often cycled on the wrong side of the road, so that they could take evasive action as necessary. Usually they just moved out of our way, but on this occasion there was a misunderstanding. Jethro and Franz, who were racing, were first to see him. Jethro stayed with Michael while Franz pedalled for all he was worth back to the lunch truck, from where they were able to phone ahead to Sharita. (Franz had won every mando

day up till now; this day, also a mando day, he lost his record through cycling back for help.) She immediately sped back in the runabout to pick Michael up while calls were being made to see what surgical services were available, maybe in Lusaka. He had badly cut lips, had lost a few teeth and had a broken vertebra. Apparently, time is of the essence in such a case. Step forward Bill. He was a 70-year-old practising surgeon, who had just joined us in Lilongwe as a sectional rider. This is how he described what happened:

"For me, my riding on the second day was diverted to the care of one rider who had experienced a head-on collision with a local cyclist. He had suffered a mid-line full thickness laceration of his upper lip, the tear extending to the base of his nose. From one side, a 7 millimetre tag of vermilion lip, devascularised, hung precariously by a thread. Both upper incisor teeth and one lower incisor had been knocked out. This was certainly a repair for a Plastic Surgeon. A phone call to Lusaka, 500 km away, informed us that their only Plastic Surgeon was away on holiday. The Italian Orthopaedic Hospital declined his care: 'We don't do that kind of thing here'.

"The on-call General Surgeon at the University Teaching Hospital in Lusaka refused to accept him, 'I don't do that sort of stuff'.'

"A call to an American Trauma Surgeon, volunteering in Lusaka, was quite instructive: 'Don't bring him here. He will likely be sutured by an Emergency physician or a Clinical Officer'.

"Well OK, then let's get him to South Africa. A further phone call informed us that the earliest flight to Johannesburg would depart the next day, leaving at least a 36 hour interval from injury to potential repair – decidedly too long a wait.

"And so it came to pass that my Plastic Surgery career was launched.

"Armed with some 5-0 sutures and some local anaesthetic taken from the Tour's medical kit box, the patient, Tour nurse Caroline and I proceeded 4 kilometres down the road to a mission hospital run by Irish nuns where we found a Spartan but spotless operating theatre, and all the tools we needed. We did a little operation - and we fixed him up!"

Bill had actually stitched Michael's lip twice. After the first stitching, the lip puckered slightly where some tissue had been lost. Bill extracted a sliver of gum and used this to fill the lip out. Michael did not know about this when I spoke to him some time afterwards. He now returned to spend some time convalescing with his parents, before rejoining us. I shall come back to Bill later: a most interesting man.

A couple of American women wandered into camp. They were volunteers from The American Peace Corps, helping local villages. One of them, Emily, had her own hut in the adjacent village, looking after herself, learning the local dialect, giving up two years of her life to help them with their problems and teaching their children. We now learnt from her that those of us who had elected to sample village life would still be tenting, but within the village. With heavy legs, we shouldered our gear to follow her. Not only did we turn our backs on all that free booze, we also passed Rod and Juliana as they prepared to make nanaimo bars for everyone, (custard on a cake base, topped with chocolate), in celebration of Juliana's birthday.

One of the villagers asked if we would like to take a shower. He even offered us warm water which we declined. The shower comprised a wattle screen about 4 feet high, in the shape of a small comma. Once inside the eye of the comma, there was a basin of water with which to "shower". I had set up my tent nearby and was changing within; well actually, I was trying to catch a little frog that had somehow joined me inside. At that moment, one of the villagers enquired if I was OK, perhaps thinking I was taking a long time. Strangely, he asked me if I was reading my bible. I had not the heart to tell him that my weight allowance had prevented me from bringing it with me.

The village was spread out through various clearings in the woodland, there being a total of 200 villagers, divided into 45 households. While other riders were attended to by other villagers, five of us sat down with the delightful headman, a straightforward and honest man in his sixties. His nephew, the next in line, also joined us. They answered our many questions in English. They explained how their village was one of 25 ruled over by a chief. This chief was one of a group of chiefs ruled over by senior chiefs. These senior chiefs were subservient to a paramount chief. Asked where the paramount chief lived, the headman shook his arm vaguely, pointing to some distant place where he had a "palace". (My mind was now see-sawing between the conversation and the incipient feast.) Malaria was killing ten babies a day in the district hospital. Aids was pandemic. The nephew's wife was HIV positive, so they had adopted three orphans and he used condoms. (I was rather surprised by this progressive attitude.) The headman insisted that he was trying hard to lift the standards of health and hygiene in the village by, for example, having toilets built, although he reluctantly admitted that villagers continued to use the bush out of habit.

Now a plate of food was set down in front of us as we washed our hands in a proffered bowl of warm water. They demonstrated to us how to pick up some of the nsima, a soggy maize dough, and use it to scoop up some of the vegetable which we think was either spinach or pumpkin leaves. This was not a side dish, this was their main meal, the same as it would be every other night of the year. Their only other meal was the porridge they ate for breakfast.

By now, the village was pitch black apart from a small fire burning in the middle of the clearing, under an open thatched hut. The headman welcomed us to stay with them for a week or two. In another lifetime, I would have loved to have accepted his offer. These people had a lot to teach us about humility, resilience and acceptance.

With stomachs half-full, which we accepted in empathy with our hosts, we retired to our tents. Poor Jacob was woken up about midnight by a crunching noise. To his horror, termites had eaten through the bottom sheet of the tent and covered his sleeping bag.

I had forgotten to bring with me my cycle computer, which I used to tell the time. Fearful of missing breakfast, with hunger pangs overcoming tiredness, I quietly took down my tent and packed away my things, unaware that it was only 4am. As I prepared to creep off, the headman appeared. He was solicitous as to my health; once reassured, he wanted to carry my bags for me, which of course I could not allow. He prayed that God go with me and I expressed my fervent hope that his village prospered.

The camp was as quiet as a graveyard. But there on a table, Juliana and Rod had left some of their delicious deserts!

Cycling time 7hrs 38mins
Average speed 26kph
Km covered 7,737 Yet to go 4,272

Friday, April 9: School camp - school camp
123 km

We descended into a valley and the temperature shot up at least 5 degrees to 33C and the humidity to at least 90%. Everyone was suffering, having problems staying cool and drinking enough. After the efforts of the previous day, the lack of nutrition and sleep, I began to feel quite low.

Our camp (67, map Zambia) was in a clearing where work was in progress to build a school for local villages. The heat, humidity and flies made any attempt to relax futile. The saving grace of this site was a borehole further into the woodland, which provided us with wonderfully cool water in which to wash ourselves and, more importantly, enjoy a fleeting sensation of coolness.

Time cycling 5hrs
Average speed 24.7kph
Km covered 7,860 Yet to go 4,149

Saturday, April 10: School camp - Jehovah camp
148 km (I cycled 103)

The spectacular sight of the Luange river at 25 km marked the start of a long climb. I had not expected to see such a wide river and the many stalls in the village selling large fish pointed to its importance. We climbed 2100m during the 75 km to lunch. Temperatures had risen very quickly in the morning. At the lunch stop, I felt rotten and could not eat much. 25 km further on, there was a small village. Immediately on arrival, I downed five cold drinks in quick succession. I was wobbling. Two locals in the bar were high on alcohol or drugs, jabbering to me about nothing. Wayne kept telling them to go away. Outside the next building, small fish had been laid out on a sheet to dry in the sun, tainting the air. The lunch truck pulled in to the village to take on water from a borehole in front of the shacks. Cheers went up from some of the locals as further down the street a woman started to beat up a man. I thought that I might be able to continue if I drank plenty. The riders that were there urged me to take the truck for the final 45 km. Patrick and Wayne took the decision out of my hands by lifting my bike into the truck.

When you felt unwell, the other riders were tremendously supportive. I was done in, so terribly dehydrated. I felt stupid to have allowed myself to get to that state, especially as I had been there before. Back in camp (68, map Zambia), Leanne got me to lie down under the truck with my camelback to drink from. Erin brought me a rehydration tablet, while Michelle, the medic, kept looking in on me. I noticed Rick cycle in, one of the last to do so. He looked all in. For a couple of days he had felt increasingly unwell. In fact he had a urine infection and it astonished me that he had been able to finish the ride.

Once I felt a little better, I took my bags out of the truck to set up the tent. Menno, who had not been well himself in recent days, gave me a hand. But one of the poles broke again and I had no sleeves left. It was opportune to use the tent I had bought from Jos.

I found it hard to eat or drink anything, feeling sickly, but I slept well, unlike some of the riders. About six tents were invaded during the night by marching ants: small black ants, and bigger ones with pincers, that were clinging on and biting. They crawled in through the zips and went on the rampage. Jeff reckons he was bitten more than fifty times. Erin moved her tent to a different spot. Paul moved out of his tent altogether and slept in the truck.

Time cycling 5hrs 23mins
Average speed 19.4kph
Km covered 8,008 Yet to go 4,001

Sunday, April 11: Jehovah camp-Lusaka
104 km (I did none)

As the dinner truck on which I was going to ride pulled out from the field, locals began a thorough search for anything we may have left behind. I napped during most of the journey. (Camp 69, map Zambia)

Km covered 8,112   Yet to go 3,897

Monday, April 12: Rest day in Lusaka

Many riders embraced the chance to stop in pleasant, even plush, hotels whenever the opportunity arose, which became more frequently the further south we cycled. Katja had arranged a lift to a hotel near Lusaka a few days in advance of us, to allow herself time to relax and from where she could sample a game drive. A dozen riders secured a reduced rate for the 5 star Protea Hotel. The remainder of us camped behind a rather run-down

hotel on the outskirts of town. The grass was a good base for our tents and the hotel staff were polite. But we all seemed to be worn out by relentless attacks on the body by multitudinous, nefarious bugs, bacteria and viruses which we found difficult to withstand or recover from in our depleted state. Although I was not fully aware of it at the time, which leaves me with some regrets, others suffered worse than I did, and I was walking round in a semi-zombie. state Instead of exploring the potential delights of city life, I hung about my tent, restless yet lifeless. Reiner provided an encouraging sight as he cycled repeatedly round the grass area, assessing as to whether he was capable of making his comeback. But I did not look at my bike; I gave my laundry to the hotel to wash.

The day was spiced up a little by a couple of ceremonies that took place in the hotel. The first entailed another TDA bike donation. A total of 28 new bikes, made locally, were handed over to volunteers of a charity group called Hands of God, local volunteers who offered help to orphans and those suffering from the ravages of Aids. Normally, these volunteers would have to walk everywhere, sometimes long distances, which naturally limited their work. So the bikes were welcomed warmly. The second event involved the surgeon Bill. He was cycling along with two of his nurses to raise funds for the Okanagan Zambia Health Initiative, which he was responsible for having set up. The objective, through a liaison between a Canadian and a Zambian university, was to teach medicinal skills and supply materials and back-up to the poor parts of western Zambia, in a manner which was sustainable. Two leading Zambian physicians, who had driven four hours to this event, joined Bill to elaborate, for the benefit of local dignitaries and the press that were present, on their aims, successes and future plans. Progress had been so successful that the Zambian government were keen to roll out the programme nationally.

Just down the road, there was a four star hotel, where riders had preferred to eat rather than in the hotel where we were camping. In the evening, I ate there with Steff, Jenny and Australian Dan. The sombre mood was most out of character as not one of us could raise a smile. I left early, unable to eat my food, while I could see the girls had a similar problem.

I retrieved my washing from reception; it was still wet. I had intended to ride the next day but decided that wearing wet gear would not be sensible at that moment in time.

Tuesday, April 13: Lusaka - Oasis camp
168 km

The five of us who rode in the dinner truck, napped or slept for the journey to Oasis Camp, except for Katja who read. The scenery apparently was nothing special. There was mainly a good tailwind. The riders found the ride surprisingly easy.

The board as we turned into the camp site (70, map Zambia) read "Oasis Camp: Honeymoon Couple Site". This gross exaggeration was not wholly apparent as you drove in. The reality would be cause for immediate divorce. There were several rondavelles (round, thatched huts) set amongst the trees. An unusable toilet was available for would-be honeymooners but the huts did *look* romantic. A local lady showed us inside them. They each contained three beds, with no other furniture. They did have power, but more importantly if you wanted to lie down, they offered shade. I wanted to lie down, but not to sweat inside my tent. Rick, really quite low after losing his EFI and still feeling wretched due to the urine infection, immediately opted to take one. At a cost of about US$10, I also paid for one. I felt a ridiculous pride in my humble mansion as other riders tried to pitch their tents away from the many lines of ants. Ant phobia had set in.

I was now able to dry my laundry and prepare my cycling gear. I intended cycling again the next day.

Km covered 8,280 Yet to go 3,729

Wednesday, April 14: Oasis camp - Ruze Chalet
185 km

No one suffered an ant invasion. But 15 TDA chairs and a bike went missing. This bike had a bamboo-frame. Two such bikes were being ridden for a few days by local mechanics, employees of Zambikes, the company which made the bamboo bikes. One of these men, by talking with the local villagers, found out who the thief was and he actually retrieved the bike.

I was one of the last to leave camp, and one of the last to finish cycling. The temperatures were thankfully quite moderate, similar to my energy levels. (Camp 71, map Zambia)

Another quite long ride awaited us on the morrow to take us into Livingstone, near the Victoria Falls. Water levels were particularly high so any rafting had been cancelled. But there were so many other things to do, from bungee jumping to elephant rides, that anyone who needed amusing, and more importantly had the energy, was spoilt for choice. We would have two rest days there and riders were planning and booking ahead. But as all of us were by now so well aware, there were no easy days on this Tour. Recovery time was insufficient, especially for us older ones. So taking a rest when you were able was essential, if you were serious about biking all the time.

Time cycling 7hrs 31mins
Average speed 24.7kph
Km covered 8,465 Yet to go 3,544

Thursday, April 15: Ruze Chalet – Livingstone 155 km

After a much-disrupted night, I was surprised that I felt much better altogether by breakfast time. The 80 km to lunch (at 9am!) passed through pleasant bush country, nothing special. 20 km of dirt followed lunch, with the remaining road severely potholed. 8 km from Livingstone, the road rose a little and there, about 14 km ahead of us, we saw the high spray of the Victoria Falls billowing upwards.

The town displayed all the trappings of prosperity built on a healthy tourist trade: modern supermarkets and fast food restaurants. But the many examples of early colonial homes also allowed one to imagine life in earlier times. The main thoroughfare was lined with trees and had an agreeable feel to it.

Quite a few riders had booked ahead to stay at the famous Victoria Falls Hotel. To get there, they had had to apply for a visa as they needed to cross the bridge over the Zambezi river and enter Zimbabwe. The hotel sits on the far bank from where an even better view of the Falls can be obtained. Other riders had chosen similarly exotic accommodation on or near the river. One of the Indaba drivers had been warning us all that the camp site earmarked for us by the TDA (72, map Zambia) was the worst there was. This encouraged a number of the group to migrate to a camp site on the river's edge.

So with no illusions, I cycled through town on the road to the Victoria Falls, turning off on a track leading for maybe a kilometre into the bush. It came as a pleasant surprise when I encountered the large central building, thatched in the traditional African style to which we had by now become accustomed, where large wicker chairs allowed you to sit in the shade with cold drinks and some simple food. Basic toilets and showers were clean. The one obvious niggle was the loud abstract music blaring out from a camp nearby.

The man who ran our camp site had the bearing of an ex-colonial officer; nothing was too much trouble for him. His staff were charmingly helpful too. He spent his afternoon cooking over a charcoal fire, helped by young local men whom he had adopted when they were young. He obviously was expecting a large clientele for his varied dishes. In the event I think there were three of us. I really felt for him though he did not appear to be too bothered.

Hours cycling 5hrs 58mins
Average speed 25.8kph
Km covered 8,620 Yet to go 3,389

Friday/Saturday, April 16/17: Livingstone rest days

The loud music continued without pause until 2 in the morning. When that stopped, we could then hear village drums that continued till 4.30. But the worst of all was the cockerel. The two African Indaba drivers had bought a cockerel a few days earlier. They kept it in a big cage attached to the back of the dinner truck, fattening it for eventual consumption. It started crowing at 2.30am and continued until daybreak at half hour intervals. So in the morning, I spoke to the TDA staff and insisted it go. They agreed, and I was reassured that it would be dealt with that very day.

Four of us - Hardy, Menno, (Swiss) Eric and myself - arranged for a taxi to take us to the Falls. The area around the Falls was maintained as a reserve, which cost us $US20 each to enter, but we unanimously agreed that it was well worth the money. Various paths lead you to stupendous lookout points. The mile-wide torrent hurtled towards the edge, crashing into the transverse

chasm some one hundred metres below, its only exit through a comparatively narrow gorge down which it sped in frothy fury as if the very devil himself was chasing it. It seemed strange to look down on that and see two rainbows below us in the mist. A helicopter passed over, barely audible for the thunderous roar of the water. We found a spot from where we could see the demented deluge enter this gorge, crash round a bend and pass under the bridge (into Zimbabwe), from where some of our intrepid riders would later be bungee jumping. My companions were keen to spend time literally soaking up the atmosphere;

meanwhile, I sat on a log to wait for them. Any movement seemed such an effort.

One of the riders had not heeded the instruction to leave the reserve before they closed the gates for the night. He found himself locked in. As the night drew in, he was scared by a group of baboons who confronted him. Perhaps the fright gave him extra strength for somehow he scaled the fence and escaped to safety.

Zambia had been a little disappointing in some ways. Perhaps we had been spoilt by the contrasting scenery of other countries but what is certainly true is that paradise itself would hold little allure to someone feeling ill. The country has so much to offer and indeed, for some, the excitement of the bungee-jumping, the marvels of the Okavango Delta or the sheer delight of three days of unadulterated rest and even luxury, had been a panacea. Botswana now beckoned.

CHAPTER 12
CATHETER COMPLICATIONS

Before starting this trip, I had had a social drink with an acquaintance who needed to catheterise in exactly the same manner as myself. Before his illness, he had been a keen traveller, but now felt restricted to moving only between the UK and Spain. For many people, an illness leads to a reappraisal and downgrading of lifestyle, frequently without need.

I will always be grateful to the urologist, Mr. Singh, who introduced me to catheterisation, thus ending two years of infections, uncontrollable wetting and useless visits to hospitals and clinics, seeing urologists who fitted me with a permanent catheter first through the penis, then through the abdomen, then back through the penis, all the time wanting to remove my prostate. Before leaving for Africa, I wanted to see Mr Singh again and I managed to obtain an appointment with him for a consultation. He was dismayed to hear of my intentions to cycle through Africa and strongly urged me to reconsider. His principal worry was the lack of cleanliness I would have to contend with, exposing me to very real infection risks. But he understood that I was already firmly intent on going.

This chapter deals with a subject which is very much of a private nature, insomuch as I would not normally wish to draw attention to it. But by doing so, I would like to think that some people who have this very problem, or who suffer some other condition that reduces their capabilities, may reach the conclusion that they can minimize the restrictions which they feel confine them, simply by a change in perspective. I shall relate the problems I encountered and how I dealt with them. While doing so, I shall be very open, at risk of perhaps seeming somewhat crude though this is certainly never my intention.

In the case of a male, catheterisation refers to the insertion of a tube through the penis and into the bladder for the removal of urine. This might sound horrific to some, but the catheters are lubricated and rarely cause any discomfort. Each of the catheters I use is in a sterile saline solution, contained in a neat aluminium foil pack. Each pack is about 18" long, which is not easy to hide. But the pack can be folded over into a much shorter overall length without breaking the seal; if left for too long like this, however, the catheter assumes that shape and makes the operation of inserting it through to the bladder rather more difficult. Once used, the catheter must be disposed of, as it can not be used again without risking infection.

Ideally, I should catheterise every three hours. Although I did not dare to admit so to Mr. Singh, I had calculated on averaging rather longer than three hours in between catheterisations, because dehydration during cycling causes the body to extract and reuse liquid sent to the kidneys, extending the time taken to fill the bladder with admittedly a higher concentration of "toxic waste". Of great significance, the hours sat on a bicycle seat, no matter the type of seat, put pressure on the urethra and the two sphincter muscles that control the passage of urine out of the bladder. The internal sphincter muscle, the one closest to the bladder, resolutely refuses entrance to the catheter for some time after getting off the bike. It can take half an hour for it to relax sufficiently. I asked Mr. Singh whether it was safe practice in such circumstances to do what I had done in the past, namely push the tube hard against the sphincter muscle until, with a most disagreeable "pop", it gives way, and allows the tube to pass into the bladder. He seemed genuinely alarmed that I should be doing that; the sphincter muscle could go into spasm. I dropped that contingency plan. Only once in the whole four months, in desperation, did I force a catheter through the sphincter muscle.

To complicate matters a little further, if the sphincter muscle prevents me from being able to use a catheter when my bladder needs emptying, the increasing pressure in the bladder can itself force the urine out, resulting in an embarrassing situation. Pressure in the bladder also exerts pressure on the bowel, and ever since I started with this condition, there are times when I can not tell if I feel uncomfortable because of a bowel that needs emptying or a bladder that needs emptying, or both.

Right from the earliest stages of planning, I realised the need for a plan to avoid having to leave the tent at night. If it was cold outside, the effect of two or three times being completely woken up would make nonsense of a night's sleep; if it was hot outside, there would be mosquitoes – and plenty of other types of nocuous insects too, I was to find out – that were ready to follow me back into my tent. If it was raining....? On top of all those considerations, I was acutely conscious of the noise made by the two zips of the tent that had to be opened and closed both when leaving and re-entering. The simplest solution was to use a one and a half litre plastic bottle. Although simple in theory, some time passed before I became adept at managing the procedure. Before going to sleep, I had to arrange several catheters, the bottle, a toilet roll and a waste bag close to me. The bags and paraphernalia in my tent had to be at the extremes of the area so as to allow me room to get out of the sleeping bag and perform the operation where, if there was a spill, I could clean it up. The tent height did not allow me to stand up, so I had to adopt a kneeling position. Once the catheter enters the bladder, the flow of urine is immediate, so it was imperative to have the bottle in place ready. The tricky part came at the end. No matter what you do, you cannot avoid a little of the urine following the catheter out and also some emptying out of the catheter itself. So you have one hand holding the catheter, the other holding the bottle; the bottle has to be released for a moment and placed on the uneven floor, with a prayer that it does not fall over, while that hand then picks up the bottle top and screws it back on the bottle sufficiently to make it safe. Then with several tissues ready at the tip of the penis, the catheter is taken out and the excess caught. With the screwed up catheter and the wet tissues safely in the waste bag, I could return to sleep.

Very occasionally, the bottle did fall over which caused me all sorts of problems. Several times, I do not know why, I made so much urine in the night that the flow was still strong when the bottle was full. On one such occasion, I had to use the water drinking bottle (from the bike) which I always kept in the tent as I was forever thirsty through the night. It was a strange coincidence that the very following morning, Michael, having lost his bottles the day before, asked me if I had a bottle that I did not use, one that he could borrow! The first night in Botswana, I also had to use the drinking bottle. I had lost my one and a half litre bottle. It was pouring with rain, so although there was a toilet block, no way would anyone want to have to leave the tent in the night; the whole site was flooded. I had asked the TDA staff if they had an empty bottle and just before turning in for the night, Allison found one for me. I was mightily relieved. If I was lucky, I normally escaped with having to pee two or three times in the night but this was one night I had to do it seven times. It was during the second pee of the night that suddenly there was pee everywhere, as an unseen crack in the bottle opened up under the pressure.

Another night, I reached for my water bottle to take a swig before having another wee. A little too late, I realised that I had picked up the wrong bottle.

The ideal situation was to empty both bowel and bladder first thing in the morning before breaking camp. This meant that bowel pressure would not influence procedures during the day. I hoped to be able to pee at the lunch stop and then again at the end of the ride. But sometimes I could do neither in the morning. Maybe I was too tense.

On the first day climbing up into the Ethiopian Highlands, I had been unable to pass water first thing in the morning, but I could feel the pressure building well before lunch. Kids were everywhere. Desperate not to have an involuntary pee, I stopped at a space by the side of the road where some quarrying had taken place. I only had to watch my back. A group of kids stared at me the whole time, but at least they kept their distance. They must have wondered how anybody could pee for so long. It took a full twenty minutes for the sphincter muscle to relax and allow the catheter entry. I could only laugh at the absurdity of it all, did it really matter? The day the dinner truck broke down and I went for a pee at lunch, the boys who brazenly stared at me, ensuring that they saw me from the front, took fright as I eased out the catheter after finishing and brandished it at them, as if to put a spell on them. On a day when I had taken a wrong road in Namibia, I was on an open hillside in almost gale conditions. For five minutes I tried to feed a catheter into the penis and each time the wind would blow it away. You should only hold the catheter by the plastic tip lest your hands contaminate it and introduce germs into the urinary tract; but this was an instance when I had no option but to break the rule. I had not seen a vehicle for an hour, but as is prone to happen, one passed right by me as I was in the middle of this delicate manoeuvre.

More embarrassing for me were the times when even after having had time to let the sphincter muscle relax while eating lunch, I still could not push the tube in. We were stopped at the lunch truck on the mountaintop in Ethiopia, where there was no shelter. Although I walked a good distance away from the truck, anyone could clearly see I had gone for a pee. Even after twenty minutes, I still could not do it and eventually gave up trying. Although no one commented on my return, I felt most uneasy. It also meant carrying on to camp with the possibility of a leakage, or at least a situation where I had not emptied for some six or seven hours. The danger then was of infection.

Of the places we would be visiting on this journey, Chitemba Beach in Malawi was one of those I most looked forward to. I was but a few minutes from our camp there, when involuntarily my bladder decided to celebrate with a great outburst. It was running down my legs as I cycled into camp. Trying unsuccessfully to avoid all the riders, I got my bags out of the truck, grabbed my towel, soap and a change of clothes and headed for the showers that thankfully were available to us.

Emptying the bowels during the day could be more difficult still and needed some thought. It was better to avoid having to do so near the lunch truck, since we invariably had onlookers. At one lunch stop, when I could not hold on, there were some disused buildings not far away and there I noticed an outside toilet. It must have been well made, as I could not see the bottom of the hole. Grateful for the privacy, I crouched over the hole in the ground, my feet firmly placed on either side. As I did so, the ground under my feet started to crumble and give way. I had visions of falling in and nobody hearing my cries. I was glad to get out of there.

Only once on the trip did I actually get a urine infection. I was not the first or the last to have one. This represented a success for me. Furthermore, I recognised the symptoms straight away: there is a constant urge to pee and indeed some dribbling is unavoidable while the whole body weakens alarmingly quickly. So I was able to start antibiotics immediately.

It could have been so much more difficult. Any number of problems could have arisen. The catheters themselves, for instance, might have got damaged as items were taken out of and replaced in the lorry. Only a very few were damaged.

My saving strength lay in knowing that whatever happened, I could deal with it. I could not cater in advance for every possible contingency, but by taking sensible precautions I reduced the risks and, most importantly, did not overly worry. I now feel I have actually expanded my horizons. Thanks to the TDA!

CHAPTER 13
BOTSWANA

Sunday, April 18: Livingstone – Kasane
83 km

Over half the riders managed to miss the turning out of Livingstone towards the Botswana border and rode an extra 12 km before finding their way back. Some (i.e. TDA staff) put it down entirely to our excessive enthusiasm and nothing to do with the fact that the expedition leader had overslept and did not flag the critical but not obvious turning; some of the riders were very annoyed. We had become so used to directions being good that we did not expect a mistake.

70 km of cycling on the flat brought us to the border. A good quarter of a mile of lorries were parked patiently, waiting to be ferried across the river. Sharita was outside the passport office to indicate where we had to go for our exit passport stamp and then it was straight onto the ferry. At this point, the river was called the Chombe, changing its name to the Zambesi a few km downstream. This section of the river holds the unique distinction of being the only place in the world where four countries meet, namely Zambia, Zimbabwe, Namibia and Botswana. The crossing took only a few minutes. There was nothing to jolt the imagination into recognising the magnitude of the moment, crossing one of the world's great waterways.

Once on the Botswana side we carried our bikes down the long ramps of the flat bottomed ferry and across the muddy shoreline. Passport control took less time than negotiating the obligatory water dip for the control of foot and mouth disease in cattle and 10 km later we entered our first camp site in Botswana (73, map Botswana), a popular spot with overlanders, replete with bar and caféteria.

If we chose to partake in no other safari or side-trip, at least pay the small fee for an evening cruise along the Chombe. This

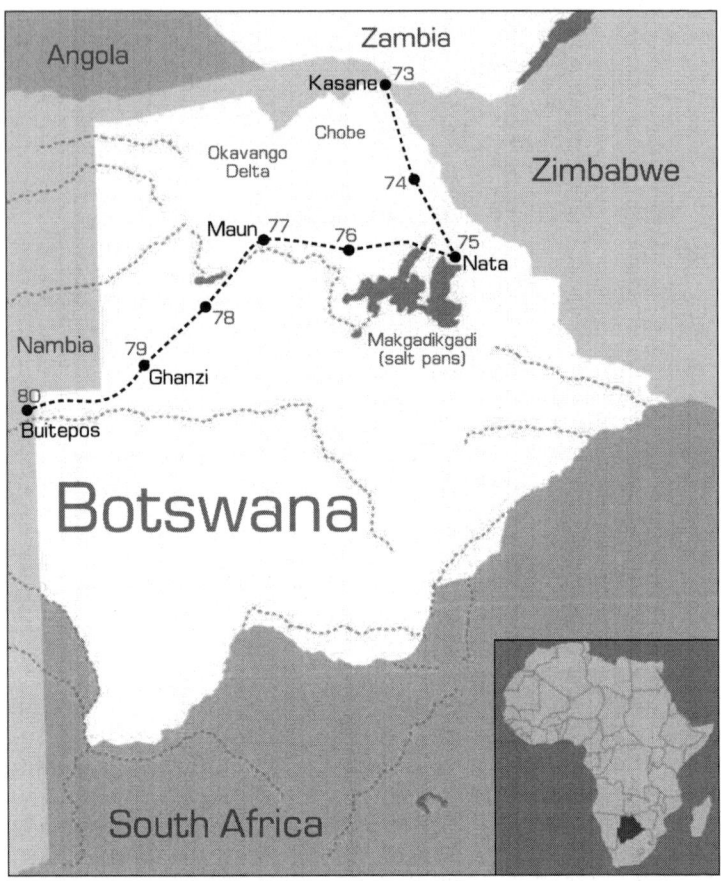

was the advice given to us days before and now taken by at least half of us. From Kasane upriver, the river widens out considerably, allowing alluvium islands to have been formed. The sun had lost little of its strength as for near what seemed like an hour we slowly chugged past a few exclusive safari hotels and into the reserve. We carefully approached the river bank with the sun on our backs. Groups of hippopotamus ignored us as we came close. Fish eagles watched quietly from high branches. Giant monitor lizards went in search of birds' eggs.

Elephants trundled about the rising riverbank, calves keeping close to their mothers. They must have already sensed, well before we saw her, a lioness quietly lying near the river's edge. She suddenly sprinted away in chase of a warthog. After her abortive attempt, she plodded gently back to the water's edge and stared at us derisively.

Heading back into a pink sunset, drained by the day's riding and the drama of the animal sightings, hardly a sound could be heard apart from the flapping of wings and the chatter of birds as they returned to their roosts. By the time the boats tied up to the jetty, night had already closed in. I had seen more wildlife in one hour than in the previous three months.

Km covered 8,703 Yet to go 3,306

Monday, April 19: Kasane - bush camp
159 km

Dawn was breaking as we trickled out on to the road. The sight and strong smell of fresh elephant dung immediately caught our attention. Not concentrating on the road, I missed a turning and cycled a couple of miles in the wrong direction.

I knew soon into the ride that I had a urine infection. The burning sensation and incontinence made for a very uncomfortable 80 km ride to lunch. With James gone for a few days break, and Gert our Indaba driver, who usually set out the lunch, having remained in Livingstone after contracting malaria, Paul himself was cooking hamburgers for us, aided by young Steve.

Early in the Tour, Steve had realised his money needed supplementing. He had made a lot of riders very happy by offering to relieve them of their evening dish duties for $5 a time. He set a minimum rate of $10 a time for washing a bike. But he also helped out around camp in various ways. He found the cycling too boring he said, and had taken to hitch hiking most days, enjoying meeting whoever came along. Sometimes one or two of the other younger lads joined him.

Thick bush gave way to open bush and then, like an infringement of the natural order, to immense flat fields of sorghum, soya beans and sunflowers. Other riders sighted giraffes, elephants, baboons and, in the case of Andra and Caroline, a pack of wild dogs. These aggressive animals were unknown in Botswana until recently. They staked out the girls ready to attack them and only the intervention of two passing cars dispersed them. When I asked Andra later about how frightened she had been, she spoke of being fascinated rather than frightened. In another incident, a group of the riders saw a troop of baboons crossing the road ahead of them. The dominant male stopped, bared his teeth and let out a loud bellow. Rod, with his typically dry humour, shouted out: "Take the women!"

My first sign of life that morning was at a lonely service station after 106 km. A number of riders were catching their breath and filling up with liquids. One of our trucks was filling up with gas. Paul pulled in with the 4x4 runabout. He put my bike inside, I sank in the seat and we sped off to camp (74, map Botswana) down one of those long, flat, straight, monotonous roads that we would forever associate with Botswana. Too late, Paul saw a police car by the roadside. He decided to bluff it and pressed the accelerator down further. But the police car, as if he had been waiting all day for this, chased and forced us to stop. Paul did a good job of explaining that he had an ill rider who needed prompt attention; my slumping shape gave credence to his story. He let us go.

A quick test confirmed my urine infection, and Caroline started me on a course of antibiotics. Since the dehydration, my tummy and bowels had been troublesome, so she suggested that the antibiotics might sort them out as well. I could eat little for dinner and retreated to my tent. During the night, the pleasant sound of rain was no impediment to sleep.

Hours cycling 4hrs 10mins
Average speed 26kph
Km covered 8.862 Yet to go 3,147

Tuesday, April 20: Bush camp – Nata safari camp 156 km

I sensibly followed Caroline's advice and rode in the truck. I did feel a sense of guilt about doing so at the time. However needless that was, no amount of reasoning with myself could obliterate it.

The riders cycled through the rain till lunch, but made good time overall. Arriving at the camp site, we were told that this place had burnt down the previous year and had been rebuilt. We drove past beautiful, recently thatched lodges and came to a standstill in the open bush at the back. As we opened the doors to get out, we were immediately surrounded by hungry mosquitoes. Everyone dived for their repellent. This perhaps more than anything else persuaded many riders to book a lodge for US$100 a night.

As we travelled south, facilities progressively improved and dramatically so. At this camp site (75, map Botswana), there was an attractive pool. But we took more interest in the availability of internet and modern showers and toilets. Arriving in camp in good time by riding the lorry, I appreciated what the fastest riders enjoyed each day - sufficient time to do the chores and relax. On my calculations, I had also gained about 45 minutes a day by buying the pop-up tent from Jos.

There was time to look over the bike and overall it was bearing up well. The mechanic had changed a brake cable for me a few weeks earlier and now the other cable needed changing. I could no longer use the top gear due to some misalignment of the derailleur, a problem that could not be rectified. A few days earlier, I had used my third and final chain. Up till now, I had been the weakest link!

Km covered 9,018 Yet to go 2,991

Wednesday, April 21: Nata - bush camp
187 km

The antibiotics had kicked in and I awoke feeling much better. On route to lunch, I enjoyed cycling with Jim, the lawyer from Ohio, who loved his biking. The inordinate amounts of money he had raised for the charity he espoused drew my envy; American kids from poor backgrounds were encouraged to cycle and provided with bikes as Christmas presents.

For the remainder of the ride, I was grateful to Jerry and Viv for allowing me to stay on their tail. Like most riders, we broke the ride by following 1.5 km of rough track to visit the safari camp called "Planet Baobab". A few younger riders liked it so much, they stayed there overnight. It was a comfortable oasis in which to take coffee and a scrumptious slice of chocolate cake. David and the group he was cycling with were greatly disappointed on arrival at finding I had taken the very last slice. After drinking their coffees, David was bewildered and upset at not being able to find his expensive sunglasses. Meanwhile we heard the whirring of a helicopter outside taking off to visit the salt pans of Makgadikgadi. With the whirring still in our ears, the pilot entered through the door to pick up his sunglasses - he had taken David's by mistake and only realised at the last minute.

Already we were in the last month with a growing realisation that Cape Town was no longer that far away, relatively speaking. I could not think of any rider who did not relish the thought of arriving there. I had been wrong in thinking that tensions might split the group in the last month, as had happened in the previous year. On the contrary, there was more open fun, teasing and good humour despite the huge weariness. The long rides through unchanging scenery in Botswana emphasised the tedium, and allowed the mind to wander, to dwell on what most was missed, the little luxuries that would

once more be in our grasp within a few weeks and the long-awaited relief from regimented routine.
(Camp 76, map Botswana)

Time cycling 6hrs 14mins
Average speed 30kph
Km covered 9,205 Yet to go 2,804

Thursday, April 22: Bush camp – Maun
136 km

On these long, flat roads, riders were tending to group up again. Ten of us in two lines of five kept up a good steady pace, the front riders dropping to the back every 10 minutes. As we passed Reiner, we all sang Happy Birthday to him. He was 69. In the afternoon, I chose to go slower and use it as a recovery ride.

Maun had a small airport from where flights over the salt pans or to the Okavango Delta were available. Not surprisingly, the town included small malls and supermarkets to service the tourist trade. Cycling in, I was so aware that tropical Africa was behind us now and more and more I expected to see the influence of an expanding South Africa.

We camped (77, map Botswana) on the grassy gardens of a small and pleasant hotel on the outskirts of town. Reiner celebrated his birthday by inviting us all to a free bar that evening in the hotel.

Time cycling 4hrs 39mins
Average speed 30kph
Km covered 9,341 Yet to go 2,668

Friday, April 23: Rest day in Maun

Torrential rain set in for the night. I blissfully enjoyed the rhythmic pounding from within my dry tent. I stretched out my arms to the side in satisfaction and...what was that, it felt wet!? Right enough, water covered the floor of my tent, not from the rain, but from my camelback. The tube end had come off and the water had completely drained out.

Some, like myself, chose to do their laundry before breakfast. Some riders had paid US$120 each to fly for an hour over the Okavango Delta or even US$280, which included a canoe trip on the Delta, so they had opted for an early, reasonably priced breakfast buffet in the hotel. When I went in after finishing my washing, a large number of riders had been and gone, eating everything in front of them, like locusts. The waitress indicated the various bowls to me: "We have eggs, bacon, beans, sausages..". "Hold on", I said, "they are all empty!" "The chef is doing more", she smiled. Behind the counter, a young man was bent casually over a frying-pan cooking two eggs. Africa does encourage you to be patient.

Certainly, everybody was trying hard to put some weight back on. Helped by the growing availability of fast food outlets on rest days, we showed great responsibility in shovelling down milk shakes, full-fat milks and burgers. Ahead of us lay five straight days of cycling to cover the 800 km to Windhoek. There was a rising swell of excitement now, knowing we were getting closer. Dared we start dreaming yet?

Saturday, April 24: Maun - (final) bush camp 160 km

Everyone seemed revived by the rest day and ready to give it some wellie. My bugs had disappeared and I felt in good shape. At the lunch stop, an English lad on an overladen bike dropped by. He had started cycling from the UK six months previously. From Gibraltar he SWAM across to Africa, then cycled down the west coast. He shared the same final destination as us, Cape

Town, where he intended to watch the World Cup and do an ultra triathlon. As Stuart, our current race leader, said: "That kinda puts us in our place, doesn't it?"

All along the highway, bullocks grazed on the long grass. They looked so healthy and well-fed. I was envious. In truth, we had been treated to an increasingly varied diet ourselves as we cycled southwards.

For over a week, I had slept very badly due to the disintegration of my Thermarest mattress. It transpired that Jim had a "cot" (like a camp bed) that he did not use. He offered me the use of it. So once in camp (78, map Botswana), I allowed the tent to put itself up (!), I cleaned myself, and put the cot together, a few minutes work. As I crawled onto the cot, a storm was breaking. I lay there, more comfortable than I had been for a long while, and just listened to nature's bad temper. All I lacked were my slippers and a packet of licorice allsorts.

Dave and Sunil had devised a competition for teams of three to test their relative speeds over 10 days, with various "challenges". As I lay there, they called out that the first event was about to take place. I just could not bring myself to rise from that cot to go out and get myself and my clothing soaking wet. One of each team had to pick up a shovel, run 12 metres over the by now swampy ground and dig a hole big enough for a washing-basin to fit in. This was conducted in the pouring rain and created much hilarity. I had joined Rick and Jacob in a group we named "The good, the bad and the ugly", without specifying who was who. As one of the future events would be to pitch and then pack away a tent as quickly as possible, I had volunteered to represent us in that event. I was more than happy to let the other two young guys represent us in the other competitions. So I lay there.

Gabrielle, our Italian rider, supervised the dinner. He made us all a mushroom risotto with lamb sausages. The rain stopped for a while, enabling us to savour the splendid food.

Time cycling 5hrs 8mins
Average speed 30.8kph
Km covered 9,501 Yet to go 2,508

Sunday, April 25: Bush camp – Ghanzi
143 km

The rain had returned with a vengeance at 8pm and continued till early morning. Some riders had been up in the night, digging moats around their tents. Not on his own, Simon had finally given up and taken shelter in the truck. He was one of the stronger riders. For a long time, he had not been feeling well, ever since he had been bitten around the feet and ankles by a spider one night in his tent. The bites had initiated inflammation and pain, becoming very infected, despite treatment. He had not felt like riding, but he was in the race and also wanted to maintain his EFI status. I saw his bites which he insisted were now much better, but the centres of the marble-sized sores were still yellow with pus.

Our camp site was flooded by morning. Taking the shovel into the bush with me, my feet sank in the mud and water rose up to my ankles. The skies remained heavily clouded all day. It came as a surprise given that we were skirting the edge of the Kalahari Desert. But I preferred the cloud cover to being exposed to the merciless sun.

The intriguing second event of the decathlon took place in camp (79, map Botswana). A well planned obstacle course had to be negotiated, some of it on bike, some on foot and, funniest of all, some by pushing a single bicycle wheel along. After the boring ride, this was a wonderful antidote, very competitive but great fun.

Time cycling 5hrs 4mins
Average speed 28kph
Km covered 9,644 Yet to go 2,365

Monday, April 26: Ghanzi – Buitepos
209 km

I slept in till 5.45am, 45 minutes late. Usually I would be one of the first out of my tent. Breakfast had started. A heavy storm during the night had abated but it was still raining. As quickly as ever I could, I stuffed everything into my holdall, dismantled my cot, and threw everything outside so I could take the tent down. Loading my bike bag with everything I might need for the day, I could not put my hands on my passport, which I needed for crossing the border. I emptied out my bag three times in the rain, each time more desperately, thinking I might have to cycle without breakfast on the day on which we would cover more kilometres than any other single day. With intense relief, I finally found it and dashed to put my bags in my locker in the dinner truck and my tent in the space allotted to me on the lunch truck. There was still breakfast on the table.

We set off in the half-light of a drizzly dawn. I teamed up with Peter and David, keeping up a good pace to the lunch stop. Encouraging signs for Namibia and South Africa brought cheers. It looked like the weather might clear up, but in fact storms flashed and threatened all day, producing the occasional cloudburst. Near the border post, some got caught in a nasty downpour that included hail. Passing through customs quite easily, a few hundred metres saw us to our camp site (80, map Namibia). The grass was saturated in most parts, whilst the paths were covered in mud and water. I found a relatively dry spot where at least the water appeared to be able to drain away. No sooner was I inside the tent than the heavens opened again. All our clothes were generally damp or wet and beginning to smell. There was nothing we could do about it. But on the plus side, our TDA dinner was a big barbecue steak with pasta and pumpkin, together with some very tasty herb-filled, garlic bread. There was also a store at the entrance to the camp, stocked with an array of goodies. Viv and Jerry had bought a good bottle of wine which they shared with me. I had forgotten how good it can be. After dinner, I went along and bought chocolates, licorice and jelly tots.

So as I wrote my blog within the privacy of my tent, with the thunder rolling and the rain hammering down, I lingered over a great nosh all by myself. There was indeed plenty to celebrate: our longest distance, done; only one more capital city before Cape Town; only one more border post; only one more bush camp; only two nights before we had a great send-off for Viv and Jerry at Joe's Steakhouse in Windhoek. Not to forget that it was also Bill's 71st birthday. He made it a day to remember by cycling the whole of the 209 km. This engaging man had made it his business to chat to everyone in the group at different times. Before joining us in Lilongwe he had followed our blogs. The day he arrived at our camp site in a taxi, I was just leaving through the gates to walk to the city centre. The taxi stopped. Bill, whom I did not know from Adam, bounced out and warmly embraced me, exclaiming delightedly "It is ericonhisbike", referring to my blog. This was the kind of outgoing personality he had.

Some riders had to move their tents in the rain as the grass turned into a swamp while some gave up and dived into one of the lorries.

We may remember Botswana more for its rains than anything else, or perhaps for its hundreds of miles of mind-numbing flat bushland, giving no hint of the rich diversity of ecological systems to be found. Cycling allows the rider to see much more than the speeding motorist, if there is something to see. I was so happy to now be entering Namibia, to go off road on easily managed tracks, to witness an under-rated wilderness of subtle beauty.

Time cycling 7hrs 40mins
Average speed 27.5kph
Km covered 9,853 Yet to go 2,156

CHAPTER 14
NAMIBIA

Tuesday, April 27: Buitepos – Witvlei
168 km

The rain retreated before daybreak, leaving us to pack up and pick our way through the quagmire to get to our breakfast. Heavy clouds grappled in the crowded grey sky. The endless bush ahead of us was shrouded in mist, apart from the south-eastern area of the sky where the lower clouds were traced with rose-pink edging. All morning, the sun tried to infiltrate the mist, sometimes piercing it but never overcoming it. There was no sign of anybody nor of any habitation until we passed through the very pleasant town of Gobabis, the meat capital of Namibia, at about 120 km. From here, it became apparent that we had left the storms behind and the sky started clearing. With so much wet clothing to dry and air, it was worth the effort to push a little harder into the headwind and gain camp as early as possible. Camp was supposed to be at Ziegy's campsite, but it had recently closed down, so we camped on open ground. (Camp 81, map Namibia)

The area was covered in the biggest thorns we had yet seen and we were advised to walk our bikes in off the road. There was a toilet block. It surprised me that nobody seemed to be doing their washing in the sinks there. Everyone felt very tired, so perhaps they had decided to wait until Windhoek. I was delighted to be able to wash all my dirty clothes and hang them out on my hastily-erected clothes line, together with the washed but not dried clothing I carried in a separate bag, to dry in the strong breeze.

Another two rounds of the decathlon were contested before dinner. One event was to time how long it took for a contestant to finish a PVM bar. Simple, even stupid, you might say, but

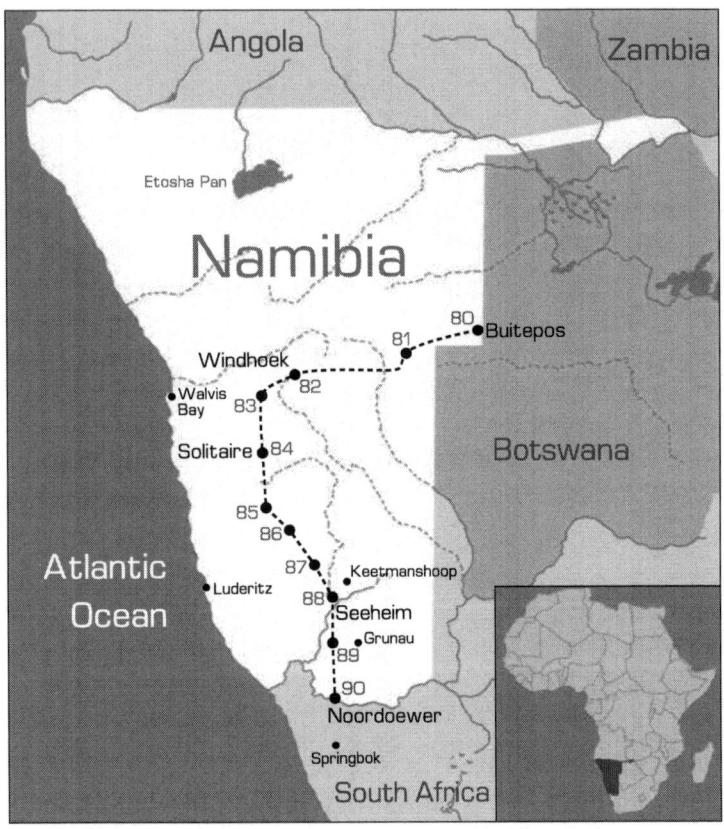

surprisingly good fun. As life becomes more simplified, so do the pleasures. PVM bars were available to us all throughout the trip. They were energy bars that came in various flavours. A couple of the flavours were quite good, though after four months even they failed to excite, while others were downright distasteful. In this event, you did not get to choose. They were very sticky, clinging to the palate and teeth. So as each blindfolded contestant picked out a bar, he would not know whether or not it was a flavour he could not stand even though he would have to chew it to the last grimace.

Dinner was really good: pork chop, potatoes and beans, with pita bread and dips. Bill, in a late celebration of his 71st birthday, bought in enough beer for everybody. As he had done all through the trip for anybody on their birthday, Dave presented him with a little cake lit with a few candles together with a bag of goodies collected from riders who had something to donate. (It might only be a PVM bar!) To top all that, Viv and Jerry had made the most delicious dessert: a chocolate, biscuit and ginger pudding, topped with caramelised oranges. It was my turn to help cleaning the pots and pans afterwards, but who cared after such a meal.

Time cycling 6hrs 50mins
Average speed 24kph
Km covered 10,021 Yet to go 1,988

Wednesday, April 28: Witvlei – Windhoek 165 km

The day was declared a non-race day but started with a fun 20 km time trial. Teams of six were chosen randomly the night before, so there had been time to discuss tactics. Starting at 6am, a team left every 2 minutes. We had decided that when our turn came we would leave room for our three strongest, namely Franz, Eric D and Andrew, to sprint ahead of us, leaving Lynn, Rick and I to work together behind them. There was a light headwind and a slight gradient to the road, so times were not super-fast. But our first three went off like rockets, and finished the 20 km in 35 minutes. We passed other riders but we still came in 8 minutes after our first three. We had to try our best in case one of our front three punctured, as it was the time of the third fastest rider that determined which group won, which happened to be our group. One of the groups who had decided to ride as six together, approached the finish in a line across the road. As we stood at the finish watching them come in, a solitary car was following them patiently, unable to pass. The road was deserted, as was the whole area, so the driver must have been most perplexed to find his way blocked, especially at that time in the morning.

During the morning, the wind picked up, holding us back with headwinds of up to 45kph, making this one tough day. One rider described the ride as a death march. With no Coke stops to break up the long ride and with many hills, we all wilted.

As in Botswana, a 25m width either side of the straight road was kept mostly free of scrub, leaving the grass to grow tall. The golden colour made me imagine I was cycling through an endless, East Anglian cornfield.

It struck me, as I very slowly passed the Windhoek Airport, watching cars occasionally driving out, that we resembled tortoises on a massive plain, our movement barely measurable relative to the motorised vehicles.

The approach to Windhoek took us parallel to a small mountain range, brown to almost mauve. We pushed up hill after hill, into the wind, until finally enjoying a long descent into the suburbs. Somewhere on that descent I lost my cycling computer. The holding mechanism had broken in Sudan, but I had managed to hold it together with duct tape through most of Africa. Coincidently, just as we entered the city, there was a first-rate bike shop, where many riders were calling in to resolve long-standing problems. Dan J, for instance, had had nearly 20 spokes break. Chris had rebuilt the wheel, but they continued to break. (Someone voted Dan "the riders' spokesperson"!) He had been wobbling along like a duck for days. Anyway, I bought a new bike computer. How strange that I should have lost it only minutes before finding the first good bike shop since Cairo.

Set amongst the hills, Windhoek seemed very pleasant. It came across as a chilled-out place, with plenty of greenery amongst the well spaced out houses. But by the time we arrived at the large camp site (82, map Namibia), set up our tents and washed, there was no time for a nap. I cycled back to the camp caféteria to use their internet for uploading my blog and to enjoy a cold drink and some food. As the staff behind the bar chatted between themselves, Rod and Juliana strolled in. Conscious of the time, I politely asked the bar staff whether they could take my order. With a smile, Rod urged me to be patient. Without meaning to snap at him, but that it is how it sounded, I told him I had no patience. He told Juliana that he could not stay there and they left.

Almost all of us joined Viv and Jerry for an early evening meal at the zany restaurant, Joe's Steakhouse. I walked over to where Rod and Juliana were seated and shook hands with Rod. On no account did I wish to cause him any upset. With game meat on the menu, many of us were trying gazelle, oryx, zebra or kudu for the first time. I so wanted to enjoy the evening and, more importantly, give Viv and Jerry a great send-off. They had contributed hugely to the dynamics of the group. But like many others, I had not the energy to finish my meal. By 9pm, I was asleep in my sleeping bag.

Km covered 10,186 Yet to go 1,823

Thursday, April 29: Rest day in Windhoek

Everyone made their way to a shopping mall, to eat, drink, have a haircut, hit the internet and absorb the unaccustomed closeness of people living "normal" lives before we left it all behind once again. Having heard of the relative smoothness of Namibia's dirt tracks, it had come as a bit of a shock to be forewarned of more loose sand and rough corrugation, the stuff of nightmares. Jason pointed out that we had already proved ourselves capable of handling anything thrown at us, so we had nothing to fear. His words articulated the thoughts of most of us while also demonstrating the steady progress he had made on the bike and the sense of accomplishment he felt.

Dark, threatening clouds filled the sky as we returned to camp. I quickly began changing the tyres on the bike, expecting the rain at any moment. In my haste, I ripped an inner tube which set me back some minutes. The first drops fell just as I completed cleaning the chain. I almost forgot my laundry; I tore the clothes off the line, threw them inside ahead of me just before the rain bore down, heralded by lightning and loud thunder claps. The time was only 5.45pm. I sat on my cot, a towel across my lap and I ate my way through a bag of bread, cheese, fruit, both dried and fresh, nuts and cake, while writing my blog. So what did I care if it poured down outside.

Friday, April 30: Windhoek - Weissenfeld camp 115 km

Eric D had pitched his tent right next to mine. I heard him up in the night trying to divert the water away from his tent. Curiously, he had warned me to build a defence around my tent but he was the unfortunate one to suffer. As we took our tents down in the morning, he looked tired, but was never one to complain about anything. I started the twisting manoeuvre necessary to fold my tent up. A pole snapped. So did my patience. I got ready to throw it, literally. Eric persuaded me not to and cooled me down. I managed to fold it up somehow and put it into its bag.

Henry Gold, the founder and owner of TDA, was introduced to us after breakfast. He would be accompanying us to Cape Town, not using his bike - though still well capable of doing so - but tenting all the way. Not the charismatic person I had expected, he was a quiet, unassuming person, very approachable, a good listener with nothing to prove. Before setting up the company, he had ridden from Cairo to Cape Town unassisted.

Then it was time to get going. My bike was ready. I just felt the tyres out of habit. The front one was nearly flat. By the time I had changed the tube, everyone had left already bar Paul who was acting as sweep. The first 10 km heading in the direction of Walvis Bay were on tarmac, taking us up higher into the hills as we climbed from Windhoek at 1700m to the Spreetshoogle Pass at over 2000m. Suddenly reaching the top after rounding a bend, the view took our breath away, forcing us to stop to allow it to register. I shared the exhilarating view with Anneke and her father, Paul. (I had shared a cabin with him crossing Lake Nasser. He had now returned to cycle the last section with his daughter.) The immensity and beauty of the lands we were about to cycle through were laid out magnificently before us.

The steep, very stony descent convinced a few wary riders to walk it. I passed Reiner sensibly walking his bike down. The terrain surprised us. We had expected it to be flat. Furthermore, there was still plenty of greenery about, as the rainy season was only just finishing. The build up of heat during the course of the day caught us unawares too. Late into the ride, Henry passed us in the 4x4, throwing a cold drink to each one of us. Maybe it was his way of telling us he understood how we felt.

Our camp site (83, map Namibia) really was in the middle of nowhere. Hidden amid small hills, we were oblivious to it until the last moment. The owners ran a small stud farm and offered accommodation. I noticed that they offered free board and lodging to anyone helping out with the horses. A feeling of homeliness, self-sufficiency and timelessness pervaded the place, as I sat with our two Norwegians, Knut and Hilda, for a couple of beers to settle us down before we did anything else.

Talk around camp centred much more on Cape Town now, discussing future plans and comparing feelings. Had we or our attitudes changed, what would we do after this?

I opened up my tent and, even with the broken pole, it remarkably took its normal shape and survived a stiff test as, once again, we were hit by a thunderstorm and savage rain. With only two weeks to go, I now knew I could manage no matter whatever was to happen.

Time cycling 6hrs 30mins
Average speed 17.8kph
Km covered 10,301 Yet to go 1,708

Saturday, May 1: Weissenfeld – Solitaire
122 km

Hail, headwinds, corrugation and wet sand, we had it all this day, but for me, this had been possibly the best day of the Tour so far. I felt more alive than I had done for many a week.

I was one of the first to leave. The turbulent clouds marauded above the desolate, rolling bush. Mountains were visible in one direction only and that was where we were steering. They could have been covered with heather, in greens and purples, such was their beauty. The sky displayed patches of blue in all its shades except over this mountain range, where the dark clouds appeared contorted in anger, in the shape of a huge oyster shell. Further to the west, the light reminded me of a painting of the Ascension of Our Lord, in which an ephemeral light shines from the heavens straight down to Earth. Lightning flashed over the mountain, as if warning us to keep away. Well before we reached there, water was gushing down the track and ponding. The sand was mostly saturated, making it a little difficult to push through. But the setting was intriguing and bewitching.

By the time we reached this mountain, the storm had moved on. We weaved our way up through the range to where our lunch truck was waiting for us, at about 60 km. Everyone was cold, somewhat apprehensive if not miserable, and a new storm was brewing. So how welcome was the sight of a hot drink, the first time on the Tour at lunch; indeed the first time we had needed it.

As riders began pulling away from the truck, the now dark skies chose to soak us once again. We had some climbing to do to take us to the top of the pass. I cannot say just why, but I was loving it. Perhaps it was the sense of freedom that the landscape gave me, the strength I felt, I don't know. There was some hail both before and after the top of the pass, but once at the top, the view was awe inspiring. In the mercurial, mysterious light the colours seemed impossible, something imagined. The wide green valley below us reached out to the distant yellow savannah through which crossed a line of pure white, broken by the triangular shape of a solitary mountain, also pure white. Steep-sided mountains embraced the valley from both sides.

A scary white-knuckle ride dropped us 500m in 4 km, propelling us from the swirling drizzle of the craggy pass to a twisting country track in relative warmth. Occasional homesteads advertised accommodation and soon five of us were turning down the track leading to the Gecko Lodge, a simple place where it was more than pleasant to feel civilised, taking tea and biscuits on a small patio, gathering our strength for the final 30 km. Joachim and Rebecca were newly-wed New Yorkers, celebrating their honeymoon, who had really proved themselves since joining us as sectional riders in Windhoek. A couple who were travelling through Africa in their 4x4 stopped to ask us about our trip. They spoke with a soft Welsh accent which I so enjoy.

Rising gently out of the valley, we ignored the right turn to Walvis Bay, and kept left to Solitaire. The setting, according to Dan J, was akin to that of Arizona. I looked for the town, but there was nothing there other than a lodge, a petrol station and a  bakery. We had been told that this bakery made the best apple crumble in Africa. So before showering, bike washing or performing any other menial duty, most of us traipsed over to the bakery for crumble and coffee. We will all testify as to its quality even if many of us felt forced to try a second just to be sure. All the other pastries and muffins were also flying off the shelf as fast as they came out of the oven. Not as many people went for seconds at dinner. (Camp 84, map Namibia)

Time cycling 6hrs 56mins
Average speed 17.7kph
Km covered 10,423 Yet to go 1,586

Sunday, May 2: Solitaire - Sossusvlei Camp
121 km (I did 80)

In eager anticipation and animated by the gathering light shining down on a hard-packed track the width of a motorway, we sped along the smooth surface. Many of us saw oryx, springbok and giraffe during this early part of the day.

On a particularly fast stretch, where I was pedalling at about 40kph, I suddenly hit deep, loose sand. The bike took a wobble. I thought I had it under control, but then I lost it again. As I fell, the handlebars smacked me in the ribs. This was the only real damage, but it hurt. Jacob checked I was OK and I gave him the thumbs-up. I carried on slowly to the lunch truck at 50 km. Bill checked me over and found nothing broken.

At the truck, some of the riders were keen to continue the TDA tradition of riding a mile while completely naked. Our driver Gert, back with us after his bout of malaria, was encouraging others and keen himself. So a few tactfully stripped off behind the lorry showing only their bums as they rode off singly or in pairs. One of them, I think it might have been Hilda, had no sooner set off than an isolated car passed her from the other direction. What a shock the driver must have had. He could not have been more surprised if he had sighted a kangaroo. Three girls had cycled off together only to suffer the indignity of a puncture. Dave so delighted in his unfettered state that he cycled nude all the way to the edge of camp.

I tried to ride after lunch, but it was too uncomfortable. For the last 25 km, I rode in the truck. The scenery continued to fascinate. The colours and contours of the hills and mountains were so varied. I could not think of anywhere else I had ever been to compare it to. Approaching our camp site (85, map Namibia), the hill behind it was actually red.

My ribcage felt so sore despite a number of painkillers that I was very grateful that the following day should be a rest day. I just hoped Bill was right and that I would be able to ride again soon. Five more days off-road lay ahead, and I badly wanted to ride them.

Km covered 10,544 Yet to go 1,465

Monday, May 3: Rest day in Sesriem (Sossusvlei)

At 4.30am I heard the vehicles leave camp to take many of our riders to the Sossusvlei dunes, 50 km away. The intention was to climb the largest dune in the world in time to see sunrise. I got up at 5.15 after an uncomfortable night. I had not dared use the cot for fear of breaking the rather fragile frame as I tried to get up whilst protecting my ribs. As the first rays of light glanced off the surrounding mountains, their vertical, fluted crevices were etched black against the purples and reds of the rock face.

We were camped just inside the gated nature reserve. By dawn, vehicles were already queuing up in anticipation of the gates opening. Other than our camp site, with its shop and restaurant, the only other buildings were both just outside the gates: the luxury Sossusvlei Lodge and the petrol station. The latter sold hot pastries and cakes as well as having four computers with a decent connection. As we did not envisage another chance to use the internet before Cape Town, except perhaps in Springbok, we had had to take turns to use the computers the previous night. But now that many had left for the morning and the station opened at 5.30, I wanted to be the first in there, to buy my breakfast and use the internet without any pressure. As I walked across the sandy earth, the footprints left by springbok and jackals during the night were clearly visible.

After washing my laundry – twice, because the first time the line came down, dropping my clothes onto the sand – I spent a lazy day, just reading. By early afternoon, those returning from the Sossusvlei dunes shared with us their two overriding memories: the incredible cold of the desert morning while driving there in a soft top 4x4, and the pure exhilaration of hurtling down the highest sand dune in the world on foot.

In the evening, I ate in the bar with Paul Porter and Reiner. We shared a bottle of wine, which felt so luxurious, even decadent, and chatted, mainly about Paul's work at Minnesota University, especially his research into viable farming systems.

As we settled in our tents, a chorus of bird-like cries rose up from jackals nearby. During the night, I tried to turn, felt a sharp pain in the ribs and heard a light snap.

Tuesday, May 4: Sesriem – Betta
139 km

I rose particularly early, to allow myself plenty of time to pack up my things. I rode in the dinner truck with Caroline, our wonderful medic, Sam, who intended riding after lunch, and Gabrielle, who was going to ride but at the last moment found his bike unfit to use.

During those first two hours, we saw more animals than I had yet seen on the whole trip, including the Chombe river cruise: herds of springbok, zebra and oryx. On one occasion, two male springbok sprinted along the track straight in front of us. Then they veered off, one to each side. The one on the left kept pace alongside us for fully one kilometre at a steady 60kph, his nostrils flared fully open, gasping for air. Black-backed jackals loped away as we approached. A pair of bat-eared foxes stared at us as we slowed down, before cautiously loping off into the bush. Ostriches skittered away in a flurry. The zebras we saw were of two types, the mountain zebra and the Burchell's zebra, which has some brown in its marking as well as the black and white.

At the lunch stop at 8.30, Caroline gave me a heavy jab in the bum with a fast-working anti-inflammatory, which eased the pain considerably.

Two hours later we arrived in Betta (86, map Namibia), to find a gas station, a shop and the small camp site, nothing more- very similar to Solitaire. Constant power was produced by a combination of wind generator and wood stove. I immediately reserved myself one of the five rooms available at 18 euros per person so that I could rest up all day. After tea and apple cake in the shop, I went to bed for an hour. What sheer indolence, indulgence, but how incredibly satisfying.

Riders found the first 70 km hard, with a choice of corrugation or loose sand, and some headwind to deal with. As a result, about 13 riders got in the lunch truck. For those that continued, they were repaid with a better surface and a heavy tailwind.

Km covered 10,683 Yet to go 1,326

Wednesday, May 5: Betta - Konkiep Lata
159 km

A mando day for the riders, following the previous day's pattern of a very tough first half followed by easier conditions after lunch, saw Marcel achieve the fastest time. He managed it in just under five and a half hours, averaging over 26kph, all off-road. After losing so much time with his sprained wrist in Ethiopia, he was no longer a contender to win the overall race and had found I think that he was having more fun taking it a day at a time, racing some days, hanging back with other riders on days when he felt like it.

I received another puncture this morning - in my bum! Caroline's injection made the day much easier for me. The dinner truck, in which I rode, made camp (87, map Namibia) for about 10am. The tiny rooms that were available were Wendy houses, just two or four beds, nothing more. But that was fine, since all I wanted to do was lie down. Unfortunately, some riders had a habit of ringing ahead to reserve themselves rooms in case of a possible short supply. All the rooms had been taken. I think it was Sharita who had a word in someone's ear and I was offered a room. Later I was asked whether I would mind sharing it with Bill, whose company was always interesting. He took another look at my ribs and straight away diagnosed a separated cartilage, i.e. the cartilage that should connect the rib had become detached, which is common amongst rugby players, but was not serious. It would just be painful for some time. Since I was clearly not going to be able to ride for a few days at best, I planned to move ahead to the border and just rest well for a couple of days. Maybe then, on the smooth tarmac of S. Africa, I could ride again.

The lovely lady who ran this camp made the most incredible chocolate cake! So before turning in for the night, a visit to her little bar was essential. With such opportunities becoming more frequent, we felt sure of starting to put weight back on.

Km covered 10,842 Yet to go 1,167

Thursday, May 6: Konkiep – Seeheim
126 km (My visit to Keetmanshoop)

While the riders continued off-road to Seeheim (88, map Namibia), Paul and James had to drive in the other direction to Keetmanshoop for supplies. They agreed to take me along so I could rest up there for two nights before hitching a lift to the Felix Unite camp at the border, where I would then spend two nights with the group, including a rest day. Hopefully I could then continue with them through S. Africa on my bike.

It was upsetting not to be riding all of Namibia, possibly my favourite country. As we hurried along the highway, I reflected on how easy it would be to forget the distressing poverty we had seen in other countries. But in fact that will be forever etched on our minds. No more will mud huts in glorious sunsets represent for us a romantic setting or way of life. They denote a cruelly hard existence, with little chance of escape.

We asked the petrol attendant in Keetsmanhoop to recommend a decent backpacker's lodge. He suggested the Shutzenhaus Guest House for comfort and good value. The guys dropped me off there with my bag and in no time at all I was installed in an immaculately clean, modern room, quiet and comfortable. For the price I paid, which was not much though I fail to remember how much, I was suspiciously wondering where the catch was, but I never found one.

The first thing I did was to buy a local paper, my favourite way to acquaint myself with fresh surroundings. This Yiddish proverb appeared on the second page: "Everyone is kneaded out of the same dough, but not baked in the same oven". It struck me quite powerfully because of a conversation with Jason the previous night. He had related the true story of a rabbi who informed his congregation that only one-tenth of the world population enjoyed the same decent standard of living as they themselves did, while the remaining nine-tenths lived a hard, precarious life, afflicted by disease, malnutrition and natural disasters. So, he asked them, if you were given the chance to be re-born at the end of your current lives, knowing the odds were so heavily in favour of you being reborn as one of the nine-tenths, would you take it? He paused. Then he added that if they would choose not to be re-born in such circumstances, they should be doing all they could in this life to help those unfortunate nine-tenths. (I mischievously wondered whether we had not moved over into the nine-tenths for four months.)

Keetmanshoop was a small town of about 22,000 people with a good variety of stores. Most people about town were coloured or black. Within an hour, I had walked right round it. If I had been feeling in better shape, I would love to have gone walking in the surrounding bush. The apparently barren landscape always throws up surprises. Instead, I contented myself with looking in what had been the mission church, but was now an interesting museum. This town was first settled by tribesmen who discovered a muddy spring. It was later the scene of conflict between the tribes people and the German colonial masters, just before the First World War.

My most wonderful surprise came in the evening when I ate in the guest house's small restaurant. The food was almost gourmet, way beyond my expectations. Afterwards, I tucked myself into bed early to read a book that has instilled in me a deep yearning to see more of Namibia. A German geologist wrote how he and a fellow geologist were working in Windhoek when WW2 broke out. To avoid being involved they drove an old truck into the Namib desert one night, lights switched off, and survived for two years there, learning survival techniques and witnessing vast herds of animals now lost to us. They returned to Germany after the war and sadly, one of them was hit by a vehicle and killed. The remaining friend then decided to publish their story. The book brought alive for me in full colour, the outline sketch I had formed of the country.

Km covered 10,968 Yet to go 1,041

Friday, May 7: Seeheim – Hobas
177 km

The riders had a long day ahead of them, starting off from alongside the Fish River, which at that point would have had little water. Their next camp at Hobas was about 10 km from the Fish River Canyon. This is said by some to be the most awe-inspiring sight in the whole of Africa, the canyon being the biggest in the world after the Grand Canyon. It was the sight I had most looked forward to on this trip. But even if I had continued with the group, I would have had to cycle to it, something I felt incapable of at that time.

With my enforced spare time, I did an evaluation of the trip so far. My main aims had been:

1 To complete the trip.

2 To avoid accident or mishap.

3 Not to lose anything.

4 To camp all the way.

5 In doing all the above, to draw attention to the tremendous work being done at Thamsanqa orphanage and in the surrounding area of the black township of Motherwell.

Well, I was confident of completing the trip, despite a few days off the bike.

I had not avoided accident and mishap completely, but given my propensity for inviting trouble, I had done well on this score I decided.

I had lost water bottles, gloves, cycle computer, a micro-fibre towel, washing line and on two occasions my temper. Also weight. Nothing of great value.

When the lorry did not turn up in Gondar with our luggage and tents, I had booked into the hotel there. At the present, I was lodging for "health" reasons.

I hoped to have encouraged followers of my blog to learn something about Thamsanqa.

(Camp 89, map Namibia)

Km covered 11,145 Yet to go 864

Saturday, May 8: Hobas - Felix Unite
175 km

The riders were to be cycling to Felix Unite, a camp site on the Orange River (90, map Namibia), some 12 km from the border crossing at Noordoewer. They would enjoy a well-earned rest day before crossing into South Africa. I had been told by TDA staff as well as the staff at the Schutzenhaus, that I would have no difficulty obtaining a lift to the border, so I booked a room (i.e. for Saturday night) at a place in Noordoewer, intending to join the group on the Sunday. All I had to do was find my way to Noordoewer.

The young man from the Schutzenhaus reception accompanied me to the petrol station and waited with me for a while. Apparently it was a common practice for drivers to offer lifts to those waiting there, people who had no other means of transport. He spoke with the petrol attendants and assured me I would soon be on my way. They would ask drivers and obtain a lift for me. Time passed and nothing happened. Meanwhile I asked him about his own background. His family lived not far away in the bush, scratching a living from rearing a few goats;

his wages supplemented their income and he helped out at home during his time off. Sensing my anxiety, he rang his boss, explained the situation to him, and then assured me that his boss would soon drive me up to the main B1 road, to a petrol station there. He now made his way back. A small group of people sat around chatting, completely relaxed while they waited and I joined in, though growing increasingly concerned.

His boss turned up not long after and very kindly deposited me by the petrol station on the main highway. Cheekily, I passed through the service station café asking for a lift and drew a complete blank. I sat on my bag next to the roadway, standing up to hitch a lift south whenever a vehicle approached. When a vehicle stopped to fill up, I walked over and politely asked if they minded giving me a lift. Each person I approached had a reason not to do so. Finally, after four hours, two young men in a lorry pulled onto the forecourt and agreed to drop me at Grunau, which is about halfway. Like most vehicles, they were heading for the more commonly used border crossing on the B3. Just after the service station at Grunau, they would turn left whereas I needed to keep straight on. They were on their way to Pretoria to pick up potatoes to take to Angola. During the two hour journey of 170 km, we stopped just once, at one of the roadside shacks selling various types of biltong (dried meat).

They dropped me at the service station near the small town of Grunau. Waiting by the roadside again, not many lorries passed and those that did drove straight past me. An attractive girl stood on the opposite side of the road hoping to hitch a lift in the other direction. She was having no luck at all either, so I wondered what chance I had, realistically. Increasingly, I felt like a hobo. It was late in the day when a driver pulled in and agreed to ferry me to Noordoewer. But not until 6am the following morning. So long as I turned up at 6am I was free to join him.

I entered the service station shop and asked if I could sleep the night inside the building, in my sleeping bag. Blow me, they had rooms available and food to eat. They allowed me to ring and cancel the lodging in Noordoewer, to sit down to a simple but nourishing meal and to use their computer. The well-equipped, en-suite room was in a separate building but I was promised a morning call at 5am. My total bill came to 24 euros. I calculated on being in Noordoewer for 8am and at camp shortly afterwards.

I went to bed amazed at how, just when you can no longer see your way forward, it drops in your lap.

Km covered 11,320 Yet to go 689

Sunday, May 9: Grunau - Felix Unite

The room had been really comfortable and I received my morning call at 5am. I left a note to thank them for their true kindness. (I decided it would be most ungracious to mention that I had managed to kill 8 mosquitoes during the night and had run out of time to finish the job.) I was through the door by 5.30 – but the lorry had already left. I petitioned every lorry that called in for fuel. Soon, one driver said he was going to Noordoewer but how much would I pay him? We agreed on 30 Namibian dollars (about 3 euros) and we were on our way. He was carrying hake from Walvis Bay, the Namibian port to the west of us. He explained that 20 lorries, each carrying 20 tonnes of filleted, iced hake, left Walvis Bay every month. From the ship, the lorry had 20 hours to reach Johannesburg airport, from where the consignment was flown to Madrid. Each load cost the Spaniards 300,000 euros. Hake was also being flown in the same way to Madrid from Cape Town, Port Elizabeth and Plattenburg Bay in South Africa.

It was still early morning when I joined the other riders at the stupendous setting of the Felix Unite site, set on a knoll overlooking a bend in the Orange River. They had thoroughly enjoyed the last five days of dirt through Namibia. Excitement at having only six more days of cycling before entering Cape Town was quite apparent. It felt good to be back with them, though strangely, such had been the comings and goings of riders during nearly four months, I in no way sensed I had been missed.

I did not know whether I had been wise to leave for a few days or not, given the difficulty of rejoining the group. At least I did get a good rest for two days and a change of adventure. I intended to try cycling again in two days time (i.e. Tuesday) for a half-day. If that passed OK, I would continue with full days. Whatever happened, I was intent on cycling into Cape Town.

Namibia had surpassed my tentative expectations, despite my not seeing Fish River Canyon. Now we had just one more border to cross to enter our final country. The final lap was upon us.

CHAPTER 15
SOUTH AFRICA

Monday, May10: Felix Unite – Springbok
121 km

On either side of the Orange river, irrigated fruit and vegetables lent colour to the flat, riverside fields. But after crossing the border into South Africa, just over the river, the road snaked up 1500m onto the naked, rocky terrain of a mountain plateau. This was treeless, desert country and although there were some interesting boulder formations, the landscape lacked the colour and contrasts that Namibia had offered. Low bushes, on the other hand, covered the ground in yellows, greens, blues and purples. The road was straight with hardly any traffic and there was a cold wind.

We camped (91, map S.Africa) at a little low-cost site a few kilometres from Springbok. As the few of us who had ridden in the truck pitched our tents, several mongoose played around us, checking us out. With time to spare, I rode the bike into town. I was delighted not to feel any exacerbation to the soreness of my ribs. The Wimpy in the main street acted as a magnet to many of the riders. I preferred something more local. After spending some time in the internet café, I cycled along the street, my bike like a new toy, to the Springbok Lodge. This was one of those places that catches you by surprise and lifts your spirit. As I entered, I passed a small room of curios and into the café proper. Displays of mineral specimens lined one wall, the walls around adorned with paintings by South African artists and interesting old photos. A whole corner of the room was taken up by books, some unobtainable anywhere else. Amidst all this, a row of back to back upholstered bench seats, in the style of the 1950s, provided seating for the half dozen tables. I could have spent hours just browsing through the

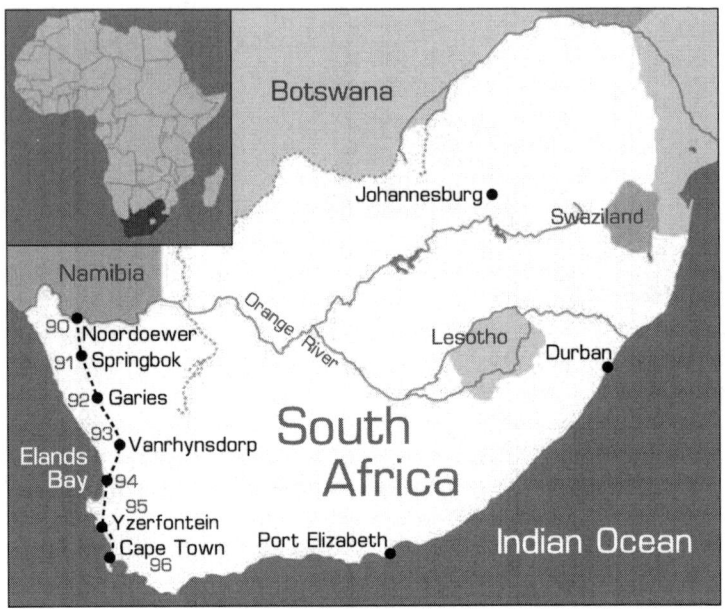

books, but eventually chose two. "The Glamour of Prospecting", an autobiography by Fred C. Cornell, brings to life the harshness and optimistic expectations of prospecting for diamonds and other precious minerals in the north-western Cape, the Kalahari and South-West Africa during the early 1900s. The other book was written by a man who became the first bishop of the area, as he tried to help and administer to local communities, at a time when many conflicts occurred between Germans, English and tribes people. As I sat leafing through these two books, waiting for the food I had ordered, two men, of whom I presumed one to be the proprietor, stood nonchalantly facing in my direction from a raised dais at the head of the room. One of them puffed all the while on a fat cigar, but little was said between them. They looked like two men happy to do nothing more than what they were doing. When I went to pay my bill, I asked the man with the cigar about the history of the place. His father had opened it in 1947 as a café/hotel and he had helped his father. When his father died, he changed the name of the place but continued the business.

Henry came in while I was there and explained that every year, on passing through with the TDA cyclists, he stopped there to buy a book. These two books that I had bought gave me much enjoyment in those last few days through South Africa.

Jennifer was celebrating her birthday. She had cycled hard to gain time for buying cheese and wine to share with the group as well as purchasing apples and pears which she cut up for us.

It beggared belief that within a few days - at 1.30pm on the Saturday - we would be forming a convoy to cycle into Cape Town, that my wife Carole and eldest son Damien would hopefully be there to greet me, as well as Tia from Thamsanqa and good friends Peter and Daphne. No one doubted how emotional a time it would be. I felt choked just thinking about it. Never again would we be together as a group and in most cases never again would we see each other, despite having spent four months living cheek by jowl.

Km covered 11,441 Yet to go 568

Tuesday, May 11: Springbok – Garies
80 km

If it had been July/August time, the land for over 100 km to the north and south of us would have been covered in low, brightly-coloured daisies, with tourists flocking from all over the world to witness the glory of nature. This was Namaqualand. It was hard for us to imagine this as we woke up to a bitterly cold morning, perhaps because we had become too accustomed to warmer climes. I wore a fleece and thick, waterproof jacket over my cycling vest, and full-length gloves. Cloud and mist hid the mountain tops and some drizzle did not appear out of place. But the rolling hills, with their unusual rock formations, pleasantly passed by.

I was much relieved that my ribs were no worse for the cycling. As I passed Steff, a vast panorama opened up and a long rather steep descent began. Speeding down, I encountered Aussie Dan climbing from the other direction. He had finished the stage, scanned in, and was trekking back to cycle in with Steff. It was for me a heart warming moment to see the open display of growing attachment between two individuals for whom I had much respect.

It was now noticeable how much weight some of the riders were putting back on with more readily available access to "naughty" foods. Catherine was the only person I know who claimed never to have lost any weight in the first place. In any case, the TDA played their part in helping us - Henry bought wine for us all and each of us received two small cakes after dinner.

All thoughts now centred on Cape Town, yet the four more days of riding equated to a chasm yet to cross before reaching our finale. The brisk beginning in Cairo could have taken place a generation earlier.

(Camp 92, map S.Africa)

Time cycling 4hrs 45mins
Average speed 25.3kph
Kms covered 11,521 Yet to go 488

Wednesday, May 12: Garies – Vanrhynsdorp 155 km

The rolling hills allowed us to warm up nicely. The magnitude of the landscape was hard to comprehend. It was semi-desert, or scrub desert, with occasional tracks meandering off to faraway homesteads, way beyond our vision. The area was so remote that the first town we came to was the one we were camping in.

(Camp 93, map S.Africa)

The race standings were mostly already decided, so even the racers could relax. Erin and Reuben had chosen this day to go for a stage win. They worked hard and achieved it.

An almost festive air permeated the camp. So many times recently I had heard riders ask each other, how can we ever explain to anyone what this trip has been like for us. It is as though each and every one of us would always have this block of memory within us that we would never properly be able to transmit. Acceptance of continued deprivation, the continual need to draw on previously unrealised strengths while watching oneself alter in mind and body, a veritable alter ego, was so far removed from any previous experience. We were warned that we would find it hard to readjust to our previously normal lives; that I could understand. But we had been enriched and strengthened emotionally and I doubt that any rider would harbour melodramatic ideas about life for people in the countries we had passed through any more. Values had been re-assessed and perhaps might be the cause of heartache for some, no longer able to turn a blind eye to the world beyond their national boundaries.

There was no time to dry my washing. The trousers I normally wore about camp had become too inflexible and stiff to wear, badly needing to be washed. I was forced by the cool evening temperature to walk around in long johns and swimming shorts. Fortunately for my blog readers, there were no photos.

The remaining good pole of my tent broke, but the tent still provided me with cover, so I could not have cared less. I felt so excited about nearly reaching Cape Town, more so than I ever had been about starting in Cairo.

Time cycling 6hrs 27mins
Average speed 23.1kph
Km covered 11,676 Yet to go 333

Thursday, May 13: Vanrhynsdorp - Elands Bay 112 km (I did 140)

Today should have been a fairly comfortable day and indeed started out so. The town of Vredendal, about 20 km from our camp, was the centre of Namaqualand's wine-growing industry. Carefully tended vineyards, sometimes edged with palm trees, scoffed at the surrounding wilderness. But more importantly for most of the riders, there was a Wimpy restaurant in town. Many of us piled in there, around 9am, for a second breakfast. I noticed Paddy demolishing a large T-bone steak with ease.

After fiddling with my bike speedometer, which I could not get to work, and then using the toilet, everyone had gone on ahead of me, apart from one rider for whom Kelsey, the morning's TDA "sweep", waited while I took off. I was enjoying the undulating ride past all the vineyards until I came to a T-junction where neither of the two options given corresponded with the direction I should be taking. After asking a number of people in a supermarket there, I finally found someone who had an inkling where the road to Lambert's Bay could be found. I had come about 20 km too far, missing a turning. (Canadian) Eric, unbeknown to me at the time, had made the very same mistake but chose to carry on regardless. We did not see him that night. Kelsey assumed we were still ahead of her on the correct route and did not know the true situation until she checked in at the lunch truck.

The sign for Lambert's Bay, when I found it, directed me up a gravel track, not a particularly bad one. But I was paranoid about shaking up my ribs or, worse still, falling. So I really took my time. I just needed to take it easy until I reached the lunch truck, at which point I could receive ongoing directions. Normally I would photograph the day's directions chalked on the blackboard; I had failed to do so in the breakfast rush, expecting to be with a group of riders all day anyway.

The track rose gradually to a plateau, from where on a clear day the ocean would have been easily visible. But this was early winter in the southern hemisphere. The wind was blowing and temperatures had dropped.

The lunch truck had turned round to come back for me. Thank goodness I had eaten in the Wimpy because they did not have any lunch for me! They wanted to carry me forward 10-15 km to wherever Michelle, the afternoon's sweep, was riding. Only two riders were sat in the truck which was impressive. Less impressive was the rain that was setting in as we approached the coast. By the time we caught up with Michelle and I mounted my bike, only a few km separated us from Lambert's Bay on the Atlantic coast. Unfortunately, the heavy mist shrouded the ocean from view. Three bikes outside an otherwise deserted restaurant persuaded me to stop. Michelle had to stop also in order to keep at the back with me. Inside, Dan, Steff and Anneke were huddled round the log fire. They hung around while I ate thick pea soup and a muffin.

Dan and Steff were riding together, so for a while I rode with Michelle. In four months, although as a medic she had treated me a few times, I had never really chatted to her. She was more intelligent and a more experienced cyclist than I had realised. The impression I now formed was that she felt her position as reserve medic gained her little respect. Her job, like that of all the staff, entailed a multitude of duties, whilst always putting on a brave face for our benefit. That would not have been easy and I sympathised with her feelings in a way I could not have done earlier.

As the mist lifted, we could see the pure white sand of the shoreline, contrasting with the red sand of the track; we could hear the roar of the ocean, smell the seaweed and the salt-laden air. Then we glimpsed the waves crashing in.

A railway line followed the shoreline. It was 861 km in length, built to carry iron ore. The interesting thing about it lay in the fact that, with the 300 trucks fully laden, it travelled south to the port of Saldanha solely by gravity.

Cycling into the little village of Elands Bay, I had already decided that I must get a room. My clothes were wet through and my tent would be too weakened for camping on the beach in the strong wind and rain. Just before joining the others on the beach, I met Franz and Carolina cycling away from the beach, carrying their gear with them. They shouted over to me that all the rooms in the village were taken and my heart sank. But as they continued cycling up the road they shouted again that they had secured a two-bedroom apartment which I was welcome to share with them. What a Godsend!

When I saw the tiny cove where the lorries had managed to park with a few tents sadly sited close by on the saturated sand and mud, I genuinely felt sorry for those who were to spend the night there. To his immense credit, Henry was one of them. I was deliriously happy to wrest my bag from the locker and set off in the rain with it precariously over my shoulder to find the apartment about 200m out of the village. Just as I was dismounting I heard a loud clanging behind me, and there was the world famous train passing right by the apartment!

Instead of eating the TDA dinner, a number of us chose a small bar that was open and offering food. Rick was in there celebrating after a momentous ride to finally win a stage. He had started in Cairo as perhaps a little on the chubby side and gradually turned into a lean athlete. At times contentious, but always humorous, he had, like all of us, experienced the whole gambit of emotions and ups-and-downs. Having lost EFI through illness, not lack of effort, what he really wanted was to be able to say that at least on one day he was the fastest in the field. This was the day he attempted it. In his blog he told how ".. historically the last 2 days of the tour are non-race days. Due to my sickness before Livingstone I had three 12 hour days in the second half (of the trip) and I was in last place for the men going into this day by an hour. Now my thoughts on this as a race are all over the board but I never want to finish last in anything I do, and even with 11 people dropping out of the race since the start I thought maybe I could push and pass Dan.

"There was a Wimpy's at 25 km from camp and a lot of people were talking about stopping there for a snack before lunch. It was a 112 km day with about 60% dirt in the middle. I decided that morning that I would see what happened if I went as hard as I could until someone passed me. I thought Stu and Gizzy would blow by me in the first 25 km and I would be able to cool it and get a milkshake, but as I approached Wimpy's I passed Gerald and Jos, 2 strong riders who I thought were maybe going for a stage win on the last day. Then going through town I passed Jethro on a hill. Jethro is the best hill climber on the tour and even though his race position was set and he was taking it easy, his easy pace is normally quite a bit faster than my hard pace. With him in the background I knew I had to go all out for the rest of the day, or until Stu caught me.

"At 30-something km we turned onto the dirt and there was a giant loose sand and gravel hill in front of me. I peddled as hard as I could and while growing tired kept the thought of people catching me from behind in my head. I was out of the saddle quite a bit on the first hill only to see many more hills when I got to the top. This was not going to be an easy day. I rode hard and passed Bill who left about 30 minutes before me. I asked if there were people going fast in front of me, he said yes. I had to ride faster! I saw a black figure on a bike up ahead. I decided I had 2 km to catch them. It was Laura and I caught her in 1.5 km. I passed her at the top of a hill and then rode down without braking, through the corrugation and into soft sand. I had a wobble but peddled through it and rode on, never looking back. At 60 km I got to the lunch truck. Paul Porter was there, I asked who was in front, just Tim and Peter. Tim was my worry and Stuart who was behind me, how far no one knew. I skipped lunch and with 45 seconds to stop with a foot down and a breathe I pushed on. Paul Porter started a fair bit before me so when he passed on the dirt I was concerned, but knew if I could stay within 15 minutes of him I would be fine. Tim started way before me as well, but crunching the numbers was too hard as I was peddling on the dirt with the 28 mm. tyres.

"From the second to last hill I saw the road we were turning right on and I saw Paul at the bottom of the last dirt hill heading towards the road. Once again I headed down the hill with reckless abandon. I didn't use my brakes all day to this point and I wasn't going to use them now. I peddled all the way down the hill and was out of the saddle most of the way up it. When I hit the tar I immediately got on the aerobars and tried to catch my breath. I was peddling as hard as I could when I lost sight of Paul, too many curves going through town, but I was close and with 40 km left maybe I could do this.

"I rode through 2 small fishing villages and then ended up facing a second dirt road. I didn't remember this from the rider meeting...I didn't go to the rider meeting. What do I do. I stopped to check the camera. It is a race, and going to be a close one and I had to stop to check directions. 30 seconds later and I saw a yellow jacket coming on a bike. Screw the directions, I either go the right way or the wrong way, but no one passes me today.

"The yellow jacket was gaining on me, I peddled harder, still gaining. I looked back and it was Tim. He was supposed to be 20 minutes in front of me. He says "Why did you stop?" I told him I had to check directions and what was he doing behind me. He said he was having a coffee, saw Paul go by then saw me and didn't want to miss it. Paid his check and came to watch the race first hand. I told him I have time on Paul but I was worried about him. He asked where Stuart was, all of a sudden I was racing the clock because I don't know when Stu left and how far back he was.

"Tim rode the rest of the way pushing me to ride harder than I had all trip. It was flattish, smoothish,hardish packed sand and we were blazing down at 36-40kph. Every time I stopped peddling to rest Tim would yell at me from behind. 18 km to go, push it out. I was out of the saddle for every hill, on the aerobars when I could, just to try and breathe. Riding over corrugation and taking the abuse with my body, all the time getting abuse from Tim. 14 km to go, you have to catch Paul. I couldn't see Paul, but I couldn't imagine he was going this fast. It was bordering on unsafe. I peddled faster, who knew who was behind me.

"We had one more right turn to make onto a road, I saw it up ahead and there was 2 yellow gates in the road, one on the left and one on the right with a space in the middle. It was a slight downhill and I was pushing 40+ I think, my speedo just stopped working in the rain. I unclipped my left foot thinking I would slow to a stop and walk through the gate. I grabbed a handful of brake and the back wheel locked up on the sand. I was not slowing down and now staring to fishtail and I was getting closer to the gate. I clipped back in, I now had 3 options, lay the bike down and slide under Dominican style. Not a great option, but I would not die. Jump the gate, all I really had to do was clear the handle bars because me and the rest of the bike would fit through the gap no problem, but jumping on a downhill at that speed is difficult, maybe impossible. Third option, do nothing. ...... I headed right for the hole in the gate, it was at the exact height of my handle bars. I watched as I cleared each side by less than an inch, back end fishtailing in fright. I made it through, checked back and Tim was rolling slow much slower. He yelled go right. I did, dodging the car that I had not noticed, still carrying my speed. Camp was close, I had to give it everything I had. We passed a building and then another. Flagging tape heading towards the beach. I got air going into the camp, landed on soft sand and rode to the truck. Threw down my bike and ran to the timing thing on the trailer. It never works in the rain and I ripped it off the trailer and yelled for Paul. After several attempts and Tim beeping in first I timed in, and almost collapsed. I have never been that tired in my life. I held myself up on a pole for the kitchen for a while, then headed into the truck to sit down and eat some candy. I got my things out and then saw Stu. I had no clue how long it had been, or when he started. I asked him his riding time, he didn't know, I guess we would have to wait for Kelsey. I set up my tent by the edge of the fence overlooking the cold wet rainy ocean and headed to the bar. The truck riders were already there, everyone was surprised to see me. I had a milkshake, calamari, fried fish, 2 Cokes, and a bottle of red wine. Jenn came in and we headed over to another bar, I had a few beers, then back to camp for dinner. It was chicken, quickly in my stomach then off for a few more beers. Kelsey wasn't going to check the times until tomorrow, I had no idea what happened, 1 or 2. I quickly forgot about the importance of the situation and just enjoyed hanging out with friends celebrating the end of the race. We partied very late (for us late is about 9pm, very late is 9:30) and stumbled back to the tent, still wet and rainy."

Rick may have left it late in the race, but he won that stage, not through default but sheer guts and determination. He had reached out and grabbed his moment of glory.

We had just one more full day of riding before our final day into Cape Town. I could barely believe it was happening, that soon we would be back with loved ones, that we would take back control of our lives, rest as much as we liked, eat what we liked, generally descend from the mountain we had climbed.
(Camp 94, map S.Africa)

Km covered 11,788 Yet to go 221

Friday May 14: Elands Bay – Yzerfontein 146 km

The heavy, cold mist which habitually rolls over this coastline from the Atlantic, had blanketed the cliffs from our view. As our wet, sandy track led us round to the other side of the cliffs, riders ahead of me kept sticking their arms out, indicating that I may want to take a different route, like I had the previous day. We passed a number of buildings anchored to the rocky edge, taking a battering from the huge, crashing waves. Fishing boats bobbled on the water alongside, protected by a small sea wall. Cranes hovered above them. Because there was no room for a slipway, the boats bringing lobster to the processing plant were hoisted in and out of the water using these cranes.

After 12 km, we were back on tarmac – no more dirt! – and with a light breeze on our backs we sailed through the scattered mist, sporadically glimpsing the mighty ocean. At 40 km, most of us stopped at a coffee shop we had been told about. After all, there was no time to be lost in trying to normalise our lives! As I was about to enter, a car stopped, and the driver enquired what was going on, where had we come from and why. I explained to him about the Tour, and why I was doing it, and he instantly put his hand in his pocket and gave me R100 for the Thamsanqa children.

At 60 km, after crossing the bridge over a charming estuary, there was the lunch truck, waiting with hamburgers, two each, which were just delicious. But the rain clouds were gathering again and it was cold. (The temperature when we left camp was 13 Celsius.) Cars had their headlights on. But seeing the signs for Cape Town brought a lump to the throat and strength to the legs.

Only as we arrived at camp in the pleasant seaside village of Yzerfontein did the weather look to be brightening up. Quite a number of riders booked rooms, to enjoy their last night. My wounded tent could support me for one last time. After a hot shower and some rearranging of bags, we had our last riders' meeting at 4.30. Everyone was in great form. Wayne had bought some wine and beer for his birthday, which helped a lot! Awards were given out for section and race winners, including an award for Rick after winning the last stage. I was so pleased for him. There were spoof awards too; I was given a "Where am I?" award. I retorted that I was not around.

We were given lots of information to ensure the final day of riding went to plan. After a 60 km cycle, we would regroup for lunch on the beach at Kreefte's Bay before travelling together in convoy for the last 30 km into Cape Town.

I had thought myself to have reached the age when one no longer gets excited over things. We older ones cope better with a more constant type of mood. Yet here I was feeling like I did at boarding school, as holidays approached, over 40 years ago, or like I had felt as an excited child on Christmas Eve. I did not know myself.

Large plastic bags were filled with a jumble of items previously deemed indispensable but which we no longer wanted to set eyes on again, everything from dirty socks to dirty dishes, from patched-up tubes to pairs of knickers. Liberation was coming.

Time stood still (speedo not working)
Average speed fairly fast
Km Covered 11,934 Yet to go 75

Saturday May 15: Yzerfountain - Cape Town
75 km

This last night was the coldest night of the whole four months. Everything was damp from the previous days' rains. For the first time on the trip, I even used both the liner and the sleeping bag. But I ended up getting up during the night to put on all the clothes and shoes I had left in the tent with me. The roof of the tent hovered just above my head due to the broken poles, and as I pulled on my already damp clothes, I must have touched the sagging tent roof and felt a stream of very cold water trickle down my back.

I was out of that tent very early. In the hope of finding some

source of warmth and wanting to enjoy one last pre-breakfast coffee with Hardy and Jacob, I packed up my belongings and besmirched a black plastic bag with my feckless tent. I was taken aback by how good that made me feel.

The temperature was 2 degrees. Many of the riders wore their cycling shoes though they were still soaking wet. I decided to use my ordinary shoes for the ride in to the finish. Each of us had been given a special Tour d'Afrique cycling shirt to wear. With television cameras awaiting us in Cape Town, it was only natural that we should wear a shirt representative of the trip and a sign of our togetherness. But I had started in my Benissa Cycling Club shirt and I wished to finish in it. Each of us had cycled through all sorts of conditions as individuals, albeit grouped together, and so I also felt it should be a celebration of the individual. Paul kindly reassured me that there was no pressure to wear the TDA shirt. So I guess that I am the only rider to own a 2010 unused TDA shirt, one that I treasure.

At first light, well-wrapped, we set off in ones and twos, still pinching ourselves that we were finally reaching the end of this four month odyssey. Though undulating, the straight road was

242

not hilly, so within 10-15 km of Kreefte's Bay, we could see Table Mountain. On our right, the Atlantic Ocean was rushing in to greet us. The sun, so often a stranger of late, came out to embrace us in its uncertain warmth, and the bright sunshine allowed us to make out the first faint images of the city, cuddled up to Table Mountain.

The dinner and lunch trucks were set up on the sandy beach of Kreefte's Bay. As I turned off the road, on to the beach, there were Peter and Daphne to greet me. I was choked.

The TDA had set out a lovely spread for us and we were hungry. Riders were running down to the surf and lifting up their bikes in the air in jubilation. An army helicopter skimmed back and forth over the incoming waves, parallel to the beach. Robben Island, where Mr. Mandela had been imprisoned for so long before his release, lay shrouded in the background, as if to mirror the moment.

The police arrived and we started out in convoy. TV camera units buzzed up and down our lines, as we started our final surge. Members of the Suburbs Cycling Club, led by Keith Ravens, brought up our rear. The occasional cyclist that met us tagged on for a while behind.

Briskly passing through the lovely suburbs, we joked and shouted to waving well-wishers, slowly closing in on the famous Cape Town Waterfront. Dark sunglasses could not hide the tears flowing down the faces of some. I needed to keep taking deep breaths, to keep my emotions in check. Sweeping round the final bend a blur of faces appeared. I saw Carole, Damien and Tia waiting. It was over.

Km covered 12,009

NB. All distances are those calculated by my own bike computer and may differ slightly from those of the TDA or of other riders.

CHAPTER 16
THE FINISH

The TDA, with its usual efficiency, had managed to arrange for a part of the Cape Town Waterfront to be sectioned off for our "arrival party". This was a glorious setting, contributing to the festive air. As we waited for the Awards Ceremony to begin, riders, friends and family laid into the range of refreshments provided by the TDA.

Yet there was something strange about that afternoon, at least for me. Most riders gravitated, naturally, to their family and friends, many of whom had travelled a long way to give us a worthy welcome. I was with Carole, Damien and Tia. Nevertheless, despite the jubilation and frothy frivolity, I felt a numbness, as if my feelings were anaesthetised by weariness and the need to maintain emotional control in front of others. In addition, questions remained unasked, explanations had not yet been sought. It was as if in recognition that the worn-out wording and trite terminology so easily fallen back on in difficult situations were not appropriate for the ending of an episode well outside the normal parameters of most of our lives.

This had a side effect. I now regret not having felt able to say proper goodbyes to my companions of four months. For instance, when I passed Steff and she said, "Eric, this is my Mum and sister", my response was totally inadequate. I could have told them what a wonderful person Steff was, how delighted I was to meet them and how much she had contributed. Similarly, the chance arose to spend a few minutes with Pete, to tell him how much I appreciated his permanently cheerful demeanour and friendliness. Rather than say something trivial using meaningless words, I chose to say next to nothing. It seemed to me that whatever I might say would be inadequate. While I had had little direct contact with some of the riders, each and every one of them had affected my journey in a different way, some leaving a deep impression (and there has not been the space in this book to recognise or mention all of these).

At that moment on the Cape Town Waterfront it was too early to confront all my own feelings let alone understand them. The result was that I could not find the means to suitably "sign off" with my companions.

After the arrival reception, which took place mid to late afternoon, there was a dinner organised by the TDA. What made the evening all the more memorable was that riders who had not shaved in four months were now almost unrecognisable. With beards replaced by white unblemished skin, smart outfits worn in the real world replacing lycra or creased casual clothing, the aspect of many riders was completely changed. The dinner was first class: I enjoyed having good food again. As dinner finished we gradually melted back to our hotel rooms. Neatly laid out by the side of each rider's bed was a tee-shirt; emblazoned on the back were the words "I survived Dinder". That thoughtful gesture touched me.

A variety of riders chose to spend a few days in the Cape. This probably gave them time to share their thoughts with each other. Others were heading straight back home. A few, unbelievably, were carrying on cycling. To the best of my knowledge, Hardy was cycling up to Durban, Lani and (Swiss) Eric were planning to join the TDA Asian cycling ride while Jeff and Diane would cycle across India with the TDA.

I had previously arranged for Carole, Damien and myself to leave the next day for Port Elizabeth to visit the Thamsanqa homes. I was keen to see what changes had taken place and it was also an opportunity for Carole and Damien to meet for the first time the people, staff and the children who, in essence and through no fault of theirs, had diverted the course of my life and indeed Carole's. This was not quite as expected. I had thought that a first visit to a black township would open their eyes. It did not. They were more surprised by how natural it felt to interact with the children and how clean and tidy the homes were and how friendly everyone was - all good impressions if not what I had anticipated.

With the chance to relax, I experienced an inordinate tiredness, such that sleep only seemed to serve as a reminder that I needed more and more of it.

A few days later we left Port Elizabeth and Africa. Our flight required us to stay a night in Dubai. The comparison between the luxury witnessed there and the scraping of leftovers we had seen African people existing on through most of four months could hardly have been more acute.

I do not feel even a tinge of embarrassment in admitting that while Carole and Damien enjoyed a look around the city, I slept, and I slept.

EPILOGUE

As I write, some twelve months after the finish in Cape Town, I am constantly surprised by how reading or talking about our final period of the Tour d'Afrique is invariably accompanied by a gush of emotion. It is as if this accumulated and still needs time to dissipate. Physically, I am now neither weaker nor stronger than before I started. Mentally and emotionally, however, I do believe I am stronger, and even capable of exercising more control over myself.

Occasionally, I fleetingly entertain the idea that were I ever to do the journey again but with the experience gained, I could acquit myself so much better and learn so much more about the places we passed through. (I remember riders recalling their first glimpse of Kilimanjaro. I had not seen it because I was looking out for it to the west of us when in fact it was in the east.) I am improving: I can now consign the idea of a re-ride to the rubbish bin it deserves. I need not fool myself. I gave it my best shot and that was exceptional. In addition, the experience has made me all the more aware of the variety of other challenges in life still waiting.

Those challenges will not include tents or tent poles. I have lost count of the number of times a pole splintered or cracked. Even pitching the tent after a day's ride could seem a momentous task sometimes. Having to repair it first was almost the last straw. Exasperation was common, especially when one's tent was the only place where privacy was guaranteed. Its thin material cut one off from one's surroundings just as effectively as bricks would have done, providing, or so it felt, a measure of home comfort. When a tent pole broke it hurt in the same manner as would a betrayal by an erstwhile trusted friend on whom one had come to rely.

On the other hand, I have become a devotee of the bike as a universal means of transport. We saw bikes used for carrying all manner of items, from huge sacks of charcoal to live animals, from stacks of fresh eggs to churns of milk. It still amazes me how much punishment our bikes were able to take. Except in a few cases, those bikes carried us over the severest of terrain, covering a continent - without needing much more than a little loving care when we felt able. A true friend and companion.

As for us riders, the continuous riding turned fat into muscle. The tissues of these new muscles were broken down and relentlessly reshaped into larger, stronger muscles during the four months of extended physical effort. But if these were the obvious physical changes, more permanent ones took place unseen. Punished, and pushed through limits we had not previously experienced or imagined, our spirit as riders was never broken. Rather it was reshaped, strengthened and changed forever.

I have written this book to serve as a memento to all my family and friends: from them I received incredible support both before and during the trip. Never will I forget the emotional cushion they so often provided when I needed it most. (It is amazing what a message or an email in a tiny internet café in the middle of nowhere can do to raise one's spirits.) In another guise, I hope the book will serve as my testimony to the tenacity of my friends, the riders who formed the Tour d'Afrique 2010. I thank all of them for their company, support and much more besides.

The TDA did more than it needed to. It was a wonderful kindness allowing me to break the rules and bring an extra 40+ kilos of catheters in a big box. Without this assistance the experience would have been impossible for me. For both the company itself and the staff who accompanied us, I have only the highest praise.

Finally, Thamsanqa is testament to the resolve and energy of Tia Wessels who reached out to help the helpless. Hers is a greater and more worthy challenge, much more so than me sitting on a bike from Cairo to Cape Town. May her efforts continue to win the support they deserve.